jQuery HOTSH⊕T

Ten practical projects that exercise your skill, build your
confidence, and help you master jQuery

Dan Wellman

BIRMINGHAM - MUMBAI

jQuery HOTSHOT

First published: March 2013

Production Reference: 2100714

Published by Packt Publishing Ltd.
Livery Place
35 Livery Street
Birmingham B3 2PB, UK.

ISBN 978-1-84951-910-6

www.packtpub.com

Cover Image by Girish Suryawanshi (girish.suryawanshi@gmail.com)

Credits

Author
Dan Wellman

Reviewers
Kaiser Ahmed

Carlos Estebes

Olivier Pons

Hajan Selmani

Christopher Stephen Sidell

Acquisition Editor
Robin de Jongh

Lead Technical Editor
Sweny M. Sukumaran

Technical Editor
Veronica Fernandes

Project Coordinator
Anurag Banerjee

Proofreader
Aaron Nash

Indexer
Tejal R. Soni

Production Coordinator
Arvindkumar Gupta

Cover Work
Arvindkumar Gupta

Foreword

I am very honored to have the opportunity to write the foreword for a *Dan Wellman* book. I've been a fan of Dan's since I first read his jQuery UI book. Then I got the opportunity to meet him in Oxford, England in February of 2012. Needless to say when he asked me to write the foreword for his latest book I didn't even think about how I wouldn't have the time to fit it in until the very last minute, but I immediately said yes.

Unlike other traditional jQuery books that dwell on how a jQuery statement is structured and functions, Dan assumes that you are already familiar with jQuery. What he is going to teach you is how to use jQuery for fun. He will walk you through a series of fun projects. Most of these projects will be very useful in your personal and professional websites. The projects include building a jQuery Mobile application, interactive Google Maps, Chrome Extensions, and Infinite Scrolling to name a few.

jQuery has been making web development easier since January 2006 when *John Resig* debuted jQuery at a New York City Barcamp with two other projects that day. Seven years later it's great to see that you can still learn to accomplish fun things with a library as simple yet as vast as jQuery.

I look forward to reading Dan's next book as I am sure this won't be his last.
At least I hope not.

Ralph Whitbeck
Modern Web Advocate at appendTo
jQuery Board Member

About the Author

Dan Wellman is an author and front-end engineer who lives on the South Coast of the UK and works in London. By day he works for Skype, writing application-grade JavaScript, and by night he writes books and tutorials focused mainly on front-end development. He is also a staff writer for the Tuts+ arm of the Envato network, and occasionally writes for .Net magazine. He's a proud father of four amazing children, and the grateful husband of a wonderful wife. This will be his seventh book.

I'd like to thank my family and friends for their continued support, you guys rock. I'd also like to thank my tireless PA, Derek Spacagna, for his persistent encouragement, and my friend Michael Chart, without whose mathematical genius some of the examples would not have been possible.

About the Reviewers

Kaiser Ahmed is a professional web developer. He has gained his B.Sc. from Khulna University of Engineering and Technology (KUET) and M.Sc. in Computer Science and Engineering from United International University, Dhaka. He is also a co-founder of CyberXpress.Net Inc (`www.cyberxpress.net`), based in Bangladesh.

He has been working as Sr. Software Developer at Krembo Interactive and D1SH.COM CORP., Canada, for 2 years.

He has a wide range of technical skills, Internet knowledge, and experience across a spectrum of online development in the service of building and improving online properties for multiple clients. He enjoys creating site architecture and infrastructure, backend development using open source toolset (PHP, MySQL, Apache, Linux and others, that is LAMP), and frontend development with CSS and HTML/XHTML.

> I want to thank my loving wife, Maria Akther, for her great support.

Carlos Estebes is the founder of Ehxioz (`http://ehxioz.com/`), a Los Angeles-based software development startup that specializes in developing modern web applications and utilizing the latest web development technologies and methodologies. He has over 10 years of web development experience and holds a B.Sc. in Computer Science from California State University, Los Angeles.

He previously collaborated with Packt Publishing as a technical reviewer in the third edition of *Learning jQuery*.

Olivier Pons is a developer who's been building websites since 1997. He's a teacher at the University of Sciences (IUT) of Aix-en-Provence, France and Ecole d'Ingénieurs des Mines de Gardanne, where he teaches PHP, jQuery, jQuery Mobile, C++, Java fundamentals, advanced VIM techniques, and Eclipse environment. He has already done some technical reviews, including one for *Ext JS 4 First Look, Packt Publishing*. In 2011, he left a full time job as a Delphi and PHP developer to concentrate on his own company, HQF Development (`http://hqf.fr`). He currently runs a number of websites, including `http://www.livrepizzas.fr`, `http://www.papdevis.fr`, and `http://olivierpons.fr`, his own web development blog. He works as a consultant, project manager, and sometimes as a developer.

Hajan Selmani is a Microsoft MVP in ASP.NET/IIS, a Microsoft Certified Trainer (MCT), and a Microsoft Certified Professional (MCP) with deep knowledge and experience in web development technologies. He works as a coordinator of CodeCademy at Seavus Education and Development Center, software development consultant, technology advisor in a few startups, and also focuses on research and innovation using cutting-edge tools and technologies. He is a regular speaker at code camps, Microsoft conferences, and local user group meetings and events where he actively promotes the latest modern web standards and development practices. He is a board member of MKDOT.NET and leader of MK Web User Group. He holds a Master's degree in Computer Science, Intelligent Systems.

He has also reviewed the books *ASP.NET jQuery Cookbook, Packt Publishing* and *Entity Framework 4.1: Expert's Cookbook, Packt Publishing*.

Christopher Stephen Sidell is a college student attending UMBC. He has been doing freelance web development work for people for the past few years, starting with HTML and CSS in 2005, JavaScript in 2007, and later adding PHP into the mix in 2008. Since then he has been working with others to create portfolio sites and self-made projects. He is self-employed and a full-time student at UMBC.

> I'd like to thank my parents for giving me a How-To guide for HTML when I was in grade school. I would like to further thank my father who helped me with any technology problems I may have had and taught me to fix them myself. My mother has given me vital support in the decisions I've made in my life.

www.PacktPub.com

Support files, eBooks, discount offers and more

You might want to visit www.PacktPub.com for support files and downloads related to your book.

Did you know that Packt offers eBook versions of every book published, with PDF and ePub files available? You can upgrade to the eBook version at www.PacktPub.com and as a print book customer, you are entitled to a discount on the eBook copy. Get in touch with us at service@packtpub.com for more details.

At www.PacktPub.com, you can also read a collection of free technical articles, sign up for a range of free newsletters and receive exclusive discounts and offers on Packt books and eBooks.

http://PacktLib.PacktPub.com

Do you need instant solutions to your IT questions? PacktLib is Packt's online digital book library. Here, you can access, read and search across Packt's entire library of books.

Why Subscribe?

- ▸ Fully searchable across every book published by Packt
- ▸ Copy and paste, print and bookmark content
- ▸ On demand and accessible via web browser

Free Access for Packt account holders

If you have an account with Packt at www.PacktPub.com, you can use this to access PacktLib today and view nine entirely free books. Simply use your login credentials for immediate access.

I'd like to dedicate this book to my father. Cheers pop!

Table of Contents

Preface

Welcome to *jQuery Hotshot*. This book has been written to provide as much exposure to the different methods and utilities that make up jQuery as possible. You don't need to be a jQuery hotshot to read and understand the projects this book contains, but by the time you've finished the book, you should be a jQuery hotshot.

As well as learning how to use jQuery, we are also going to look at a wide range of related technologies including using some of the more recent HTML5 and related APIs, such as localStorage, how to use and create jQuery plugins, and how to use other jQuery libraries such as jQuery UI, jQuery Mobile, and jQuery templates.

jQuery has been changing the way we write JavaScript for many years. It wasn't the first JavaScript library to gain popularity and widespread usage among developers, but its powerful selector engine, cross-browser compatibility, and easy-to-use syntax quickly propelled it to be one of the most popular and widely-used JavaScript frameworks of all time.

As well as being easy-to-use and abstracting complex and powerful techniques into a simple API, jQuery is also backed by an ever-growing community of developers, and is possibly the only JavaScript library protected by a not-for-profit foundation to ensure that development of the library remains active, and that it remains open source and free for everyone for as long as it's available.

One of the best things is that anyone can get involved. You can write plugins for other developers to use in order to complete common or not-so-common tasks. You can work with the bug tracker to raise new issues, or work with the source to add features, or fix bugs and give back in the form of pull requests through Git. In short, there is something to do for everyone who wants to get involved, whatever their background or skillset.

Getting started with jQuery

Every project in this book is built around jQuery; it's the foundation for everything we do. To download a copy of jQuery, we can visit the jQuery site at `http://jquery.com/`. There are download buttons here to obtain production and development versions of the library, as well as a wealth of other resources including full API documentation, tutorials, and much, much more to help you familiarize yourself with using the library.

One of the core concepts of jQuery is based on selecting one or more elements from the **Document Object Model (DOM)** of a web page, and then operating on those elements somehow using the methods exposed by the library.

We'll look at a range of different ways of selecting elements from the page throughout the projects in the book, as well as a wide selection of the different methods we can call on elements, but let's look at a basic example now.

Let's say there is an element on a page that has an `id` attribute of `myElement`. We can select this element using its `id` with the following code:

```
jQuery("#myElement");
```

As you can see, we use simple CSS selectors in order to select the elements from the page that we wish to work with. These can range from simple `id` selectors as in this example, `class` selectors, or much more complex attribute selectors.

As well as using `jQuery` to select elements, it is also common to use the `$` alias. This would be written using `$` instead of `jQuery`, as follows:

```
$("#myElement");
```

Once the element has been selected in this way, we would say that the element is wrapped with jQuery, or that it's a jQuery object containing the element. Using the `jQuery` (or `$`) method with a selector always results in a collection of elements being returned.

If there are no elements that match the selector, the collection has a length of `0`. When `id` selectors are used, we would expect the collection to contain a single element. There is no limit as to how many elements may be returned in the collection; it all depends on the selector used.

We can now call jQuery methods that operate on the element or elements that have been selected. One of the great features of most jQuery methods is that the same method may be used to either get a value, or set a value, depending on the arguments passed to the method.

So to continue our example where we have selected the element whose `id` attribute is `myElement`, if we wanted to find out its `width` in pixels, we could use jQuery's `width()` method:

```
$("#myElement").width();
```

This will return a number which specifies how many pixels wide the element is. However, if we wish to set the `width` of our element, we could pass the number of pixels that we'd like the element to have its width set to as an argument to the same method:

```
$("#myElement").width(500);
```

Of course, there is much more to using jQuery than these simple examples show, and we'll explore much more in the projects contained in this book, but this simplicity is at the heart of the library and is one of the things that have made it so popular.

What this book covers

Project 1, *Sliding Puzzle*, helps us build a sliding puzzle game. We'll use jQuery and jQuery UI together to produce this fun application and also look at the localStorage API.

Project 2, *A Fixed Position Sidebar with Animated Scrolling*, helps us implement a popular user interface feature – the fixed-position sidebar. We focus on working with the CSS of elements, animation, and event handling.

Project 3, *An Interactive Google Map*, teaches us how to work with Google's extensive Maps API in order to create an interactive map. We look at a range of DOM manipulation methods and look at how to use jQuery alongside other frameworks.

Project 4, *A jQuery Mobile Single-page App*, takes a look at the excellent jQuery Mobile framework in order to build a mobile application that combines jQuery with the Stack Exchange API. We also look at jQuery's official template engine, JsRender.

Project 5, *jQuery File Uploader*, uses jQuery UI once again, this time implementing a Progressbar widget as part of a dynamic front-end file uploader. We also cover writing jQuery plugins by making our uploader a configurable jQuery plugin.

Project 6, *Extending Chrome with jQuery*, shows us how we can extend the popular Chrome web browser with an extension built with jQuery, HTML, and CSS. Once again we make use of JsRender.

Project 7, *Build Your Own jQuery*, takes a look at how we can build a custom version of jQuery using a range of key web developer's tools including Node.js, Grunt.js, Git, and QUnit.

Project 8, Infinite Scrolling with jQuery, takes a look at another popular user-interface feature – infinite scrolling. We focus on jQuery's AJAX capabilities, again use JsRender, and look at the handy imagesLoaded plugin.

Project 9, A jQuery Heat Map, helps us build a jQuery-powered heat map. There are several aspects to this project including the code that captures clicks when pages are visited, and the admin console that aggregates and displays the information to the site administrator.

Project 10, A Sortable, Paged Table with Knockout.js, shows us how to build dynamic applications that keep a user interface in sync with data using jQuery together with the MVVM framework Knockout.js.

What you need for this book

Some of the projects covered in this book can be completed using nothing but a browser and a simple text editor. Of course, a complete IDE is always going to make things easier, with features such as code completion, code coloring, and collapsible blocks. So using an IDE over a simple text editor is recommended.

Other projects rely on additional JavaScript frameworks or community-built plugins. Several projects use third-party services hosted on the Internet in order to consume data. One project requires the use of several additional and highly specialized applications.

Where additional software or scripts are required, or API access is needed, these requirements are discussed in the relevant projects and information is included on where to obtain the required code or applications, how to install them, and how to use them sufficiently for the project to be completed.

Who this book is for

This book is aimed primarily at front-end developers that have some knowledge and understanding of HTML, CSS, and JavaScript. Some jQuery experience is desired, but not essential. All code, whether it be HTML, CSS, or JavaScript (including jQuery) is discussed in full to explain how it is used to complete the project.

Conventions

In this book, you will find several headings appearing frequently.

To give clear instructions of how to complete a procedure or task, we use:

Mission Briefing

This section explains what you will build, with a screenshot of the completed project.

Why Is It Awesome?

This section explains why the project is cool, unique, exciting, and interesting. It describes what advantage the project will give you.

Your Hotshot Objectives

This section explains the major tasks required to complete your project.

> ▸ Task 1
>
> ▸ Task 2
>
> ▸ Task 3
>
> ▸ Task 4, and so on

Mission Checklist

This section explains any prerequisites for the project, such as resources or libraries that need to be downloaded, and so on.

Task 1

This section explains the task that you will perform.

Prepare for Lift Off

This section explains any preliminary work that you may need to do before beginning work on the task.

Engage Thrusters

This section lists the steps required in order to complete the task.

Objective Complete - Mini Debriefing

This section explains how the steps performed in the previous section allow us to complete the task. This section is mandatory.

Classified Intel

The extra information in this section is relevant to the task.

You will also find a number of styles of text that distinguish between different kinds of information. Here are some examples of these styles, and an explanation of their meaning.

Code words in text are shown as follows: "First of all we define a new variable called `correctPieces` and set its value to 0."

A block of code is set as follows:

```html
<!DOCTYPE html>

<html lang="en">
  <head>
    <meta charset="utf-8" />
    <title></title>
    <link rel="stylesheet" href="css/common.css" />
  </head>
  <body>
    <script src="js/jquery-1.9.0.min.js"></script>
  </body>
</html>
```

Two independent lines of code will appear as follows:

```html
<div data-role="header">
    <a href="bounty-hunter.html" data-icon="home"
```

A line of code that has overflown to the next due to space constraints would appear as follows:

```
filter: "!)4k2jB7EKv1OvDDyMLKT2zyrACssKmSCX
    eX5DeyrzmOdRu8sC5L8d7X3ZpseW5o_nLvVAFfUSf"
```

When we wish to draw your attention to a particular part of a code block, the relevant lines or items are set in bold:

```
pieces.appendTo(imgContainer).draggable("destroy");

if (timer) {
  clearInterval(timer);
```

```
    timerDisplay.text("00:00:00");
}

timer = setInterval(updateTime, 1000);
currentTime.seconds = 0;
currentTime.minutes = 0;
currentTime.hours = 0;

pieces.draggable({
```

Any command-line input or output is written as follows:

```
cd C:\\msysgit\\msysgit\\share\\msysGit
```

New terms and **important words** are shown in bold. Words that you see on the screen, in menus or dialog boxes for example, appear in the text like this: "Clicking on the **Next** button moves you to the next screen".

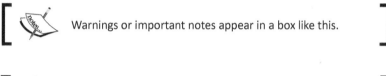

Warnings or important notes appear in a box like this.

Tips and tricks appear like this.

Reader feedback

Feedback from our readers is always welcome. Let us know what you think about this book— what you liked or may have disliked. Reader feedback is important for us to develop titles that you really get the most out of.

To send us general feedback, simply send an e-mail to feedback@packtpub.com, and mention the book title via the subject of your message.

If there is a topic that you have expertise in and you are interested in either writing or contributing to a book, see our author guide on www.packtpub.com/authors.

Customer support

Now that you are the proud owner of a Packt book, we have a number of things to help you to get the most from your purchase.

Downloading the example code

You can download the example code files for all Packt books you have purchased from your account at `http://www.packtpub.com`. If you purchased this book elsewhere, you can visit `http://www.packtpub.com/support` and register to have the files e-mailed directly to you.

Errata

Although we have taken every care to ensure the accuracy of our content, mistakes do happen. If you find a mistake in one of our books—maybe a mistake in the text or the code—we would be grateful if you would report this to us. By doing so, you can save other readers from frustration and help us improve subsequent versions of this book. If you find any errata, please report them by visiting `http://www.packtpub.com/submit-errata`, selecting your book, clicking on the **errata submission form** link, and entering the details of your errata. Once your errata are verified, your submission will be accepted and the errata will be uploaded on our website, or added to any list of existing errata, under the Errata section of that title. Any existing errata can be viewed by selecting your title from `http://www.packtpub.com/support`.

Piracy

Piracy of copyright material on the Internet is an ongoing problem across all media. At Packt, we take the protection of our copyright and licenses very seriously. If you come across any illegal copies of our works, in any form, on the Internet, please provide us with the location address or website name immediately so that we can pursue a remedy.

Please contact us at `copyright@packtpub.com` with a link to the suspected pirated material.

We appreciate your help in protecting our authors, and our ability to bring you valuable content.

Questions

You can contact us at `questions@packtpub.com` if you are having a problem with any aspect of the book, and we will do our best to address it.

Project 1

Sliding Puzzle

In our first project we'll get to see a variety of techniques in action, in a fun and relaxed setting. Consider this a gentle warm up for the rest of the book.

We'll see how to make elements draggable using jQuery UI and how we can configure the behavior of the draggable elements. We'll also look at other subjects including sorting algorithms, and client-side storage using the localStorage API.

Mission Briefing

In this project we'll be building a simple but fun puzzle game in which a picture is scrambled and has to be unscrambled back to the original picture by sliding the different pieces around the board – a modern web-based take on a classic game from yesteryear.

Typically there is one blank space on the board and pieces can only be moved into this blank space so we will need to build a system that keeps track of where the blank space is, and only allows pieces directly adjacent to it to be dragged.

To give the player an incentive, we can also look at keeping track of how long it takes the player to solve the puzzle so that the player's best time can be recorded. The following is a screenshot that shows the final result of this project:

Why Is It Awesome?

Games are fun and they can keep people coming back to your site, especially a younger audience. Non-flash browser-based games are taking off in a big way, but getting into the action at the top end of the scale can have a steep learning curve.

A simple drag-based game like this is the perfect way to ease yourself into the gaming market without jumping straight in at the deep end, allowing you to hone your skills with some of the simpler concepts of game development.

This is also a great way to learn how to build a draggable interface in a precise and engaging format that is well suited to its intended purpose and intuitive to use. We can also look at some more advanced draggable concepts such as collision avoidance and precise positioning. We will also be learning how to interact with the localStorage API in order to store and retrieve data between sessions.

Your Hotshot Objectives

This project will be broken down into the following tasks, which we'll work through sequentially in order to produce a working end result:

- ▸ Laying down the underlying HTML
- ▸ Creating a code wrapper and defining variables
- ▸ Splitting an image into pieces
- ▸ Shuffling the puzzle pieces
- ▸ Making the puzzle pieces draggable
- ▸ Starting and stopping the timer
- ▸ Determining if the puzzle has been solved
- ▸ Remembering best times and adding some final styling

Mission Checklist

As well as jQuery, we'll also be using jQuery UI in this project, so now is the time to grab these libraries and put them in place. We can also take a moment to set up our project folder, which is where we can store all of the files that we'll create over the course of the book.

Create a new folder somewhere called `jquery-hotshots`. Within this folder create three new folders called `js`, `css`, and `img`. All the HTML pages we create will go into the root `jquery-hotshots` folder, while the other files we use will be distributed amongst the subfolders according to their type.

For the projects covered throughout the book we'll use a local copy of the latest version of jQuery, which at the time of writing is the brand new 1.9.0. Download a copy of the minified version from `http://code.jquery.com/jquery-1.9.0.min.js` and save it in the `js` folder.

It's considered best practice to use Google's **content delivery network (CDN)** to load jQuery and to link to the file without specifying a protocol. Using a CDN means the file is more likely to be in the visitor's browser cache, making the library much quicker to load.

It is also advisable to provide a fallback in the event that the CDN is not accessible for some reason. We can very easily use the excellent **yepnope** to load a local version of the script if the CDN version is not found. See the yepnope site, `http://yepnopejs.com/`, for more information on this and other resource-loading tips and tricks.

To download the jQuery UI components we'll require, visit the download builder at `http://jqueryui.com/`. We'll be using various other components in later projects, so for simplicity we can just download the complete library using the **Stable** button. The current version at the time of writing is 1.10.0.

Once the build has been downloaded, you'll need to grab a copy of the `jquery-ui-x.x.x.custom.min.js file` (where `x.x.x` is the version number) from the `js` directory inside the archive, and paste it into your `js` folder.

Recent versions of jQuery UI, as well as some of the more popular pre-built themes generated with Themeroller, are also available via Google's CDN.

Laying down the underlying HTML

First of all we need to build out the page that'll contain our sliding puzzle. The initial page will be a shell with mostly just a few containers; the draggable elements that will make up the individual pieces of the puzzle can all be created dynamically when required.

Prepare for Lift Off

We'll use a standard starting point for all of the different projects throughout this book, so we'll look at this briefly now to save showing it in every project:

```
<!DOCTYPE html>

<html lang="en">
    <head>
        <meta charset="utf-8" />
        <title></title>
        <link rel="stylesheet" href="css/common.css" />
    </head>
```

```
<body>
    <script src="js/jquery-1.9.0.min.js"></script>
</body>
</html>
```

Downloading the example code

You can download the example code files for all Packt books you have purchased from your account at http://www.packtpub.com. If you purchased this book elsewhere, you can visit http://www.packtpub.com/support and register to have the files e-mailed directly to you.

Each project we cover will be contained in a page that starts out exactly like this. Save a copy of the previous file now in your local project folder and call it template.html. At the start of each project I'll say something like "save a copy of the template file as project-name.html". This is the file I'll be referring to.

So in this case, save a copy of the previous HTML (or template.html if you wish) in the main project directory (jquery-hotshots) and call it sliding-puzzle.html.

We'll also be using a common style sheet for basic styling that each project will utilize. It contains things such as an HTML5 reset, clearfix, and other utilities, as well as some basic typographical fixtures and theming for consistency between projects. While I won't go into detail on that here, you can take a look at the common.css source file in the accompanying download of this book for more information.

Each project will also need its own style sheet. These will be covered where applicable and will be discussed on a per-project basis as and when required. We can create the custom style sheet we'll be using in this project now.

Create a new file and call it sliding-puzzle.css, then save it in the css folder. We can link to this file in the <head> of the page using the following code:

```
<link rel="stylesheet" href="css/sliding-puzzle.css" />
```

This should appear directly after the common.css style sheet reference.

We can also link to the script files that we'll be using in this project. First, the jQuery UI file we downloaded and copied into the js folder can be linked to using the following code:

```
<script src="js/jquery-ui-1.10.0.custom.min.js"></script>
```

Remember to always add the script for jQuery UI on the next line after the script for jQuery itself.

Lastly we can add the script file we'll use for this project. Create a new file and save it as `sliding-puzzle.js` in the `js` folder. We can link to it by adding the following `<script>` element directly after the jQuery UI reference:

```
<script src="js/sliding-puzzle.js"></script>
```

Engage Thrusters

Save a copy of the template file as `sliding-puzzle.html` in the root project folder and then add the following mark-up to the `<body>` element (before the jQuery `<script>` element):

```
<div id="puzzle" class="clearfix">
    <figure>
        <img src="img/Flower.png" />
    </figure>
    <div id="ui">
        <p id="time">Current time: <span>00:00:00</span></p>
        <button id="start">Start!</button>
    </div>
</div>
```

Objective Complete - Mini Debriefing

This simple HTML is all that's required to start with. As this is a book about JavaScript, I won't cover the HTML in much detail unless absolutely critical to the project at hand. In this case most of the elements themselves aren't significant.

The main thing is that we have a series of containers with `id` attributes that make selecting them fast and easy. The only really important element is the `<img>`, which displays the original image that we'll be turning into the puzzle.

Creating a code wrapper and defining variables

All of our code will need to be contained within a wrapper function that is executed once the page has finished loading.

Prepare for Lift Off

The steps that we'll complete in this part of the project are as follows:

▸ Add a wrapper function for our code that will execute as soon as the page has finished loading

▸ Define the variables that we'll use throughout the script

Engage Thrusters

The first step is to create a wrapper function for our code that will be executed as soon as the page has loaded. Add the following code to a new script file called `sliding-puzzle.js`, which should be saved in the `js` directory we created earlier:

```
$(function () {

    //all our code will be in here...

});
```

Most jQuery code that we see in the wild resides within some kind of wrapper like this. Using `$(function(){});` is a shortcut to jQuery's `document.ready` function, which is fired once the DOM for the page has loaded.

Using $

We wouldn't normally use $ in the global scope like this if we were sharing our code with other developers, as there may be other libraries on the page also using it. Best practice is to alias the $ character within an automatically invoked anonymous function, or an immediately invoked function expression if you prefer. This can be done using the syntax `(function($) { ... } (jQuery));`.

Next we can set some variables near the top of the script file. This is so that we don't have lots of values that we may want to change later distributed throughout the file. Organization is one of the keys to writing maintainable code, and we should always strive to make our code, as well as our intentions, as clear as possible.

Next add the following code inside the function we just defined, replacing the comment shown in the previous code sample:

```
var numberOfPieces = 12,
    aspect = "3:4",
    aspectW = parseInt(aspect.split(":")[0]),
    aspectH = parseInt(aspect.split(":")[1]),
    container = $("#puzzle"),
    imgContainer = container.find("figure"),
    img = imgContainer.find("img"),
    path = img.attr("src"),
    piece = $("<div/>"),
    pieceW = Math.floor(img.width() / aspectW),
    pieceH = Math.floor(img.height() / aspectH),
    idCounter = 0,
    positions = [],
    empty = {
        top: 0,
        left: 0,
        bottom: pieceH,
        right: pieceW
    },
    previous = {},
    timer,
    currentTime = {},
    timerDisplay = container.find("#time").find("span");
```

These aren't all of the variables that we'll use, just the majority of them. The list also includes any variables that we'll need to use inside callback functions so that we don't run into scope issues.

Objective Complete - Mini Debriefing

The variables we defined first are a combination of simple (primitive) values and objects or arrays that we'll use throughout the code, and cached jQuery elements. For best performance when using jQuery, it's best to select elements from the page and store them in variables instead of repeatedly selecting them from the page.

Although none of our variables are directly assigned to `window`, and are therefore not actually global, because we are defining them right at the top of our outermost function, they will be visible throughout our code and we can consider them as global. This gives us the visibility of globals, without actually cluttering the global namespace.

It is best practice to define variables at the top of the function they are scoped to because of a phenomenon known as **hoisting**, in which variables defined deep inside a function, inside a `for` loop for example, are "hoisted" to the top of the function in some situations, potentially causing errors that are hard to track down.

Defining variables at the top of the function where possible is a simple way to avoid this occurring and is considered a good practice when writing jQuery, or JavaScript in general.

Most of the variables are quite straightforward. We store the number of puzzle pieces we'd like to use and the aspect ratio of the image being used. It's important that the number of pieces can be equally divided by both the `width` and `height` components of the ratio.

We split the aspect ratio into its component parts using JavaScript's `split()` function and specifying the colon as the character to split on. We also use the JavaScript `parseInt()` function to ensure we end up with actual numbers and not strings in the `aspectW` and `aspectH` variables.

The next three variables are all different elements selected from the page that we need to manipulate. Following this is a new element that we create using jQuery.

Next we calculate the `width` and `height` each piece of the puzzle will need to be sized to, based on the `width` and `height` of the original image and the aspect ratio, and we initialize a counter variable that we'll use to add a unique, ordered `id` attribute to each puzzle piece. We also add an empty array called `positions`, which we'll use to store the `top` and `left` positions of each new piece.

We'll need a way of keeping track of the empty space as the pieces are moved around the board, so we create an object called `empty` and give it `top`, `left`, `bottom`, and `right` properties so that we'll know exactly where the blank is space at any given moment. We'll also want to keep track of the previous location of any given piece so we create an empty object called `previous` that we'll populate with properties when required.

The remaining three variables are all concerned with keeping track of the time it takes to solve the puzzle. We defined, but didn't initialize the `timer` variable that we'll use to store a reference to a JavaScript `setInterval()`-based timer later in the script. We also created an empty object called `currentTime`, which again we'll populate when required, and cached a reference to the element that we'll use to display the current time.

Splitting an image into pieces

Our next task is to divide the image into a specified number of squares to represent the individual pieces of the puzzle. To do this we'll create a series of smaller elements which each show a different part of the image and which can be manipulated individually.

Prepare for Lift Off

The single step required to complete this task is to create a specified number of puzzle pieces and give each a unique background-position and position in order to recreate the image.

Engage Thrusters

We now want to generate the different pieces that make up the puzzle. We can do this with the following code, which should be added directly after the variables we just defined in `sliding-puzzle.js`:

```
for (var x = 0, y = aspectH; x < y; x++) {
    for (var a = 0, b = aspectW; a < b; a++) {
        var top = pieceH * x,
            left = pieceW * a;

        piece.clone()
            .attr("id", idCounter++)
            .css({
                width: pieceW,
                height: pieceH,
                position: "absolute",
                top: top,
                left: left,
                backgroundImage: ["url(", path, ")"].join(""),
                backgroundPosition: [
                    "-", pieceW * a, "px ",
                    "-", pieceH * x, "px"
                ].join("")
        }).appendTo(imgContainer);

        positions.push({ top: top, left: left });
    }
}
```

Objective Complete - Mini Debriefing

We used a nested set of `for` loops to create the new puzzle pieces in a grid pattern. The first loop will run for as many rows as required; with a 3:4 aspect-ratio image such as that used in this example, we will need four rows of squares. The inner loop will for run for as many columns as required, which in this case is three.

Within the inner loop we first create two new variables `top` and `left`. We need to use these values in a couple of places so it makes sense to create them once and reuse them each time they're required.

The `top` position is equal to the `height` of the piece multiplied by the current value of the outer loop's counter variable (x), while the `left` position is equal to the `width` of the piece multiplied by the current value of the inner loop's counter variable (a). These variables are used to make the puzzle pieces line up in a grid.

We then copy our stored `<div>` element using jQuery's `clone()` method and use the `attr()` method to set a unique `id` attribute using the `idCounter` variable that we initialized in the first part of the project. Notice that we increment the variable at the same time as setting it directly within the `attr()` method.

We could increment the variable either inside the method as we have done here, or outside of the method; there's no real difference in performance or anything else. I just feel that it's more succinct to update it in situ.

Next we use the `css()` method to set a `style` attribute on the new element. We set the `width` and `height` of the puzzle piece and position it using our `top` and `left` variables, as well as set its `backgroundImage` and `backgroundPosition` style properties.

 Any style properties that are usually defined using hyphenated words, such as `background-image`, should be camel-cased when used with jQuery's `css()` method in conjunction with an object.

The `backgroundImage` property can be set using our `path` variable and the rest of the string components of the style, but the `backgroundPosition` property will need to be calculated individually for each puzzle piece.

The horizontal component of the `backgroundPosition` style property is equal to the `width` of the piece multiplied by the value of the inner loop's counter variable (a), while the vertical component is equal to the `height` of the piece multiplied by the value of the outer loop's counter variable (x).

Once the new element has been created we can add its position to our `positions` array using JavaScript's `push()` method, passing in an object containing the `top` and `left` positional properties of the element for later use.

Classified Intel

Instead of using standard string concatenation to construct the `backgroundImage` and `backgroundPosition` strings, we put the values into an array literal and then joined the array using JavaScript's `join()` method. By specifying an empty string as the value to use to join the string, we ensure that no additional characters are added to the string.

Joining an array of substrings to form a single string is much faster than building a string using the + operator on substrings, and as we're working repetitively inside a loop, we should optimize the code within the loop as much as possible.

Shuffling the puzzle pieces

In this step we need to randomly shuffle the pieces to make it a puzzle so that the visitor can unscramble them. We can also remove the original image as it's no longer required, and remove the first piece to create an empty space so that the other pieces can be moved around.

Prepare for Lift Off

The steps we'll cover in this task are:

- ▸ Removing the original image from the page
- ▸ Removing the first piece of the puzzle
- ▸ Removing the first item in the positions array
- ▸ Shuffling the pieces randomly

Engage Thrusters

Completing the first step requires just the following line of code, which should be added directly after the closing curly-bracket of the outer `for` loop we added to `sliding-puzzle.js` in the last task:

```
img.remove();
```

The second step is equally as simple; the following can be added directly after the previous line of code:

```
container.find("#0").remove();
```

We can also use a single line of code for the next step. Add the following directly after the previous line of code:

```
positions.shift();
```

Shuffling the pieces will be slightly more complex; you'll remember from the first part of the project when we added the underlying HTML that one of the elements was a start button. We'll use this button to trigger the shuffle. Add the following code directly after the first two lines we just added (make sure they are still within the outer function wrapper):

```
$("#start").on("click", function (e) {
    var pieces = imgContainer.children();

    function shuffle(array) {
        var i = array.length;

        if (i === 0) {
            return false;
        }
        while (--i) {
            var j = Math.floor(Math.random() * (i + 1)),
                tempi = array[i],
                tempj = array[j];

                array[i] = tempj;
                array[j] = tempi;
        }
    }

    shuffle(pieces);

    $.each(pieces, function (i) {
        pieces.eq(i).css(positions[i]);
    });

    pieces.appendTo(imgContainer);

    empty.top = 0;
    empty.left = 0;

    container.find("#ui").find("p").not("#time").remove();

});
```

Objective Complete - Mini Debriefing

jQuery's `remove()` method is used to remove the original image element from the page, which we already selected when we declared our variables at the start of the script. We use the same method to remove the first puzzle piece, which we should do *before* the pieces are shuffled to avoid removing a key piece, such as a face. As with the image used in this example, an image where the main item of interest is not in the top-left corner is beneficial.

As we've removed the first piece from the board, we should also remove the first item in the `positions` array. We'll use this array when we come to check whether the puzzle has been unscrambled and as there won't be a piece at the first position, we don't need to store its position. We use JavaScript's `unshift()` method to do this, which simply removes the first item in the array it is called on.

Adding an event handler to the button using on()

We added a click event handler for the button by selecting it and calling the jQuery `on()` method. The `on()` method takes two arguments in this example (although it can take three when event delegation is required).

The first argument is the event to listen for and the second is the handler function to be executed each time the event is detected. We are listening for the `click` event in this case.

The all-encompassing on() method

jQuery's `on()` method, introduced in version 1.7, replaces the `bind()`, `live()`, and `delegate()` methods, which are now deprecated. Using `on()` is now the recommended way of attaching event handlers in jQuery.

Within the handler function we first define a variable which stores the children of the `<figure>` element. Although we need to select the pieces from the page again, we can still use our cached `imgContainer` variable to avoid creating a new jQuery object.

Shuffling the pieces

Next we define a function called `shuffle()`, which accepts the array to shuffle as an argument. This function performs a **Fisher-Yates** shuffle, which is an established pattern for creating a random ordering of a given set of values.

Within the function, we first get the length of the array that was passed in, and return `false` (exiting the function) if the array is empty. We then use a `while` loop to cycle through the array. A `while` loop in JavaScript is similar to a `for` loop but executes while the condition specified in brackets has a truthy value (or while it evaluates to true), instead of executing a specified number of times. A pre-decrementing loop condition is used to avoid an unnecessary iteration of the loop once the items have all been shuffled.

In JavaScript, as well as the `true` or `false` Boolean values, other types of variables can be said to be `truthy` or `falsey`. The following values are all considered falsey:

- The Boolean value `false`
- The number 0
- An empty string
- `null`
- `undefined`
- NaN

All other values are considered truthy. This is so that non-Boolean values can be used as conditionals. The similarities between the terms falsey and false may lead to confusion; just remember that false is an actual value, and falsey is an aspect of a value, which values other than false also have.

For more information on this subject, see `http://james.padolsey.com/javascript/truthy-falsey/`.

Within the loop, which will be executed once for each item in the array except the first item, we want to pick a random item from the array and swap its position in the array with another item. To generate a random number to use as the index of the item to swap, we first generate a random number using JavaScript's `Math.random()` function and multiply the random number (which will be between 0 and 1) by the length of the array plus 1. This will give us a random number, between 0 and the length of the array.

We then pull the item with the current index out of the array, along with the item at the randomly generated index, and swap them. It may seem complex but this is almost universally regarded as the most efficient way to randomly shuffle the items in the array. It gives us the most random result for the least amount of processing.

Once we have defined the function, we then invoke it, passing in the `pieces` array as the array to shuffle.

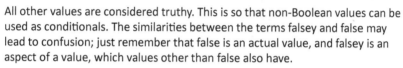

For more information on the JavaScript implementation of the Fisher-Yates shuffle, see `http://sedition.com/perl/javascript-fy.html`.

Positioning the pieces

Once the array of elements has been shuffled, we iterate it using jQuery's `each()` method. This method is passed the array to iterate over, which in this case is the `pieces` array we have just shuffled. The second argument is an iterator function that will be called for each item in the array.

Within this function we use our `positions` array to put the shuffled elements in the right place on the page. If we didn't do this, the elements would be shuffled, but would still appear in the same place on the page because of their `absolute` positioning. We can use the `positions` array that we updated when creating the new elements to get the correct `top` and `left` positions for each of the shuffled elements.

Once the collection of elements have been iterated and their positions set, we then append them back to the page using jQuery's `appendTo()` method. Again we can specify our `imgContainer` variable as the argument to `appendTo()` in order to avoid selecting the container from the page once more.

Positioning the empty space

Lastly we should make sure that the empty space is definitely at `0` top and `0` left, that is the top-left square of the board. If the button is clicked, some pieces are moved and then the button is clicked again, we have to ensure that the empty space is in the right place. We do this by setting both the `top` and `left` properties of the `empty` object to `0`.

We can also remove any previous messages that may be displayed in the UI area (we'll cover adding these messages towards the end of this project). We don't want to remove the timer though, so we filter this element out of the selection using jQuery's `not()` method, which accepts a selector for which matching elements are discarded and therefore not removed from the page.

At this point we should be able to run the page in a browser and shuffle the pieces by clicking on the **Start!** button:

Making the puzzle pieces draggable

Now it's time to kickstart jQuery UI to make the individual pieces of the puzzle draggable.

jQuery UI is a suite of jQuery plugins used to build interactive and efficient user interfaces. It is stable, mature, and is recognized as the official, although not the only UI library for jQuery.

Prepare for Lift Off

In this task we'll cover the following steps:

▶ Making the puzzle pieces draggable using jQuery UI's Draggable component

▶ Configuring the draggables so that only pieces directly next to the empty space can be moved

▶ Configuring the draggables so that pieces can only be moved into the empty space

Engage Thrusters

First we'll make the pieces draggable and set some of the configuration options that the component exposes. This code should be added to `sliding-puzzle.js`, directly after the code added in the previous task:

```
pieces.draggable({
    containment: "parent",
    grid: [pieceW, pieceH],
    start: function (e, ui) {

    },
    drag: function (e, ui) {

    },
    stop: function (e, ui) {

    }
});
```

The next few steps in this task will see additional code added to the `start`, `drag`, and `stop` callback functions in the previous code sample.

We also need to configure the draggability so that the pieces can only be moved into the empty space, and not over each other, and so that only pieces directly adjacent to the empty space can be moved at all.

Next add the following code in to the `start` callback function that we just added:

```
var current = getPosition(ui.helper);

if (current.left === empty.left) {
    ui.helper.draggable("option", "axis", "y");
} else if (current.top === empty.top) {
    ui.helper.draggable("option", "axis", "x");
} else {
    ui.helper.trigger("mouseup");
    return false;
}

if (current.bottom < empty.top ||
    current.top > empty.bottom ||
    current.left > empty.right ||
    current.right < empty.left) {
        ui.helper.trigger("mouseup");
        return false;
    }

    previous.top = current.top;
    previous.left = current.left;
```

Next, add the following code to the `drag` callback function:

```
var current = getPosition(ui.helper);

ui.helper.draggable("option", "revert", false);

if (current.top === empty.top && current.left === empty.left) {
    ui.helper.trigger("mouseup");
    return false;
}

if (current.top > empty.bottom ||
    current.bottom < empty.top ||
    current.left > empty.right ||
    current.right < empty.left) {
        ui.helper.trigger("mouseup")
                .css({
                    top: previous.top,
                    left: previous.left
                });
        return false;
}
```

Finally, we should add the following code to the `stop` callback function:

```
var current = getPosition(ui.helper);

if (current.top === empty.top && current.left === empty.left) {

    empty.top = previous.top;
    empty.left = previous.left;
    empty.bottom = previous.top + pieceH;
    empty.right = previous.left + pieceW;
}
```

In each of our callbacks we've used a helper function that returns the exact position of the current draggable. We should also add this function after the `draggable()` method:

```
function getPosition(el) {
    return {
        top: parseInt(el.css("top")),
        bottom: parseInt(el.css("top")) + pieceH,
        left: parseInt(el.css("left")),
        right: parseInt(el.css("left")) + pieceW
    }
}
```

Objective Complete - Mini Debriefing

We wrote a lot of code in that last task, so let's break it down and see what we did. We started by making the pieces draggable using the jQuery UI draggable component. We did this by calling the `draggable()` method, passing in an object literal that sets various options that the draggable component exposes.

First we set the `containment` option to `parent`, which stops any of the pieces being dragged out of the `<figure>` element that they are within. We also set the `grid` option, which allows us to specify a grid of points that the piece being dragged should snap to. We set an array as the value of this option.

The first item in this array sets the horizontal points on the grid and the second item sets the vertical points on the grid. Setting these options gives the movement of the pieces a more realistic and tactile experience.

The next and final three options that we set are actually callback functions that are invoked at different points in the life-cycle of a drag. We use the `start`, `drag`, and `stop` callbacks.

When the drag begins

The start callback will be invoked once at the very start of the drag interaction following a mousedown event on a draggable. The stop callback will be invoked once at the very end of a drag interaction, once a mouseup event has registered. The drag callback will fire almost continuously while a piece is being dragged as it is invoked for every pixel the dragged element moves.

Let's look at the start callback first. Each callback is passed two arguments by jQuery UI when it is invoked. The first of these is the event object, which we don't require in this project, while the second is an object containing useful properties about the current draggable.

At the beginning of the function we first get the exact position of the piece that dragging has started on. When we call our getPosition() function, we pass in the helper property of the ui object, which is a jQuery-wrapped reference to the underlying DOM element that has started to be dragged.

Once we have the element's position, we first check whether the element is in the same row as the empty space by comparing the left property of the current object (the object returned by getPosition()) with the left property of the empty object.

If the two properties are equal, we set the axis option of the draggable to y so that it can only move horizontally. Configuration options can be set in any jQuery UI widget or component using the option method.

If it isn't in the same row, we check whether it is in the same column instead by comparing the top properties of the current and empty objects. If these two properties are equal, we instead set the axis option to x so that the piece may only move vertically.

If neither of these conditions is true, the piece cannot be adjacent to the empty space, so we manually trigger a mouseup event to stop the drag using jQuery's trigger() method, and also return false from the function so that our stop handler is not triggered.

We need to make sure that only squares in the same row or column as the empty space are draggable, but we also need to make sure that any pieces that are not directly adjacent to the empty space cannot be dragged either.

To stop any pieces not adjacent to the empty space being dragged, we just check that:

- The *bottom* of the current piece is *less* than the *top* of the empty space
- The *top* of the current piece is *greater* than the *bottom* of the empty space
- The *left* of the current piece is *greater* than the *right* of the empty space
- The *right* of the current piece is *less* than the *left* of the empty space

If any of these conditions are true, we again stop the drag by triggering a `mouseup` event manually, and stop any further event handlers on the draggable being called (but only for the current drag interaction) by returning `false`.

If the callback function has not returned at this point, we know we are dealing with a draggable that is adjacent to the empty space, thereby constituting a valid drag object. We therefore store its current position at the start of the drag for later use by setting the `top` and `left` properties of the `previous` object that we initialized at the start of the project.

The position of ui.helper

The `ui` object passed to our callback function actually contains an object called `position`, which can be used to obtain the current draggable's position. However, because we are using the `grid` option, the values contained in this object may not be granular enough for our needs.

During the drag

Next we can walk through the `drag` callback, which will be called every time the position of the current draggable changes. This will occur during a `mousedown` event.

First of all we need to know where the piece that's being dragged is, so we call our `getPosition()` helper function again.

Then we want to check whether the piece being dragged is in the empty space. If it is, we can stop the drag in the same way that we did before – by manually triggering a `mouseup` event and returning `false`.

During the drag, only valid pieces will be draggable because we've already filtered out any pieces that are not directly adjacent to the empty space. However, we still need to check that the piece being dragged is not being dragged away from the empty space. We do this in the same way that we filtered out pieces not adjacent to the empty space in the `start` callback.

When the drag ends

The `stop` callback is the simplest of the three callbacks. We get the position of the piece that was dragged, and if it's definitely in the empty space, we move the empty space so that it is in the position the dragged piece was in when the drag began. Remember we stored this information in an object called `previous`.

Starting and stopping the timer

At this point, our game is fully functional and the puzzle can be unscrambled; however to make it more fun we should introduce an element of competitiveness by incorporating a timer.

Prepare for Lift Off

In this task we'll need to complete the following steps:

▸ Check the timer isn't already running when the **Start** button is clicked

▸ Start the timer from 0

▸ Increment the timer every second

▸ Update the display on the page so that the player can see how long the current game has taken so far

Engage Thrusters

To check whether the timer is already running when the **Start** button is clicked we should add the following code directly after where we appended the shuffled pieces to the page, and directly before the call to `draggable()`:

```
pieces.appendTo(imgContainer).draggable("destroy");

if (timer) {
    clearInterval(timer);
    timerDisplay.text("00:00:00");
}

timer = setInterval(updateTime, 1000);
currentTime.seconds = 0;
currentTime.minutes = 0;
currentTime.hours = 0;

pieces.draggable({
```

Next we can add the function that increments the timer and updates the display. This code should come directly after where we update `currentTime.hours` in the previous code:

```
function updateTime() {

    if (currentTime.hours === 23 && currentTime.minutes === 59 &&
currentTime.seconds === 59) {
```

```
        clearInterval(timer);
    } else if (currentTime.minutes === 59 && currentTime.seconds ===
59) {

        currentTime.hours++;
        currentTime.minutes = 0;
        currentTime.seconds = 0;
    } else if (currentTime.seconds === 59) {
        currentTime.minutes++;
        currentTime.seconds = 0;
    } else {
        currentTime.seconds++;
    }

    newHours = (currentTime.hours <= 9) ? "0" + currentTime.hours :

    currentTime.hours;
    newMins = (currentTime.minutes <= 9) ? "0" + currentTime.minutes :

    currentTime.minutes;
    newSecs = (currentTime.seconds <= 9) ? "0" + currentTime.seconds :

    currentTime.seconds;

    timerDisplay.text([
        newHours, ":", newMins, ":", newSecs
    ].join(""));


}
```

Objective Complete - Mini Debriefing

The first thing we have to do in this task is check whether a timer is already running. The timer will be stored in one of our "global" variables so we can check it easily. We use an `if` statement to check whether `timer` contains a truthy value (see the previous information on JavaScript's truthy and falsey values).

If it does, we know the timer is already running, so we cancel the timer using JavaScript's `clearInterval()` function, passing in our `timer` variable as the timer to clear. We can also reset the timer display if the timer is already running. We selected the timer display element from the page and cached it when we initially declared our variables at the start of this project.

Next we start the timer using JavaScript's `setInterval()` method and assign it to our `timer` variable. When the timer begins this variable will contain the ID of the timer, not the value of the timer, which is how `clearInterval()` knows which timer to clear.

The `setInterval()` function accepts a function to execute after the specified interval as the first argument, and the interval as the second argument. We specify `1000` milliseconds as the interval, which is equal to 1 second, so the function passed as the first argument will be called every second until the timer is cleared.

Once the timer has started we can also reset the values stored in the object we'll use to keep track of the timer – the `currentTime` object. We set the `seconds`, `minutes`, and `hours` properties of this object to `0`. We need an object to keep track of the time because the `timer` variable itself just contains the ID of the timer.

Next we added the `updateTime()` function that will be called by our interval every second. All we do in this function is update the relevant properties of the `currentTime` object, and update the display. We use an `if` conditional to check which parts of the timer to update.

We first check that the timer has not reached 24 hours. I would hope that no one would actually spend that long playing the game, but if the browser is left open for some reason for this length of time, we don't want the time display to say, for example, 24 hours and 1 minute, because at that point, we really should update the display to say 1 day, 0 hours, and 1 minute. But we aren't bothering with days so instead we just stop the timer.

If the timer has not reached this length of time we then check whether the current minutes equal `59` and the current seconds equal `59`. If they do we need to increment `currentTime. hours` by `1` and reset the `currentTime.minutes` and `currentTime.seconds` properties back to `0`.

If this check fails we then check whether the seconds equal `59`. If they do, we increment the `currentTime.minutes` property and then reset `currentTime.seconds` back to `0`. If this second test also fails we know that all we have to do is increment `currentTime.seconds`.

Next we need to check whether we need to pad any of the time components with a leading `0`. We could use another `if else` conditional for this, but the JavaScript ternary construct is neater and more compact so we use this instead.

First we test whether `currentTime.hours` is equal to or less than `9` and if so we add `0` to the start of the value. We do the same for `currentTime.minutes` and `currentTime.seconds`.

Finally, we build the string which we will use to update the timer display. Instead of using boring and slow string concatenation, we again use an awesome array comprising the various parts of the display and then join the array.

The resulting string is set as the value of the `<span>` element contained in the `timerDisplay` variable and the element on the page is updated using jQuery's `text()` method.

At this point we can now click on the button to shuffle the puzzle pieces, and watch as the timer starts to increment.

Determining if the puzzle has been solved

In this task we'll focus on determining whether the pieces have been put back into their correct locations, unscrambling and therefore solving the puzzle.

Prepare for Lift Off

The following steps will be covered in this task:

▸ Checking the order of pieces to see if they match the starting order of the pieces

▸ Stopping the timer

▸ Displaying a congratulatory message

Engage Thrusters

First of all we need to decide when we should check whether the puzzle has been completed. A good place to do the check would be on the `stop` event of the drag.

First add the following new variable directly after the existing `current` variable at the top of the `stop()` callback:

```
var current = getPosition(ui.helper),
    correctPieces = 0;
```

Don't forget to add a trailing comma after the first variable, as shown in the previous code sample. Next add the following code directly after the `if` statement:

```
$.each(positions, function (i) {
    var currentPiece = $("#" + (i + 1)),
        currentPosition = getPosition(currentPiece);

    if (positions[i].top === currentPosition.top && positions[i].left
    === currentPosition.left) {

        correctPieces++;
    }
});

if (correctPieces === positions.length) {
    clearInterval(timer);
    $("<p/>", {
        text: "Congratulations, you solved the puzzle!"
    }).appendTo("#ui");
}
```

Objective Complete - Mini Debriefing

First of all we defined a new variable called `correctPieces` and set its value to `0`. We then used jQuery's `each()` method to iterate the `positions` array that we populated much earlier in the code, when we initially shuffled the pieces.

What we need to do at this point is get each piece from the puzzle and check whether the pieces are in the correct order. However, we can't just select the elements from the page using jQuery's `children()` method, for example, or `find()`, because jQuery does not return the elements in the order that they are found in the DOM, especially as we have already dragged them all around their parent container.

What we have to do instead is select each element by its `id` attribute, and check to see what `top` and `left` CSS properties it has in its `style` attribute. The length of the `positions` array is the same as the number of pieces so we can iterate this array and use the index argument that jQuery automatically passes to the iterator function.

Within the iterator we first select the current element. The `id` attributes for each piece will start at `1` instead of `0` because we already removed the first piece from the puzzle, so we add `1` to the index value when selecting each piece. We also get the position of the current element using our existing `getPosition()` function, passing in the element we just selected.

Next we compare the current piece's `top` and `left` properties with the equivalent item from the `positions` array, and if both the `top` and `left` properties match, we increment the `correctPieces` variable.

Once each piece from the page and each item in the positions array have been compared and the `each()` method has finished iterating, we then check whether the value of the `correctPieces` variable is equal to the length of the `positions` array. If it is, we know that each piece is in the correct place.

We can stop the timer at this point in the same way that we did before – using the `clearInterval()` function, and then create the congratulatory message and append it to the element with an `id` of `ui`.

Remembering best times and adding some final styling

The game is now pretty playable as it stands. We can shuffle the pieces, only allow them to be dragged according to the rules, and the game will detect when the puzzle has been solved. Using a simple timer we can tell the player how long it took for them to solve it, but then what? What is the player supposed to do, just remember his/her best score?

Of course, we now need a way to save the player's best time. It would also be handy if we could display an additional message if they beat their stored best time. We'll use the JavaScript localStorage API to store the best time.

We can also add a little extra styling to finish the appearance of the game and lay out the different elements a little better.

Prepare for Lift Off

The steps that we'll cover in this task are as follows:

- ▶ Checking whether a best time has been saved
- ▶ Checking whether the current best time is better than the saved best time
- ▶ Updating the saved best time when the current best time is better than it
- ▶ Displaying an additional message when the saved best time is beaten
- ▶ Tidying up the presentation of the game with CSS

Engage Thrusters

Everything we need to do in this task can be done in the `if` statement that is executed once the pieces are back in the correct order. Directly after where we displayed the congratulatory message in the last task add the following code:

```
var totalSeconds = (currentTime.hours * 60 * 60) +
(currentTime.minutes * 60) + currentTime.seconds;



if (localStorage.getItem("puzzleBestTime")) {

    var bestTime = localStorage.getItem("puzzleBestTime");

    if (totalSeconds < bestTime) {

        localStorage.setItem("puzzleBestTime", totalSeconds);

        $("<p/>", {
            text: "You got a new best time!"
        }).appendTo("#ui");
    }
} else {
    localStorage.setItem("puzzleBestTime", totalSeconds);

    $("<p/>", {
        text: "You got a new best time!"
    }).appendTo("#ui");
}
```

We already created the style sheet that we'll use for this – `sliding-puzzle.css`, so we just need to add the following selectors and style rules to this file:

```css
#puzzle {
    width:730px; padding:5px; margin:auto;
    border:1px solid #aaa; border-radius:5px;
    background-color:#eee;
}
#puzzle figure {
    width:510px; height:676px; border:1px solid #aaa;
    position:relative; float:left; background-color:#fff;
}
#ui { padding:10px 0 0 10px; float:left; }
#ui button { margin-bottom: 2em; }
#ui p { font-size:1.7em; }
#start { width:204px; height:50px; font-size:1.75em; }
```

Objective Complete - Mini Debriefing

First of all we convert the current time into seconds so that we have only a single value to work with and store. The seconds are calculated using the `hours`, `minutes`, and `seconds` properties of the `currentTime` object used to update the visible timer on the page.

The `hours` property is multiplied by 60 to convert to minutes, and then by 60 again to convert to seconds. The `minutes` property is multiplied by 60 a single time, then these two values are added to the seconds remaining in the `seconds` property to give the final total, which we store in the `totalSeconds` variable.

Next we check the localStorage to see if a key exists with the name `puzzleBestTime`. If it does, we store the value held in `localStorage` in the `bestTime` variable. If the value of our `totalSeconds` variable is less than the `bestTime` variable, we have a new high score, which we save in localStorage with the `puzzleBestTime` name in order to overwrite the old best time. We then display a second congratulatory message to say a new high score has been achieved.

If localStorage doesn't contain a key with this name, this must be the first time the game has been played in this browser, so we set the name of the key and store the value of the `currentTime` variable as the new best time, and again display the second congratulatory message.

There's nothing really crucial in the CSS that we added; it was just a little bit of light styling to tidy up the various elements we've used and present the game in a cleaner style.

Classified Intel

The localStorage API is one of the more stable JavaScript APIs that fall within the general umbrella term of HTML5, and enjoys wide support by all of the latest versions of all common browsers.

Old browsers, which we may still need to support, such as IE7 or Firefox 2, do not support localStorage. Luckily there are plenty of polyfills and workarounds that exist to add a basic level of support in these legacy browsers.

See `https://github.com/Modernizr/Modernizr/wiki/HTML5-Cross-Browser-Polyfills` for a wide range of polyfills and patches that add support for modern APIs to legacy browsers.

Mission Accomplished

We used a wide range of jQuery and plain-vanilla JavaScript over the course of this project to create this simple game. We also looked at using jQuery UI's draggable component as well as the localStorage API.

We covered a lot of code so let's briefly look back at what we did.

We first declared most of the variables that we used throughout the project right at the start of our `document.ready` function. It's useful to do this so that variables can be used throughout our code without making them global in scope. For performance reasons, it's also best to cache jQuery objects so that they can be manipulated frequently without having to keep selecting them from the page.

We then saw how we can easily split an image of a known aspect-ratio into a number of equally-sized pieces laid out in a grid using nothing but some nested `for` loops and some simple mathematics. We also saw that using an array of substrings to create a string instead of using string concatenation is a very easy optimization that can help speed up our applications when long strings need to be constructed.

We then saw how to shuffle the individual pieces into a random order using an accepted algorithm for randomizing – the Fisher-Yates shuffle. We didn't actually use jQuery at all to do this, but don't forget that the code to produce the shuffle was executed inside an event handler added using jQuery's `on()` method.

Next we looked at how to make the pieces of the puzzle draggable using jQuery UI. We looked at some of the configurable options exposed by the component, as well as how to react to different events generated when the pieces were dragged. Specifically, we used the `start`, `drag`, and `stop` callbacks to enforce the rules of the game concerning which pieces could be moved, and how they could be moved during game play.

After this we looked at using a standard JavaScript timer to keep track of how long it took to solve the puzzle, and how to keep the visible timer on the page updated so that the player could see the time that has elapsed since they started.

Detecting when the puzzle was solved was also a crucial ability of the code. Our main obstacle here was the fact that the pieces weren't selected from the page in the visible order we could see on the screen, but this was easily overcome by selecting the pieces using their numbered `id` attributes and then manually checking their CSS position.

Lastly we looked at how to keep a record of the player's best time in solving the puzzle. localStorage is the obvious choice here, and it was a small step to check whether a score was already stored, and then compare the current time with the stored time to see if the record had been beaten.

You Ready To Go Gung HO? A Hotshot Challenge

There is still much more functionality we could add to our simple game. Why not update the game so that it has different skill levels available for the player to choose from?

All we'd need to do to achieve this would be to provide some kind of interface to allow the visitor to select the skill level, and then think of a way in which the game could be made more difficult.

If we assume that the game in its current format is the easiest skill level, one very simple way to make it harder is to increase the number of pieces that the original image is split into. Have a go at doing this yourself. Those of you with a deep understanding of mathematics may realize that our game has another flaw – some random combinations of the pieces will simply not be solvable. Storing or computing all of the possible combinations that are solvable is probably beyond practical, but there is another option.

Instead of randomly shuffling the array of pieces and then writing their positions to the board, we could instead shuffle the pieces by programmatically moving them around the board. A puzzle shuffled according to the rules of the game by which the player is bound would result in a solvable puzzle every time.

Project 2

A Fixed Position Sidebar with Animated Scrolling

The `position:fixed` CSS style adds an interesting effect that allows a targeted element to retain its position on the screen even when the page it is on is scrolled. However, its effectiveness is limited by the fact that no matter how deep the element is nested within other elements, it is always fixed relative to the document as a whole.

Mission Briefing

In this project we'll create a sidebar that emulates the `position:fixed` CSS style but doesn't suffer from the same limitations as a pure CSS solution. We can also add an attractive animation to the page so that when navigation items in the sidebar are clicked, different parts of the page are scrolled into view.

The following is a screenshot that shows the final result of this project:

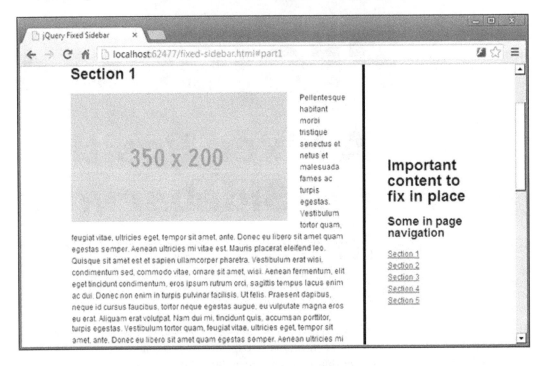

Why Is It Awesome?

Being able to fix an element in place on the page is an incredibly popular UI design pattern used by many large and popular websites.

Keeping the visitor's main tools or calls-to-action within reach at all times improves the user experience of the site and can help keep your visitors happy. Making things convenient is important, so if a visitor has to scroll down a long page, then scroll all the way up just to click something, they will soon lose interest in the page.

This same principle is also an emerging trend on mobile devices. Actual `position:fixed` styling has pretty poor support on mobile devices in general, but the idea of keeping important tools in hand, so to speak, without requiring excessive scrolling or a change of screen is being picked up and implemented in some of today's most well-known apps.

Your Hotshot Objectives

To complete this project we will need to work through the following tasks:

- ▸ Building a suitable demo page
- ▸ Storing the initial position of the fixed element
- ▸ Detecting when the page has scrolled
- ▸ Handling browser window resizes
- ▸ Automating scrolling
- ▸ Restoring the browser's back button
- ▸ Handling the hash fragment on page load

Building a suitable demo page

In this task we'll prepare the demo page and the other files we'll need ready for the script.

To make the benefits of this technique obvious, we'll need to use a number of extra elements that strictly speaking aren't part of the required elements for the sidebar that we'll be fixing in place.

The sidebar that we'll use as the focus of this example will need to sit within the structure of a complete page, and to see the fixed position effect, the page will also need to be quite long.

We'll be using a range of HTML5 elements when building our demo page and you should be aware that these are not supported in older versions of some browsers. If you find that you do need to support legacy browsers, you'll need to use the `html5shiv` script available at Google Code (`http://code.google.com/p/html5shiv/`).

Prepare for Lift Off

We should first save a new copy of the template file to the root folder of our project and call the new file `fixed-sidebar.html`. We can also create a new style sheet called `fixed-sidebar.css`, which we can save in the `css` folder, and a new JavaScript file called `fixed-sidebar.js`, which should be saved to the `js` folder.

We can link to the new style sheet in the `<head>` part of the HTML page using the following new `<link>` element, which should be added directly after the link to `common.css`:

```
<link rel="stylesheet" href="css/fixed-sidebar.css" />
```

Remember that the `common.css` style sheet is used to provide useful things such as a reset, a simple typography framework, and some common layout styles in order to minimize the CSS each project requires.

We can link to the new JavaScript file using the following new `<script>` element, which should be directly after the jQuery `<script>` file in the `<body>` part of `fixed-sidebar.html`:

```
<script src="js/fixed-sidebar.js"></script>
```

The underlying page is now set up ready for us to add the elements that are required for this project.

Engage Thrusters

We'll use a basic layout for our page consisting of the following elements, which should be added to `fixed-sidebar.html`:

```
<header>
    <h1>jQuery fixed sidebar example page</h1>
</header>

<div class="wrapper">
    <article>
        <h1>Example content area</h1>
        <section id="part1">
        </section>
        <section id="part2">
        </section>
        <section id="part3">
        </section>
        <section id="part4">
        </section>
        <section id="part5">
        </section>
    </article>
    <aside>
        <h2>Important content to fix in place</h2>
        <nav>
            <h3>Some in page navigation</h3>
            <ul>
                <li><a href="#part1">Section 1</a></li>
                <li><a href="#part2">Section 2</a></li>
                <li><a href="#part3">Section 3</a></li>
                <li><a href="#part4">Section 4</a></li>
                <li><a href="#part5">Section 5</a></li>
            </ul>
        </nav>
    </aside>
</div>
```

These elements should be added to the `<body>` of the page, directly before the `<script>` element that links to jQuery.

We'll also need some basic CSS for our example page in order to create the layout that this example requires. In the `fixed-sidebar.css` style sheet that we created for this example, add the following styles:

```
header, .wrapper { width:80%; max-width:1140px; margin:auto; }
header {
    padding-bottom:2em; border-bottom:4px solid;
    margin-bottom:3em;
}
header h1 { margin-top:.75em; }
article {
    width:70%; padding-right:4%; border-right:4px solid;
    margin-right:5%; float:left;
}
aside { width:20%; float:left; }
```

As before, none of this code is actually required, we're using it just to lay out the demo page as we need to for the purposes of this example.

Objective Complete - Mini Debriefing

We've added a very simple layout to create our demo page. The HTML5 `<article>` is filled with five different HTML5 `<section>` elements, each with their own `id` attributes. We'll use these a little later in the project to allow animated navigation between them.

In the previous code sample each `<section>` element is empty. But if you're following along and writing the example code as you go, you should fill each of them with a variety of random elements in order to increase the length of the page.

None of the elements we're using in this example matter at all. The HTML5 `<aside>` is the element that we'll be fixing in place, but the fact that it's an `<aside>` element is not important – any element can be used with this technique.

Inside the `<aside>` element is an HTML5 `<nav>` element. As I mentioned, this will allow us to add another cool feature later on, but again, is not essential for the basic technique to be used. Any content can be used in the element that is to be fixed in place.

Notice also that in the CSS we don't use `position:fixed` anywhere at all. The reason for this is simple. An element that has a fixed position is positioned relative to the document as a whole, not to its parent container.

If no pixel coordinates are supplied, a fixed position element is rendered where the flow of elements on the page dictates depending on its DOM position (although it is still technically out of the normal flow of the page).

If we try to do this with our example layout, it ends up at the far-left of the outer `.wrapper` element, because the `float` specified on the `<article>` element also removes the `<article>` element from the normal document flow. This is not good.

If pixel coordinates are supplied, these are interpreted by the rendering engine to be relative to the window, just like absolutely positioned elements. In some situations it may be acceptable to specify pixel coordinates, but when using a liquid layout such as in this example, the required coordinates to set the `left` and `top` style properties of the `<aside>` element will vary depending on the resolution of the screen used to view the page, hence the conundrum we face and hence the reason to use jQuery to achieve it instead of simple CSS.

Classified Intel

To save time when creating example layouts, like the one used in this project, we can use services such as Placehold It (`http://placehold.it/`) for placeholder images of any dimensions, and HTML Ipsum (`http://html-ipsum.com`) for a range of common HTML elements pre-filled with Lorem Ipsum placeholder text.

Storing the initial position of the fixed element

Before we can fix the element in place, we'll need to know where that place is. In this task we'll obtain the current starting position of the `<aside>` element that we're going to be fixing in place.

Engage Thrusters

In `fixed-sidebar.js` we should start with the following code:

```
$(function() {

});
```

We can cache a couple of jQuery-selected elements at the top of our function, and to store the initial position of the fixed element, we can then add the following code within the function we just added:

```
var win = $(window),
    page = $("html,body"),
```

```
wrapper = page.find("div.wrapper"),
article = page.find("article"),
fixedEl = page.find("aside"),
sections = page.find("section"),
initialPos = fixedEl.offset(),
width = fixedEl.width(),
percentWidth = 100 * width / wrapper.width();
```

Objective Complete - Mini Debriefing

We've used the same outer wrapper for our code that we used in the first project. As I mentioned then, it's a very common way to execute code once the page has finished loading. We'll probably use it in every project throughout the book.

We then cache references to the elements that we're going to be referring to so that we don't have to keep selecting them from the DOM. We'll be querying these elements inside event handlers a little later so it's much better for performance to select them from the page once and then refer to the saved, or cached, version throughout our code, instead of repeatedly selecting elements from the page.

We store references to the window object as we'll be attaching several event handlers to it. We'll be scrolling the entire page a little later on and for full cross-browser compatibility we should select and store a reference to both the `<html>` and `<body>` elements, as different browsers use either the `<html>` or `<body>` element, so this covers all bases.

We'll need to select the element with the class name wrapper, the containing `<article>`, all of the different `<section>` elements, and of course the `<aside>` element, which we'll be working with frequently throughout the remaining code.

We also store the initial position of the fixed element so that we know the coordinates on the page to fix the element to. We use jQuery's `offset()` method, which returns an object containing top and left properties that show the current position relative to the document, exactly what we require.

Depending on the styles applied to the surrounding elements, the width of the element being fixed may change. To alleviate this we also store the initial width of the element using jQuery's `width()` method, which returns an integer expressing the width in pixels.

Lastly, we can also compute and store the width as a percentage. We'll need to know this later when we want to react to the browser window being resized. Working it out is easy by multiplying 100 by the width of the fixed element, then dividing this figure by the width of its container, which again we use jQuery's `width()` method to obtain. This also means that the width of the fixed sidebar can easily be changed in just the CSS file, and the script will continue to work.

Detecting when the page has scrolled

Our next task is to detect when the page has been scrolled and fix the element in place when that occurs. Detecting the scroll event is made easy for us by jQuery, as is setting the `position` to `fixed`, because there are simple jQuery methods we can call to do these exact things.

Engage Thrusters

Add the following code to the script file directly after the variables we initialized in the last task:

```
win.one("scroll", function () {
    fixedEl.css({
        width: width,
        position: "fixed",
        top: Math.round(initialPos.top),
        left: Math.round(initialPos.left)
    });
});
```

Objective Complete - Mini Debriefing

We can use jQuery's `one()` method to attach an event handler to the `window` object that we stored in a variable. The `one()` method will automatically unbind the event handler as soon as the event is detected for the first time, which is useful because we only need to set the element to `position:fixed` once. In this example we are looking for the `scroll` event.

When the event is detected, the anonymous function we pass as the second argument to `one()` will be executed. When this occurs we use jQuery's `css()` method to set some `style` properties. We set the `width` of the element to counter situations where the `width` of our target element increases because of `float` and/or `margin` on surrounding elements.

We set the `position` to `fixed` and also set the `top` and `left` style properties using the initial position of the element that we stored in the `initialPos` variable at the start of the project. We use JavaScript's `Math.round()` method in order to round the `top` and `left` pixel positions to whole numbers, which helps to avoid any cross-browser issues with subpixel rounding.

Handling browser window resizes

At the moment, our `<aside>` element will be fixed in place as soon as the page scrolls, which suits our needs while the browser remains the same size.

However, if the window is resized for some reason, the `<aside>` element will fall out of its fixed position and could be lost outside of the boundaries of the viewport. In this task, we'll fix that by adding an event handler that listens for the window's resize event.

Engage Thrusters

To maintain the fixed element's correct location relative to the rest of the page, we should add the following code directly after the `one()` method that we added in the last task:

```
win.on("resize", function () {
    if (fixedEl.css("position") === "fixed") {
        var wrapperPos = wrapper.offset().left,
            wrapperWidth = wrapper.width(),
            fixedWidth = (wrapperWidth / 100) * percentWidth;

        fixedEl.css({
            width: fixedWidth,
            left: wrapperPos + wrapperWidth - fixedWidth,
            top: article.offset().top
        });
    }
});
```

Objective Complete - Mini Debriefing

This time we use jQuery's `on()` method to attach our event handler. We pass two arguments to this method; the first is the event we are listening for, which in this task is the window's `resize` event, and the second is the function that we wish to execute when the event is detected.

We only want to reposition and resize the `<aside>` element if the page has already been scrolled and the element has had its `position` set to `fixed`, so before we do anything else we first check that this is the case.

If the element's `position` is set to `fixed`, we first determine the current `left` style property of the wrapper element using the `left` property of the object returned by jQuery's `offset()` method. We also get the wrapper element's `width` using jQuery's `width()` method.

Because our layout is liquid we also need to adjust the width of the fixed element. In the CSS we originally set the width to 20%, so we can ensure that it stays at 20 percent of its container by dividing the container's current width by 100 and then multiplying it by the percentWidth variable we stored in the first task.

We then use jQuery's css() method to set the width of the fixed element and it's top and left style properties to make sure that it stays in the correct location when the window is resized.

Automating scrolling

At this point, we should be able to click on any of the links in the navigation menu we added to the fixed element, and the page will jump to bring the corresponding section into view. The fixed element will still be fixed into place.

The jump to the section is quite jarring however, so in this task we'll scroll each section into place manually so that the jump to each section is not so sudden. We can also animate the scroll for maximum aesthetic effect.

Engage Thrusters

For this task we should add another event handler, this time for click events on the links in the navigation list, and then animate the page scroll to bring the selected <section> into view.

First, we can add a general function for scrolling the page which accepts some arguments and then performs the scroll animation using those arguments. We should define the function using the following code directly after the one() method that we added in the last task:

```
function scrollPage(href, scrollAmount, updateHash) {
    if (page.scrollTop() !== scrollAmount) {
        page.animate({
            scrollTop: scrollAmount
        }, 500, function () {
            if (updateHash) {
                document.location.hash = href;
            }
        });
    }
}
```

Next, we can add a handler for click events on the navigation in our fixed element. This should be added directly after the `scrollPage()` function that we just added:

```
page.on("click", "aside a", function (e) {
    e.preventDefault();

    var href = $(this).attr("href"),
        target = parseInt(href.split("#part")[1]),
        targetOffset = sections.eq(target - 1).offset().top;

    scrollPage(href, targetOffset, true);
});
```

Objective Complete - Mini Debriefing

First we defined the `scrollPage()` function which accepts three arguments. The first is `href`, the second is an integer that represents the figure that the `scrollTop` property of the page will need to be animated to, and the third is a Boolean that will tell the function whether or not to update the hash fragment in the location bar of the browser.

The first thing we do in this function is check whether the page actually needs to be scrolled. To ensure it does, we just check that the current scroll of the page, obtained using jQuery's `scrollTop()` method, is different from the amount that we wish to scroll to.

The jQuery `animate()` method also accepts three arguments. The first is an object where each key is a property to animate, and each value is the value to animate it to. In this case we want to animate the `scrollTop` property using the `scrollAmount` argument which is passed to our function.

The second argument to the `animate()` method is the duration that the animation should run for. It accepts an integer that represents the duration in milliseconds. We specify 500 so the animation will take half a second to complete.

The third argument is a callback function that we would like executed as soon as the animation ends. If the `updateHash` argument passed to our function is set to `true`, we can update the location bar of the browser to show the `id` of the desired `<section>` element.

We can do this by updating the `hash` property of the `document.location` object with the `href` argument passed to our `scrollPage()` function. This updates the location bar but because it is just a hash fragment, it doesn't cause the page to reload.

After adding the scrollPage() function, we then added a handler for click events on the navigation inside the fixed element. We use jQuery's on() method once again to attach this event, but this time we pass three arguments to the method, which enables event delegation. The handler is attached to the <body> of the page that we have already stored in a variable.

The first argument is the event that we want to bind the handler to, which in this case is the click event. The second argument is a selector; the on() method will filter all click events so that only those originating from elements that match the selector will invoke the bound handler function.

In this case we are only interested in clicks on the <a> elements in our fixed element – <aside>. The third argument is the function to bind as the handler, which is automatically passed the original event object by jQuery.

Within this function we first stop the browser navigating to the corresponding <section> element, using the preventDefault() method of the event object that is passed to our handler function.

Next, we set a variable that tells us which <section> the user would like to navigate to. Inside our event handler function the $(this) object is scoped to the link that was clicked, so we can easily get the required section id by getting the href attribute of the clicked link using jQuery's attr() method. We store this in a variable called href.

We need to know where on the page the required <section> element is, which we obtain by using JavaScript's split() method to split the string stored in the href variable that we just set.

If we specify #part as the string to split on, the split() method will return an array consisting of two items, where the second item is a string version of the section number that was clicked. By wrapping this statement in JavaScript's parseInt(), we end up with an integer. We store this integer in the target variable.

The last variable we set is the offset of the desired <section> element. To select the correct <section> element, we can use the sections array that we stored at the start of the project.

To pull the correct element from this array, we use jQuery's eq() method and pass it the value that we just saved in the target variable minus 1. We need to subtract 1 because arrays in JavaScript start at 0, but our <section> id attributes start at 1.

Once we have this information we can then call our scrollPage() function, passing in the values we have just computed to animate the page scroll in order to bring the desired <section> element into view.

Restoring the browser's back button

At this point, we can click any of the links in the `<aside>` element and the page will be smoothly scrolled to the desired location on the page. The address bar of the browser will also be updated.

However, if the user tries to go back to a previous `<section>` using the back button of his/her browser, nothing will happen. In this task we'll fix that so that the back button works as expected, and can even use smooth scrolling when the back button is used to go back to the previous `<section>`.

Engage Thrusters

We can enable the back button very easily by adding another event handler directly after the one for click events that we just added:

```
win.on("hashchange", function () {

    var href = document.location.hash,
        target = parseInt(href.split("#part")[1]),
        targetOffset = (!href) ? 0 : sections.eq(target - 1).offset().
        top;

    scrollPage(href, targetOffset, false);
});
```

Objective Complete - Mini Debriefing

We use jQuery's `on()` method to attach our event once again, and this time we don't need to make use of event delegation, so we revert to the two-argument form of the method.

This time we are listening for the `hashchange` event, which as before is passed as the first argument and occurs whenever the `hash` property of the `document.location` object is changed.

In our handler function, which is passed as the second argument, we set the variables for the different values that we need to pass to the `scrollPage()` function in order to perform the scroll. We don't need to prevent the default behavior of the browser this time, and the `href` variable is set using the `document.location.hash` property as it will be the back button that will trigger the event, not one of the links in the `<aside>`.

Actually, this handler will also be triggered when one of the links is clicked, because the links also update the hash, but the conditional check inside the `scrollPage()` function will prevent unnecessary calls to jQuery's `animate()` method.

The `target` variable is computed in exactly the same way as it was in the last event handler, but this time, the `targetOffset` variable needs to handle cases where there is no hash fragment in the address bar of the browser. To handle this, we use a JavaScript ternary construct that checks whether the `target` variable that we just defined has a falsey value, which would indicate an empty string. If it does, we want to just animate the scroll back to zero. If it doesn't, we determine the required scroll amount in the same way as we did before.

We should now be able to load the page, scroll to a part of the page by clicking on one of the links in the `<aside>` element, and then scroll back to the top of the page using the browser's back button.

Handling the hash fragment on page load

At the moment the functionality of the browser's back button has been restored, and the visitor can see the bookmarkable URL in the address bar.

If the page is requested with a hash fragment in it, the page will automatically jump to the specified `<section>` when the page loads. In this part we'll add some code that checks the hash property of the `document.location` object and if a hash is detected, it will scroll to the corresponding part of the page smoothly.

Engage Thrusters

To enable this, we should add the following code directly after where we define our starting variables near the top of the script file, and directly before where we listen for the scroll event:

```
if (document.location.hash) {

    var href = document.location.hash,
        target = parseInt(href.split("#part")[1]),
        targetOffset = sections.eq(target - 1).offset().top;

    page.scrollTop(0);
    document.location.hash = "";
    scrollPage(href, targetOffset, true);

}
```

Objective Complete - Mini Debriefing

In this bit of code, which will be executed as soon as the page has loaded, we first check whether the `document.location` object contains a `hash` (or at least, contains a `hash` that is not an empty string).

If it does, we obtain the `hash`, get the number of the `<section>`, and calculate the offset from the top of the page in the same way that we have done in previous tasks. We then set the `scrollTop` of the page to `0` to force the browser to the top of the page. We also remove the hash at this point.

Finally we can call our `scrollPage()` function, passing in the new `href` fragment, the amount of scroll required, and set the final argument to `true` so that the correct hash fragment is added back to the browser's location bar. It should all happen so quickly that the user does not notice that the page load has been intercepted and the behavior modified.

Mission Accomplished

In this project we looked at a very simple way of mimicking CSS's `position:fixed` styling to fix an important element into place. The technique to only apply the fixed positioning when the page starts to scroll is simple but effective, and is an excellent way to circumvent the shortcomings of actual `position:fixed` when working with complex or liquid layouts.

We saw how to handle window resizes and added a smooth scrolling facility that scrolled the page between different named sections of the page.

We also looked at how we can read and write to the `document.location.hash` property of the `window` object, and how to manually scroll to the requested section when the page is loaded. We also fixed the browser's back button to work with our smooth-scrolling animations.

You Ready To Go Gung HO?
A Hotshot Challenge

Very often, with the kind of in-page navigation we've used in this project, it is useful to show an on-state on the navigation links when a section is scrolled to, either manually, or by clicking on one of the links. Have a go at adding this simple but effective addition to the code that we've looked at over the course of this project.

Project 3

An Interactive Google Map

In this project we'll create a highly interactive Google map that works with the latest version of Google's API to produce a map with custom overlays and markers, geocoded addresses, and computed distances. We'll also look at how to keep our simple UI in sync with the locations added to the map using a combination of Google and jQuery event handlers.

Mission Briefing

For the purposes of this project, we'll have a scenario where we need to build a map-based application for a company that takes things from one place to another. They want a page that their customers can visit to calculate the cost of, and maybe order, the transport of something from one place to another by clicking on different areas of a localized map.

We'll see how to listen for clicks on the map so that markers can be added and the precise locations of each marker can be recorded. We can then update the UI to show the actual street addresses of the locations that were clicked and allow the visitor to generate a quote based on the computed distance between the two addresses.

Why Is It Awesome?

Google Maps is a fantastic API to build on. Already highly interactive and packed with features, we can build robust and highly functional applications on top of the solid foundation it provides. Google provides the mapping data and interactivity with the map, while jQuery is used to build the UI – a winning combination.

The page that we'll end up with will resemble the following screenshot:

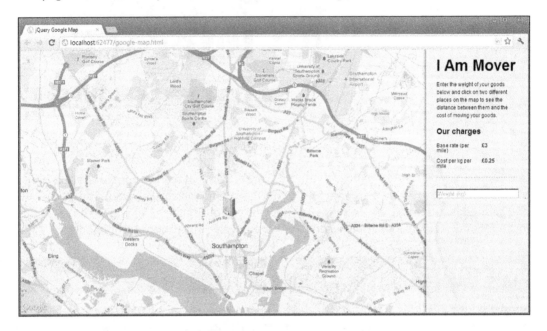

Your Hotshot Objectives

This project will be broken down into the following tasks:

- ▶ Creating the page and interface
- ▶ Initializing the map
- ▶ Showing the company HQ with a custom overlay
- ▶ Capturing clicks on the map
- ▶ Updating the UI with the start and end locations
- ▶ Handling marker repositions
- ▶ Factoring in weights
- ▶ Displaying the projected distance and cost

Mission Checklist

We'll need to link to a script file provided by Google in order to initialize the map and load in the API. We can also create the new files that we'll be using in the project at this point.

Don't worry, we don't need an API key from Google or anything like that for this project to work, we can just use the script by linking directly to it.

 The Google Maps API is feature-rich and stable, and contains entry points for all of the best known mapping features, including Street View, geolocation, and the directions service. As well as the configuration options we used here, there are many, many others. For further information, see the documentation site at `http://developers.google.com/maps/`.

First we should save a new copy of the template file to our root project folder and call it `google-map.html`. Also create a `google-map.css` file and a `google-map.js` file and save them in the `css` and `js` folders respectively.

We can link to the style sheet for this example by adding the following `<link>` element to the `<head>` of the page, directly after the `<link>` element for `common.css`:

```
<link rel="stylesheet" href="css/google-map.css" />
```

 Don't forget, we're using `common.css` with each project so that we can focus on the styles we actually need for the project, without all of the boring reset, float-clears, and other common CSS styling required for most web pages.

We can link to Google's script file, as well as the JavaScript file we just created, using the following `<script>` elements, directly after the `<script>` element for jQuery:

```
<script src="http://maps.googleapis.com/maps/api/js?sensor=false">
</script>
<script src="js/google-map.js"></script>
```

We'll also be using a couple of images in this project, `hq.png` and `start.png`, which can both be found in the accompanying code download for this book. You should copy them into the `img` directory in your local `jquery-hotshots` project directory. Our page is now set up ready for the first task.

Creating the page and interface

In our first task we can add the different containers for the map, and the initial UI elements needed by the page. We can also add some basic styling to lay things out as we want.

Engage Thrusters

We should add the following elements to the `<body>` element in the `google-map.html` page that we just set up:

```
<div id="map"></div>
<div id="ui">
    <h1>I Am Mover</h1>
    <p>Enter the weight of your goods below and click on two
    different places on the map to see the distance between
    them and the cost of moving your goods.</p>
    <h3>Our charges</h3>
    <dl class="clearfix">
        <dt>Base rate (per mile)</dt>
        <dd>&pound;3</dd>
        <dt>Cost per kg per mile</dt>
        <dd>&pound;0.25</dd>
    </dl>
    <input id="weight" placeholder="Weight (kg)" />
</div>
```

For some basic styling and to lay out the page ready for when we initialize the map, we can add the following selectors and styles to the `google-map.css` file that we just created:

```
#map { width:100%; height:100%; }
#ui {
    width:16%; height:99.8%; padding:0 2%;
    border:1px solid #fff; position:absolute; top:0; right:0;
    z-index:1; box-shadow:-3px 0 6px rgba(0,0,0,.5);
    background-color:rgba(238,238,238,.9);
}
#ui h1 { margin-top:.5em; }
#ui input { width:100%; }
#ui dl {
    width:100%; padding-bottom:.75em;
    border-bottom:1px dashed #aaa; margin-bottom:2em;
}
#ui dt, #ui dd { margin-bottom:1em; float:left; }
#ui dt { width:50%; margin-right:1em; clear:both; }
#ui dd { font-weight:bold; }
```

Objective Complete - Mini Debriefing

In this task we're just getting started by adding the underlying HTML elements that we'll populate properly over the next few tasks. A slightly boring, but somewhat necessary, first step in getting the example page up and running, and the project under way.

The first element we added is the container that the Google Maps API will render the map tiles into. We give it an `id` of `map` so that it can be efficiently selected, but it is completely empty to start with.

The next element is the container for the various UI elements the example requires. It too has an `id` of `ui` for easy selecting from our script, as well as for adding the CSS styling with.

Styling with IDs

Avoiding the use of ID selectors to add CSS styling is well on its way to becoming a general best practice, with tools such as **CSSLint** advising against its use.

While the arguments for doing this and sticking to classes, element, or attribute selectors are compelling, we'll be working with them in some of the projects throughout this book for simplicity.

CSSLint is an open source CSS code quality tool that performs static analysis of source code and flag patterns that might be errors or otherwise cause problems for the developer. See `http://csslint.net/` for more information.

Within the interface container we have the name of the fictional company, some basic instructions for using the page, a list of the different charges, and an `<input>` element to allow weights to be entered.

Most of the CSS that we added in this task was purely decorative and specific to this example. It could easily be wildly different if a different look and feel was required. We've made the map container take up the full width and height of the page, and styled the interface so that it appears to float over the right-hand side of the page.

Initializing the map

Getting a zoomable and panable interactive Google map up and running takes a ludicrously small amount of code. In this task we'll add that code, as well as set up some of the variables that we'll use later in the script.

Prepare for Lift Off

In this task we'll initialize the variables needed to configure the map and make a call to the Google Maps API. We should start by adding the standard jQuery wrapper to the empty `google-map.js` file that we created earlier:

```
$(function () {
    //all other code in here...
});
```

Remember, the `$(function () { ... });` construct is a shortcut for jQuery's `document.ready` event handler.

Engage Thrusters

Within the wrapper we just added, we should add the following code:

```
var api = google.maps,
    mapCenter = new api.LatLng(50.91710, -1.40419),
    mapOptions = {
        zoom: 13,
        center: mapCenter,
        mapTypeId: api.MapTypeId.ROADMAP,
        disableDefaultUI: true
    },
    map = new api.Map(document.getElementById("map"), mapOptions),
    ui = $("#ui"),
    clicks = 0,
    positions = [];
```

Objective Complete - Mini Debriefing

In this task we start by creating some variables that we'll need to initialize the map. We'll be addressing the `google.maps` namespace throughout our code so the first variable we set is the contents of the top two namespaces for convenience.

Having a locally scoped copy that reaches right into the actual API that we want to use will make our code marginally more efficient because it is easier for our code to resolve a single variable. It's also much quicker to type in the first place.

All properties and methods used by the Google Maps API are namespaced. They all sit within the `maps` namespace, which itself sits in the `google` namespace. Google has such a large code-base for use in so many different applications that it makes sense to keep everything isolated and organized using namespaces.

For an excellent in-depth discussion on the intricacies of namespacing in JavaScript, see the excellent article on the subject by JavaScript supremo *Addy Osmani* (http://addyosmani.com/blog/essential-js-namespacing/).

Next we store the latitude and longitude that we'd like to center the map on. This is done using the Google Maps API's LatLng() method, which takes two arguments, the latitude and longitude values, and returns a LatLng object for use with other API methods. Notice how we call the LatLng constructor using our local api variable.

We can then create an object literal containing some of the configuration options that our map will need. These options include the zoom level, the location the map should be centered on, the type of map, and an option which disables the default map type and zoom/pan controls. We can use the LatLng object contained in mapCenter for the center configuration option.

Following this we create a new map instance using the map API's Map() constructor function. This function accepts two arguments: the first is the DOM element that the map should be rendered into and the second is the object literal containing the configuration options that we wish to set.

The first argument takes an actual DOM element, not a jQuery-wrapped DOM element. So although we could select the element from the page using jQuery and then extract the raw DOM element, it is more efficient to use JavaScript's native getElementById() function to retrieve the map container we added to the page in the previous task and pass it to the Map() constructor.

Next, we cache a jQuery selector for the UI container so that we can access it from the page repeatedly without having to actually select it from the DOM each time, and define a variable called clicks, which we'll use to record how many times the map has been clicked. We need to define it here in the top-level function scope so that we can reference it from within a click handler later in the code.

Lastly, we add an empty array literal in the variable positions, which we'll populate later on when we need to store the different areas of the map that have been clicked on. The array needs to be in the scope of the top-level function so that we can access it from within different event handlers later in the code.

Showing the company HQ with a custom overlay

In this task we'll put the company HQ on the map, literally, by adding a custom marker complete with an overlay that provides some basic information about the company, and perhaps an image of the premises.

Prepare for Lift Off

In this task we'll cover the following subtasks:

► Adding a marker to the map

► Adding a hidden element containing information about the company

► Adding a custom overlay to display the company information when the new marker is clicked

► Adding a click handler to show the overlay when the marker is clicked

Engage Thrusters

Adding a custom marker to the map can be achieved with the following simple code block, which should be added directly after the variables we added in the previous task:

```
var homeMarker = new api.Marker({
    position: mapCenter,
    map: map,
    icon: "img/hq.png"
});
```

To create an information overlay, or info window to use the correct Google terminology, for our new marker, we should first add an HTML element that contains the content we wish to display in the overlay. We can add the following new collection of elements to `google-map.html` directly after the UI container:

```
<div id="hqInfo">
    <img class="float-left" src="http://placehold.it/140x100"/>
    <h1>I Am Mover</h1>
    <p>This is where we are based.</p>
    <p>Call: 0123456789</p>
    <p>Email: info@i-am-mover.com</p>
</div>
```

We're using the `placehold.it` service again so that we don't have to worry about sourcing or creating an actual image for this bit of example content. It's a great service to use when mocking up prototypes quickly.

To tell the map about the new info window, we can use the following code, which should be added directly after the `homeMarker` code back in `google-map.js`:

```
var infoWindow = new api.InfoWindow({
    content: document.getElementById("hqInfo")
});
```

We also need some extra CSS to style the contents of the info window and to hide it until it is required. Add the following code to the bottom of `google-map.css`:

```
body > #hqInfo { display:none; }
#hqInfo { width:370px; }
#hqInfo h1 { margin-bottom:.25em; line-height:.9em; }
#hqInfo p { margin-bottom:.25em; }
```

Finally, we can add a simple click handler that displays the info window using the following code, which should be added after the `infoWindow` variable that we added a moment ago in `google-map.js`:

```
api.event.addListener(homeMarker, "click", function(){
    infoWindow.open(map, homeMarker);
});
```

Objective Complete - Mini Debriefing

First of all we defined a new marker, which is done using Google's `Marker()` constructor. This function takes a single argument, which is an object literal that defines different properties of the marker.

We set the `position` of the marker to be the center of the map for simplicity, although when defining other markers you'll see that any `LatLng` object can be used. We should also define the map that the marker belongs to, which we set to the `map` variable that contains our map instance. To specify the image to use as the marker, we can supply a relative path in string format to the `icon` option.

We then added a new container to the page which contains the information we want to display in our custom info window. The content here is not important; it's the technique that matters. We also added some additional styling for the contents of the info window.

In order to add the info window to our map instance, we used Google's `InfoWindow()` constructor. This method also takes a single argument, which again is an object literal which contains the options we wish to set. In this example we just set the `content` option to the element containing the content we just added to the page.

This should be an actual DOM element, hence we use JavaScript's `document.getElementById()` to get the element, instead of selecting it with jQuery.

Lastly we added an event handler to the map using Google's `addListener()` method. This method takes the element to attach the event handler to, which in this case is the marker we added, as the first argument, the event we wish to listen for as the second argument, and the callback function to handle the event as the third argument. The signature of this method is very similar to the event handling methods found in other common JavaScript libraries, although it is slightly different to how events handlers are added in jQuery.

Within the anonymous function we pass as the third argument to the `addListener()` method, all we do is call the `open()` method of our info window. The `open()` method takes two arguments; the first is the map that the info window belongs to, and the second is the location the info window is added to, which we set to our marker.

At this point we should be able to run the page in a browser, click on our custom marker, and have the contents of our hidden `<div>` displayed in the info window, as shown in the following screenshot:

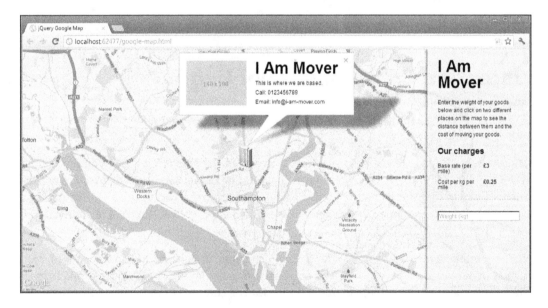

Capturing clicks on the map

In this task we need to add a click handler for our map so that visitors can set the start and end of their transportation journey.

Engage Thrusters

First of all we need to add the function that will be executed when the map is clicked. Directly after the listener that we added in the last task, add the following function expression:

```
var addMarker = function (e) {

    if (clicks <= 1) {

        positions.push(e.latLng);

        var marker = new api.Marker({
            map: map,
            position: e.latLng,
            flat: (clicks === 0) ? true : false,
            animation: api.Animation.DROP,
            title: (clicks === 0) ? "Start" : "End",
            icon: (clicks === 0) ? "img/start.png" : "",
            draggable: true,
            id: (clicks === 0) ? "Start" : "End"
        });

        api.event.trigger(map, "locationAdd", e);

    } else {
        api.event.removeListener(mapClick);
        return false;
    }
}
```

Then, to attach a listener for clicks on the map which fires this function, we can add the following code directly after it:

```
var mapClick = api.event.addListener(map, "click", addMarker);
```

Objective Complete - Mini Debriefing

First of all we added the function that will be executed every time the map is clicked. The function will automatically be passed the event object by the `addListener()` method, which will contain a `latLng` object for the coordinates on the map that were clicked.

The first thing we do in the function is store the `latLng` property of the event object in our `positions` array. We'll need to know both of the locations that were clicked so it is useful to add them both to the `positions` array, which is visible throughout our code.

Then we check whether the `clicks` variable that we defined earlier is less than or equal to 1. Provided it is, we go ahead and create a new marker using Google's `Marker()` constructor. We used the constructor earlier when we added a marker to show the company's headquarters, but this time we set some different properties.

We set the `map` property to be our map instance, and this time set the `position` of the marker to the `latLng` object contained in the event object, which will match the point on the map that was clicked.

We'll use a green marker image for the first click, which will represent the start of the journey. The image we'll use already has its own shadow, so when we add the first marker, which we can determine using a JavaScript ternary that checks whether `clicks` is equal to 0, we set the `flat` property to `true` to disable the shadow that Google will otherwise add.

We can easily add a nice drop animation so that when the map is clicked, the new marker drops into place. The animation features a bounce easing effect, which is also visually pleasing. The animation is set using the `animation` property, which is set to `DROP` using the `Animation` API.

We can also set a `title` for the marker, which is displayed when the cursor hovers over it, using the `title` property. Again we use a simple JavaScript ternary to set either the `Start` or `End` as the string depending on value of our `clicks` variable.

We use the `icon` property to specify the path to the image that we'll use for the start marker. When `clicks` is not equal to 0 we just specify an empty string, which causes the default red marker to be added.

We also set the `draggable` property to `true` to make the markers draggable. This will let users modify the start or end locations of the journey if they wish. We can add the code that will handle this a little later on.

Next we can use Google's `event` API to trigger a custom event. We use the `trigger()` method, specifying the `map` instance as the object that the event will originate from, `locationAdd` as the name of our custom event, and pass the event object that we've worked with in our `addMarker()` function (stored in `e`) as a parameter to any handlers that may be listening for our custom event. We add a handler for this event in the next section.

Lastly we can set a unique `id` attribute on the marker so that we can differentiate each marker. We'll need this when we want to update our UI following a marker drag, which we'll look at a little later on.

This is everything we want to do at this point while the `clicks` variable is still less than or equal to 1. The second branch of the outer conditional in our `addMarker()` function deals with situations when `clicks` is greater than 1.

In this case, we know the map has already been clicked twice, so when this occurs we want to stop listening for clicks on the map. We can unbind our handler using the `event` API's `removeListener()` method. This method simply takes a reference to the `eventListener` returned by the `addListener()` method.

When we bind the click event on the map to our `addMarker` function, we store what is returned in the `mapClick` variable, which is what is passed to the `removeListener()` method.

At this point we should be able to run the page in a browser and add new markers to the map by clicking at different locations.

Classified Intel

We used a **function expression** in this task, by assigning the event handler to a variable, instead of perhaps the more familiar **function declaration**. This is generally considered a good practice, and while not essential in this situation, it is certainly a good habit to get into. For a thorough understanding of why function expressions are generally better than function declarations, see *John Resig's* blog post at `http://ejohn.org/blog/javascript-as-a-first-language/`.

Updating the UI with the start and end locations

Once the two markers have been added to the map, we want to display their locations in the UI sidebar at the right of the page ready for when we compute the cost of the journey.

We'll want to show the full street address of each location that is clicked and also add a button that triggers the computation of a quote based on the locations that the visitor has chosen on the map.

Prepare for Lift Off

In the last task we used Google's `trigger()` method to trigger a custom event each time a new marker was added to the map following a click. In this task we'll add a handler for that custom event.

So far in this project, we've stuck almost entirely to Google's map API and haven't really used jQuery at all other than to add the initial `document.load` wrapper for the rest of code. In this part of the project we'll rectify that and fire up jQuery in order to update our UI.

Engage Thrusters

The handler for our custom `locationAdd` event should be as follows, which can be added directly after the `mapClick` variable from the last task:

```
api.event.addListener(map, "locationAdd", function (e) {

    var journeyEl = $("#journey"),
        outer = (journeyEl.length) ? journeyEl : $("<div>", {
            id: "journey"
        });

    new api.Geocoder().geocode({
        "latLng": e.latLng },
        function (results) {

            $("<h3 />", {
                text: (clicks === 0) ? "Start:" : "End:"
            }).appendTo(outer);
            $("<p />", {
                text: results[0].formatted_address,
                id: (clicks === 0) ? "StartPoint" : "EndPoint",
                "data-latLng": e.latLng
```

```
        }).appendTo(outer);

        if (!journeyEl.length) {
            outer.appendTo(ui);
        } else {
            $("<button />", {
                id: "getQuote",
                text: "Get quote"
            }).prop("disabled", true).appendTo(journeyEl);
        }

        clicks++;
    });
});
```

As we'll be adding some new elements to the page, we'll also need to update our style sheet for this project. Add the following new styles to the bottom of `google-map.css`:

```
#journey { margin-top:2em; }
#journey h3 { margin-bottom:.25em; }
```

Objective Complete - Mini Debriefing

We add the event handler for our custom `locationAdd` event in the same way that we added our click events, using Google's `addListener()` method.

Within the event handler we first define some variables. The first is a cached jQuery object that represents the element that displays the start and end points.

The next variable we set is then one of two things. If the jQuery object we set as the first variable has length, we know the journey element exists on the page, so we just store a reference to it. If it doesn't exist, we create a new element to use as the journey element and set its id to `journey`.

When the map is clicked for the first time, the journey element won't exist and will be created. The second time the map is clicked, the element will exist, so it will be selected from the page instead of being created.

Next we use the `geocode()` method of Google's `Geocoder()` API, which allows us to reverse-geocode a `latLng` object to get a street address. This method takes two arguments. The first is a configuration object, which we can use to specify the `latLng` object that we want to convert.

The second argument is a callback function that is executed once the geocoding is complete. This function is automatically passed a `results` object that contains the address.

Within this callback function we can use jQuery to create new elements to display the address and then append them to the journey element. The complete street address is found in the `formatted_address` property of the `results` object, which we can set as the text of one of the new elements. We can also set an `id` attribute on this element so that we can easily select it programmatically when required, and store the `latLng` object of the location using a custom `data-latLng` attribute.

The `results` object also contains a range of other useful properties about the address, so be sure to check it out in the object explorer of your favorite browser-based developer toolkit.

If the journey element doesn't exist we can then append it to the UI in order to display the address of the location. If it does exist, we know that it is the second click and can then create a new `<button>` that can be used to generate a quote based on the distance between the two locations.

We disable the `<button>` element using jQuery's `prop()` method to set the `disabled` property. We can enable the button later when a weight is added to the `<input>` in the UI.

Once we have added the new elements showing the journey start and end points in the UI, we can then increment the `clicks` variable so that we can keep track of how many markers have been added.

Now when we run the page and click on the map twice to add both the markers, the address of the points that we clicked should be displayed in the UI area at the right of the page. We should also now see the red end marker and be limited to adding only two markers now that we're incrementing the `clicks` variable.

Handling marker repositions

We've made our map markers draggable, so we need to handle address changes following a marker drag. This task will show just how easily that can be done. This will take just two steps:

- ▸ Binding each marker to the `dragend` event
- ▸ Adding the handler function for the event

Engage Thrusters

First we need to bind each marker to the `dragend` event when the marker is created. To do this, we should add the following highlighted line of code to the `addMarker()` function, directly after the marker's constructor:

```
var marker = new api.Marker({
    map: map,
    position: e.latLng,
```

```
        flat: (clicks === 0) ? true : false,
        animation: api.Animation.DROP,
        title: (clicks === 0) ? "Start" : "End",
        icon: (clicks === 0) ? "img/start.png" : "",
        draggable: true,
        id: (clicks === 0) ? "start" : "end"
    });
```

```
    api.event.addListener(marker, "dragend", markerDrag);
```

Next we should add the `markerDrag()` function itself. This can go directly after the `locationAdd` handler that we added in the last task:

```
var markerDrag = function (e) {
    var elId = ["#", this.get("id"), "Point"].join("");

    new api.Geocoder().geocode({
        "latLng": e.latLng
    }, function (results) {
        $(elId).text(results[0].formatted_address);
    });
};
```

Objective Complete - Mini Debriefing

In this task we first updated the `addMarker()` function to bind each new marker to the `dragend` event, which will be fired once the marker stops being dragged. We specify the marker as the first argument to Google's `addListener()` method, which is the object to bind to the event. The name of the event, `dragend`, is specified as the second argument, and `markerDrag` as the name of the function that will handle the event.

Then we added `markerDrag()` as a function expression. Because it's an event handler it will automatically be passed to the event object, which once again contains the `latLng` that we need to pass to a `Geocoder()` to get the new address that the marker was dragged to.

Inside the handler we first set a new variable that will be used as the selector for the element in the UI we want to update. Instead of concatenating a string together, we use the `array.join()` technique for performance reasons. The first and last items in the array we join are simply text.

The second item will be a string containing either `start` or `end` depending on which marker was dragged. Inside our event handler this refers to the marker, so we can use it get the custom `id` property that we added to each marker when it was created, allowing us to update the right element in the UI.

Once we have constructed the selector we just get the street address using Google's `geocode()` method exactly as we did before, which will give us the new address of the marker after the drag.

Inside the callback function for `geocode()` we use the selector we just created to select the `<p>` element in the UI and update its text content to the newly geocoded address.

Now when we view the page, we should be able to add the markers to the map as before, then drag them around and see the new address in the UI area at the right of the page.

Factoring in weights

We now have two addresses – the start and end markers for the journey. All the visitor needs to do now is enter a weight and we'll be able to calculate and display the distance and cost.

Engage Thrusters

All we need to do in this task is add a handler for the `<input>` element in the UI area so that once a weight is entered the `<button>` becomes clickable. We can achieve this with the following code, which can be added directly after the `markerDrag()` function from the previous task:

```
$("#weight").on("keyup", function () {
    if (timeout) {
        clearTimeout(timeout);
    }

    var field = $(this),
        enableButton = function () {
            if (field.val()) {
                $("#getQuote").removeProp("disabled");
            } else {
                $("#getQuote").prop("disabled", true);
            }
        },
        timeout = setTimeout(enableButton, 250);
});
```

Objective Complete - Mini Debriefing

We can add the event handler for the user-generated `keyup` DOM event using jQuery's `on()` method. Using the `on()` method is now the standard way of attaching event handlers in jQuery. Old methods such as `live()` or `delegate()` have now been deprecated and should not be used.

Within the event handler we first check whether a timeout has been set, and if it has, we clear it.

We then cache a selector for the `<input>` element so that we can see it inside our `enableButton()` function. We add the `enableButton()` function, again as a function expression.

All this function does is check whether the `<input>` element has a value, and if it does, we set the `disabled` property to `false` using jQuery's `prop()` method. If it doesn't have a value, we just disable it once more by setting the `disabled` property to `true`. Lastly we set a timeout using the JavaScript `setTimeout()` function, passing it the `enableButton()` function as the first argument. We set `250`, or a quarter of a second, as the timeout length. The timeout is stored in the `timeout` variable, ready for us to check the next time the function is executed.

Classified Intel

The reason we use the timeout here is to rate-limit the number of times the `enableButton()` function is executed. The function will be invoked after every character is entered into the field.

A quarter of a second is a barely discernible delay, but if someone types a long number into the field quickly, it can drastically reduce the number of times the function runs. Within the function, we select an element from the page and create a jQuery object. That's not too intense and in this example we probably don't even need to worry about it. But using a timeout like this is a robust solution that can help out when doing more intense operations inside a frequently fired event handler.

We could have just used jQuery's `one()` method to attach an event handler that simply enables the `<button>` and then removes itself. However, this wouldn't allow us to disable the `<button>` once more if the figure entered into the field is removed.

Displaying the projected distance and cost

Our last task in this project is to get the distance between the two markers and calculate the cost of the journey. Once calculated, we should probably display the results to the visitor too.

Engage Thrusters

First we should attach a click event handler for our `<button>`. Add the following code directly after the handler for the `keyup` event that we added in the last task:

```
$("body").on("click", "#getQuote", function (e) {
    e.preventDefault();

    $(this).remove();
});
```

Next we can get the distance between the two points. Directly after the `remove()` method we just added (but still inside the click handler function), add the following code:

```
new api.DistanceMatrixService().getDistanceMatrix({
    origins: [$("#StartPoint").attr("data-latLng")],
    destinations: [$("#EndPoint").attr("data-latLng")],
    travelMode: google.maps.TravelMode.DRIVING,
    unitSystem: google.maps.UnitSystem.IMPERIAL
}, function (response) {

});
```

Now we just need to compute and display the cost, which we can do by adding the following code to the empty callback function we just added. First we can add the variables we'll need:

```
var list = $("<dl/>", {
        "class": "clearfix",
        id: "quote"
    }),
    format = function (number) {
        var rounded = Math.round(number * 100) / 100,
            fixed = rounded.toFixed(2);

        return fixed;
    },
    term = $("<dt/>"),
    desc = $("<dd/>"),
```

```
distance = response.rows[0].elements[0].distance,
weight = $("#weight").val(),
distanceString = distance.text + "les",
distanceNum = parseFloat(distance.text.split(" ")[0]),
distanceCost = format(distanceNum * 3),
weightCost = format(distanceNum * 0.25 * distanceNum),
totalCost = format(+distanceCost + +weightCost);
```

Next we can generate the HTML structure that we'll use to display the computed figures:

```
$("<h3>", {
    text: "Your quote",
    id: "quoteHeading"
}).appendTo(ui);

term.clone().html("Distance:").appendTo(list);
desc.clone().text(distanceString).appendTo(list);
term.clone().text("Distance cost:").appendTo(list);
desc.clone().text("£" + distanceCost).appendTo(list);
term.clone().text("Weight cost:")
            .appendTo(list);

desc.clone().text("£" + weightCost).appendTo(list);
term.clone().addClass("total").text("Total:").appendTo(list);
desc.clone().addClass("total")
            .text("£" + totalCost)
            .appendTo(list);

list.appendTo(ui);
```

Lastly, we should probably add some additional styling for the new elements that we just created and added to the page. At the bottom of `google-map.css`, add the following new styles:

```
#quoteHeading {
    padding-top:1em; border-top:1px dashed #aaa;
    margin-top:1em;
}
#quote dt { margin-right:0; }
#quote dd { width:50%; }
#quote .total {
    padding-top:.5em; border-top:1px dashed #aaa;
    margin-bottom:0; font-size:1.5em;
}
```

Objective Complete - Mini Debriefing

We started out by binding a click event handler to the body of the page using jQuery's on() method. This time we use the 3-argument form of the method where the first argument is still the name of the event, the second argument is a selector to filter the event by, and the third argument is the function to trigger when the event occurs.

Events in JavaScript bubble up through their containers and when the event hits the body, it will be filtered by the selector used as the second argument and the function will only be executed if it was dispatched by an element that matches the selector. In this example, only events dispatched by the <button> will trigger the function.

Using the on() method in this form gives us a means of employing powerful event delegation that allows us to bind events for elements which may or may not exist at the time of the binding.

Within the handler function, we first prevent the default behavior of the browser. There shouldn't be any default behavior because we don't have a <form> on the page so there is nothing for the <button> to submit. But if someone were to try and run this on an ASPX page, which usually does have a <form> enclosing most, if not all, of the elements on the page, it could behave in unexpected ways. Unless strictly necessary, preventDefault() should always be used.

We then remove the <button> from the page. Note that even though the event handler is bound to the <body>, the this object inside the handler function still points at the <button> element that triggered the event.

We then used another of Google's APIs – the DistanceMatrixService(), which allows us to compute the distance between two or more points on the map. Because we don't need to reference the object returned by the DistanceMatrixService() constructor, we can chain the getDistanceMatrix() method directly onto it.

This method takes two arguments with the first being a configuration object and the second a callback function to execute when the method returns. The callback function will automatically be passed an object containing the response.

We set several configuration options using the first argument. The origins and destinations options both take arrays where each item in each array is a latLng object. We can easily get the latLng objects for both of the markers using the custom data-latLng attribute that we set when we showed the addresses.

We also set the travelMode option to the distance it would be via road using the google. maps.TravelMode.DRIVING constant, and set the unitSystem option to google.maps. UnitSystem.IMPERIAL to give a distance in miles instead of kilometers, for no other reason than because I'm a Brit, and I'm used to using miles.

The callback function we supply is automatically passed a results object that contains, of course, the results returned by the distance matrix. The first half of the callback function is concerned with creating variables and computing values. The second part of the function deals with displaying the information that has been computed.

We first create a new `<dl>` element and give it a `class` that is required for use with our `common.css` style sheet, and an `id` attribute, mostly for decorative styling. Then we add a simple function expression that receives a number as an argument, rounds it, and then fixes it to two decimal places before returning it. We'll use this function to ensure that our financial figures are in the required format.

We also create a new `<dt>` element and a new `<dd>` element that we can clone as many times as required without having to repeatedly create new instances of jQuery, and then store the value entered into the weight text field using jQuery's `val()` method.

Next we extract the `distance` property from the object passed to the callback function. Its structure may look complex, as the object we are actually interested in for this example is buried within a multidimensional array, but as the method's name suggests, it is able to return a complex matrix of results for multiple origins and destinations.

Following this we concatenate a string that includes the `text` property of the `distance` object that we just stored and the full word `miles`. The distance matrix returns imperial results as `mi` instead of the full `miles`, so we add the string `les` to the end of the value.

We then get the numerical distance by splitting the string on the space between the number of miles and the letters `mi`. JavaScript's `split()` function will return an array of two items containing the part of the string up to, but not including, the split-character and the part after the split-character. We are only interested in the first item in this array, and also use JavaScript's `parseFloat()` function to ensure that this value is definitely a number and not a string.

Now we have enough information to actually work out the cost of the journey. We've specified the charge per mile to be £3 so we multiply the distance by 3 and pass the result to our `format()` function so that the number is in the correct format.

We can also work out the charge per kilogram per mile in a very similar way, first multiplying the weight by the cost per kilogram, then multiplying by the distance. Again we pass this figure into our `format()` function. Then we can work out the total cost by adding these two figures together. The figures that we've been working with somehow become strings. To fix this, we can still use our `format()` function, but we prefix each of the values we want to add with the + character, which will force them to be numbers and not strings.

Once we have created the figures we wish to display, we can then create the new elements that we need to use to display them, starting with a nice heading to help clarify the new set of information we're adding to the UI.

We can then create the clones of the `<dt>` and `<dd>` elements which hold each label and figure. Once these have been created, we append them to the `<dl>` element we created, before finally appending the new list as a whole to the UI, as shown in the following screenshot:

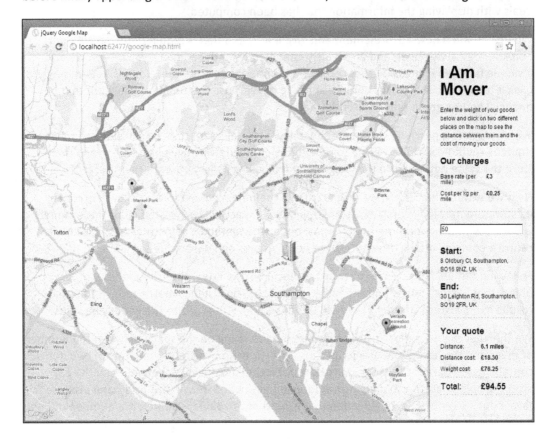

Classified Intel

The astute of you will notice that the number rounding solution we've used in this example isn't that robust, and won't round all fractions as precisely (or correctly) as would be required for a genuine system that deals with real currency.

JavaScript does not handle floating point arithmetic as gracefully as some other languages do, and so creating the perfect rounding system that rounds correctly 100 percent of the time is beyond the scope of this book.

For those who are interested, the stackoverflow site has some extremely illuminating answers posted to questions around currency formatting in JavaScript. For example, see: `http://stackoverflow.com/questions/149055/how-can-i-format-numbers-as-money-in-javascript`.

Mission Accomplished

We've covered a lot of both Google and jQuery functionality in this project. Specifically we looked at the following subjects:

- Adding markers and overlays to the map using the `Marker()` and `InfoWindow()` constructors.

- Reacting to map-driven events such as clicks on markers or marker drags. Event handlers are attached using the `addListener()` method of the `google.maps` API. We also saw how to fire custom events using the `trigger()` method.

- Using Google's services to manipulate the data generated by the map. The services we used were the `Geocoder()` to reverse-geocode the `latLng` of each point on the map that was clicked in order to obtain its address, and the `DistanceMatrixService()` to determine the distance between the points.

- Taking advantage of jQuery's event capabilities to add both standard and delegated events using the `on()` method to detect when different parts of our UI were interacted with, such as the `<button>` being clicked or the `<input>` being typed into.

- Using jQuery's powerful DOM manipulation methods to update the UI with addresses and the quote. We used a range of these methods including `clone()`, `html()`, `text()`, and `prop()`, as well both selecting and creating new elements.

You Ready To Go Gung HO?
A Hotshot Challenge

In this example, visitors are only able to generate a single quote. Once the `getQuote` `<button>` is clicked, the results are displayed and no further interaction is possible. Why don't you change it so that a reset button is added to the UI when the quote is generated? The visitor can then clear the quote and the markers from the map and start over from scratch.

Project 4

A jQuery Mobile Single-page App

jQuery mobile is an exciting project that brings the power of jQuery to the world of handheld and mobile experience. Like jQuery UI, it builds on and extends the jQuery core with a series of UI widgets and helpers. In this case these are optimized for mobile display and a touch interface.

We're also going to use JsRender, the official templating solution for jQuery and the successor to the jQuery template plugin `tmpl`.

Mission Briefing

In this project we'll build a simple application that looks for questions on stack overflow that have an un-awarded bounty on them. We'll call it Bounty Hunter. It will contain just a few individual pages, but will be made to feel like a native application rather than as a standard website.

Although sites and apps built with jQuery Mobile will work perfectly fine on a laptop or desktop, jQuery Mobile subscribes to the mobile-first philosophy of building the smallest layouts first.

This is the layout that we'll be focusing on throughout this project. If you don't have a smartphone or other capable mobile device, the example app we'll be building will still work in a normal desktop browser.

The app we'll be building in this project will look as shown in the following screenshot:

Why Is It Awesome?

jQuery Mobile offers full support and, importantly, consistency across all of the major modern smartphones and tablets. It also offers limited support to a much wider sphere of common, but perhaps older, and definitely less capable mobile devices. It builds on the solid foundation of jQuery itself and borrows a lot of best-practices from jQuery UI, certainly with regard to how widgets are initialized and configured.

jQuery Mobile offers two ways in which widgets can be initialized; we can use the extensive HTML5 `data-` attribute system, which will trigger the initialization of widgets automatically without any additional configuration, or we can create widgets dynamically and invoke them purely via script.

Both techniques have their advantages and disadvantages and we'll get to look at both techniques over the course of this project, so you'll be able to decide which way suits you best.

Your Hotshot Objectives

These are the tasks that this project will be broken down into:

- ▸ Building the welcome screen
- ▸ Adding a second page
- ▸ Creating the script wrapper
- ▸ Getting some bounties
- ▸ Adding a JsRender template
- ▸ Building the list view
- ▸ Building an item view
- ▸ Handling paging

Mission Checklist

The jQuery Mobile site provides a page template to use as a starting point when developing with the framework. We can use that template as the basis for this project. To get set up we should visit `http://jquerymobile.com/demos/1.2.0/docs/about/getting-started.html`.

Copy the template shown in the **Create a basic page template** section and save it as `bounty-hunter.html` in our main working directory. This template contains everything we need to get started.

We should also link to JsRender at this point; add the following code directly after the `<script>` element that links to jQuery Mobile in the template we just saved:

```
<script src="http://borismoore.github.com/jsrender/jsrender.js">
</script>
```

 At the time of writing, the current version of jQuery Mobile is not compatible with jQuery 1.9. The template that we'll get from the jQuery Mobile site will already link to a compatible version of jQuery, and 1.9 support will shortly be available once jQuery Mobile hits the 1.3 milestone.

In order to test our mobile app, we should also use a web server for this project so that the test page is viewed using a proper `http://` URL and not a `file:///` URL. You may already have an open source web server, such as Apache, installed on your computer, and if so that should be fine.

If you don't have a web server already installed and configured, I'd recommend downloading and installing Microsoft's **Visual Web Developer Express** (**VWDE**). This is a free version of Microsoft's industry-standard IDE Visual Studio, and as well as including a built-in development web server, it's also a very capable IDE with Intellisense support for JavaScript and jQuery and a range of features for frontend developers.

For developers who prefer open source software, the Apache web server, along with PHP and MySQL, can be installed on both Mac and Windows systems. To make installation and configuration easier, a range of packages have been created which install the software together and configure it automatically, such as XAMPP.

VWDE can be installed by visiting `http://www.microsoft.com/visualstudio/en-us/products/2010-editions/visual-web-developer-express`.

The XAMPP downloads are available at `http://www.apachefriends.org/en/xampp.html`.

Building the welcome page

Many apps have a welcome or home screen that the user can return to in order to select common actions. In our first task of this project, we'll build the welcome screen, which will consist of some simple page furniture such as a header, footer, a logo, and will also feature a search box and button that will trigger a call to Stack Exchange's API.

Prepare for Lift Off

At this point we can create the additional resources that we'll be using in the project. We should create a new style sheet called `bounty-hunter.css` in the `css` folder, and a new script file called `bounty-hunter.js` in the `js` folder.

We should add a `<link>` element to the `<head>` of the page for the style sheet. The following code should be added directly after the jQuery mobile style sheet (and before the jQuery mobile `<script>` elements):

```
<link rel="stylesheet" href="css/bounty-hunter.css" />
```

We can add the `<script>` element in the usual place right before the closing `</body>` tag:

```
<script src="js/bounty-hunter.js"></script>
```

Since jQuery Mobile provides its own baseline styling that includes a reset and typography defaults, we won't need to link to our `common.css` file in this example.

Engage Thrusters

The jQuery Mobile template that we downloaded contains the recommended basic structure that most jQuery Mobile pages should be built from. We'll use the recommended structure, but we'll be adding some extra attributes to the existing markup.

We should add an `id` attribute to the `<div>` element that has the `data-role="page"` attribute in `bounty-hunter.html`; set the `id` attribute to `welcome`:

```
<div data-role="page" id="welcome">
```

Next we should change the original markup so that it appears as follows. First we can add a header area:

```
<div data-role="header">
    <h1>Bounty Hunter</h1>
</div>
```

Next we can add the main content area directly after the header area:

```
<div data-role="content">
    <p>
        Enter tag(s) to search for bounties on.
        Separate tags with a semi-colon, or leave blank to get
        all bounties.
    </p>
    <div class="filter-form">
        <label for="tags" class="ui-hidden-accessible">
            Search by tag(s):
        </label>
        <input id="tags" placeholder="Tag(s)" />
        <button data-inline="true" data-icon="search">
            Search
        </button>
    </div>
</div>
<img src="img/boba.png" alt="Bounty Hunter" />
```

Lastly we can add a footer area after the main content area:

```
<div data-role="footer" data-position="fixed"
    data-id="footer">

    <small>&copy; 2012 Some Company Inc.</small>
    <a href="bounty-hunter-about.html" data-icon="info"
        data-role="button" data-transition="slide">About</a>

</div>
```

We can also add a few styles for our welcome screen. Add the following selectors and rules to `bounty-hunter.css`:

```
.filter-form .ui-btn { margin:10px 0 0 0; float:right; }

.ui-footer small { display:block; margin:10px; float:left; }
.ui-footer .ui-btn { margin:2px 10px 0 0; float:right; }
```

Objective Complete - Mini Debriefing

First we updated the text inside the `<h1>` element within the container `<div>` that has the `data-role="header"` attribute.

We then added some content to the content container, including a paragraph of introductory text and a container `<div>`. Inside the container we added the `<label>`, `<input>`, and `<button>` elements.

jQuery Mobile recommends using a `<label>` element with a valid `for` attribute for all `<input>` elements for accessibility reasons, so we add one, but then hide it using the `ui-hidden-accessible` class. This will allow assistive technologies to still see it, without it cluttering up the page visually.

The `<input>` is just a simple text field with an `id` attribute for easy selection from scripts and a `placeholder` attribute, which adds the specified text inside the `<input>` as placeholder text. This is nice to use to give a visual cue now that the label is hidden, but may not be supported in older browsers.

The `<button>` element has several custom jQuery Mobile `data-` attributes and will be enhanced automatically by the framework when the page initially loads. jQuery Mobile automatically enhances a range of different elements based on which element they are and any `data-` attributes they have. Enhancements usually include wrapping the original element in a container or adding other additional elements to sit alongside it.

The `data-inline="true"` attribute sets the container that is wrapped around the `<button>` to `inline-block` so that it doesn't span the full width of the viewport. The `data-icon="search"` attribute gives it a search icon.

We added some extra `data-` attributes to the container `<div>` element in the original template with the `data-role="footer"` attribute. The `data-position="fixed"` attribute works in conjunction with the `data-id="footer"` attribute to fix the element to the bottom of the viewport, and to ensure that is not transitioned when we change pages.

Inside the footer container, we added a `<small>` element with some fake copyright info, such as would usually be found in a web page's footer. We also added a new `<a>` element that links to another page, which we'll add in the next task.

This element is also given several custom `data-` attributes. The `data-icon="info"` attribute gives the enhanced element an icon. The `data-role="button"` attribute triggers enhancement by the framework and gives this simple link its button-like appearance. The `data-transition="slide"` attribute uses the slide transition when navigating to the new page.

Lastly we added some basic styling to the style sheet for this project. We floated the search button to the right and changed the margin given to it by jQuery Mobile. The style is added using the class we added to our container and a class added by the framework. We need to use both classes to ensure that our selector is more specific than the one used by the framework.

We also styled our footer elements to float them left and right and position them as desired. Again we have to beat the specificity of the selector used by the default jQuery Mobile theme.

At this point, we should be able to run the page in a browser and see the home page with the header and footer at the top and bottom respectively, the super-simple search form, and the big orange image that gives the application a basic identity.

Classified Intel

jQuery Mobile is built upon a custom `data-` attribute system in which we can give certain attributes to elements and have the framework initialize widgets based on them. This custom `data-` attribute framework isn't mandatory; we can manually initialize and configure widgets if we want.

But using the attributes is convenient and allows us to focus on the custom script code to add the behavior we want without worrying about the setup and initialization of the jQuery Mobile widgets we wish to use.

Adding a second page

In this task we'll add the page that the **About** hyperlink we added to the footer container of the welcome page links to. This allows us to experience jQuery Mobile transitions in action, configured purely via the `data-` attributes system.

 For more information, see the jQuery Mobile `data-attributes` reference at `http://jquerymobile.com/demos/1.2.0/docs/api/data-attributes.html`.

Prepare for Lift Off

Save a new copy of the jQuery Mobile page template that we used in the last task but this time call it `bounty-hunter-about.html` and save it in the main project directory (alongside the `bounty-hunter.html` page).

We also still need to link to our `bounty-hunter.css` file, our `bounty-hunter.js` file, and JsRender as we did before.

 For more information on JsRender, see the documentation at `https://github.com/BorisMoore/jsrender`.

Engage Thrusters

In our new `bounty-hunter-about.html` page, change the markup inside the `<div>` with a `data-role="page"` to the following:

```
<div data-role="header">
    <a href="bounty-hunter.html" data-icon="home"
    data-shadow="false" data-iconpos="notext"
    data-transition="slide" data-direction="reverse"
    title="Home"></a>

    <h1>About Bounty Hunter</h1>
</div>

<div data-role="content">
    <p>
        Bounty Hunter is an educational app built for the
        jQuery Hotshots book by Dan Wellman
    </p>
    <a href="http://www.danwellman.co.uk">
        danwellman.co.uk
    </a>
</div>

<div data-role="footer" data-position="fixed"
    data-id="footer">

    <small>&copy; 2013 Some Company Inc.</small>
    <a class="ui-disabled" href="#" data-icon="info"
        data-role="button">About</a>

</div>
```

Objective Complete - Mini Debriefing

This time, along with setting some different text in the `<h1>` inside the header container, we also added a new link. This links back to the welcome screen of the app and uses several custom `data-` attributes.

The `data-icon`, as before, sets the icon that should be used for the button. We can disable the default shadow applied to the outer container element of the icon using `data-shadow="false"`, and set the `data-iconpos="notext"` attribute to make the button an image-only button.

We also specified the `data-transition="slide"` attribute, so that the page transitions nicely back to the welcome page, but this time we also set the `data-direction="reverse"` attribute so that the page appears to go *backwards* (that is, it slides in the opposite direction) to the home page. Because we put this link before the `<h1>` element it will be automatically floated to the left by the framework.

We added some basic content to the `content` container. This isn't important, and as you can see, I've added a shameless plug for my personal website. This external link isn't completely useless however, because it does show that when a link is prefixed with `http://`, jQuery Mobile knows that it's an external link and doesn't hijack the click and try and transition it into view.

You'll notice that the footer container has the same `data-` attributes as before, including the same `data-id="footer"` attribute. This is what gives the footer container persistence. When the page transitions into view, the footer will appear outside of the transitioned area and remain fixed at the bottom of the page.

We've modified the `<a>` element in the footer container slightly. We've removed the `data-transition` attribute and added the `ui-disabled` class instead. We've also changed the `href` to a simple hash. As we're already on the About page, the **About** link will do nothing, so we disable it to avoid the page being reloaded if it is clicked.

Classified Intel

jQuery Mobile adds its beautiful page-to-page transitions by hijacking any relative links. When a relative link is clicked, jQuery mobile will fetch the page via AJAX, insert it into the DOM of the current page, and transition it into view.

Generally when using a jQuery Mobile site, you will never move away from the page that you started on because the framework will silently hijack same-domain links and dynamically insert the content into the page. You might therefore think that each page need not link to all of the CSS and script resources.

This is not the case however – what if someone lands directly on one of the internal pages? Or what if an external link is followed, but then the visitor returns using their browser's back button? In both of these scenarios, they will be greeted with an unenhanced, dysfunctional page that looks and feels nothing like the page they expected to see.

Now we should be able to reload the home page, then click on the **About** button in the footer, and see the About page.

Creating the script wrapper

We won't be making use of jQuery's `$(document).ready() { }` function (or the `$(function() { })` shortcut) to execute our code when the page has loaded. However, we still need to protect our top-level variables and functions from the global scope so we still need a wrapper of some kind. In this task we'll create that wrapper, as well as our top-level variables.

Engage Thrusters

In the empty `bounty-hunter.js` file, we can start by adding the following code:

```
(function() {

    var tags = "",
        getBounties = function(page, callback) {

        $.ajax({
            url: "https://api.stackexchange.com/2.0/questions/
            featured",
            dataType: "jsonp",
            data: {
                page: page,
                pagesize: 10,
                tagged: tags,
                order: "desc",
                sort: "activity",
                site: "stackoverflow",
                filter: "!)4k2jB7EKv1OvDDyMLKT2zyrACssKmSCX
                eX5DeyrzmOdRu8sC5L8d7X3ZpseW5o_nLvVAFfUSf"
            },
            beforeSend: function () {
                $.mobile.loadingMessageTextVisible = true;
                $.mobile.showPageLoadingMsg("a", "Searching");
            }
```

```
        }).done(function (data) {

            callback(data);

        });
    };

}());
```

Objective Complete - Mini Debriefing

Our script wrapper consists of a self-executing anonymous function (or an immediately-invoked function expression if you prefer). This outer function is wrapped in parentheses, and has an extra pair of brackets at the end which cause the anonymous function to execute and return immediately. This is an established JavaScript pattern often used in large-scale applications.

This creates a closure which encapsulates all of the code within it and shields it from the global namespace, which makes the code more robust and less likely to break or fail when used in conjunction with other libraries or plugins.

 If you aren't sure of what a closure is or what it can do, there is an excellent discussion about it on the Stack Overflow website (http://stackoverflow.com/questions/111102/how-do-javascript-closures-work).

It also allows us to run code almost as soon as the document has loaded. As the <script> element it lives within is right at the bottom of the <body>, it will not be executed until the rest of the page has been parsed by the browser.

Within the anonymous outer function we first define some variables. The first, called tags, will be used in various functions over the course of this project, so it needs to be accessible everywhere. Initially it can be set to an empty string.

The next variable is a function called getBounties(), which again we define in our top-level scope so that it can be called from elsewhere in the code without issue. We'll use the function to issue AJAX requests at different points in the app's lifecycle, and most of the parameters of the request will not need to change.

We make an AJAX request to the Stack Exchange API using jQuery's ajax() method. This method is jQuery's de facto method for making AJAX requests and is what the library's helper methods, such as getJSON(), delegate to.

The `ajax()` method accepts an object literal that can be used to configure any of the standard AJAX options supported by jQuery in order to control how the request is performed.

The `url` property sets the URL that the request is made to, which we set to the entry point of the Stack Exchange API that we'd like to use. We set the `dataType` to `JSONP` so that we can get the data from the Stack Exchange domain without triggering the browser's cross-domain security restrictions.

JSON (JavaScript Object Notation) is a data format, with an extremely similar syntax to object literals in JavaScript, and it is used to exchange data across different platforms or systems. **JSONP (JSON with padding)** is a technique that dynamically injects new scripts into the page, which exposes JSON data to the JavaScript parser in the browser. It is necessary because of the browser's same-origin security policy, which restricts the domains that data can be loaded from to the current domain.

The Stack Exchange API can be configured, and the data we receive filtered in very specific ways, using standard query string parameters to enable or disable particular functionality. We can use jQuery's `data` AJAX property to add the query string parameters we wish to set.

 For more information on the Stack Exchange API, see the documentation at `https://api.stackexchange.com/`.

We use the `page` parameter to specify which page of the results we'd like to get, which will be received by the function as a parameter. We set the number of questions returned to `10` to page the amount of data shown at any one time. This is set using the `pagesize` parameter.

The `tagged` parameter uses the value of the tags variable, which we can manipulate when required later in the project. The Stack Exchange API won't complain if we send this parameter without a value, so we can safely set it regardless of whether there are actually any tags or not.

We specify that we'd like the results in descending order, and sort by activity, so questions with the most recent activity will be listed first. The `site` is set to `stackoverflow`, so that questions are not received from the entire Stack Exchange network of sites.

The last configuration property is a predefined filter that I have already created and saved on Stack Exchange. There is a tool included for doing this when browsing any of the API methods. The purpose of the filter is to control exactly which fields are returned in the response, to ensure that we aren't receiving more data than we need.

In this example we're just using the Stack Exchange API anonymously. For full production-ready applications intended for public use, we must always register the application with Stack Applications, and use an API key with any requests we make.

Some fields that we want are not included in the default filter (which is used if no filter is provided when making the request), and a lot of fields that we don't need are returned. The filter we will use here gives us just the fields we need for this project, and does not require authentication to use.

These are most of the AJAX options that we need to set for this request; those which are not known at this point can be passed to the function when it is invoked. We'll see how to do this in the next task.

We can make use of jQuery's `beforeSend` AJAX event to show the jQuery Mobile AJAX spinner directly before the request is made. jQuery Mobile uses a spinner every time a page is transitioned, but we can subvert it for our own requirements when making the AJAX request.

The framework will automatically attach a `mobile` object to the instance of jQuery running on the current page. This object contains various properties used to configure the jQuery Mobile environment, and various methods to trigger different behavior with the framework. We can use some of these now.

To ensure the message we wish to add is displayed, because by default the spinner uses accessibly-hidden text, we set the `loadingMessageTextVisible` property of the `mobile` object to `true`.

At page load, jQuery Mobile creates an object called `mobile`, which contains a range of useful properties and methods.

To actually show the spinner, we can use the jQuery Mobile `showPageLoadingMsg()` method. This method takes the theme swatch to use as the first argument, which in this case we can set to the default theme `a`, and the text to display inside the spinner as the second argument.

After the `ajax()` method, we chain the `done()` method. This is the new way of handling successful AJAX requests as of jQuery 1.8 and replaces jQuery's `success()` method. We pass an anonymous function to this method to be executed when the request object returns, and this function receives the response as an argument. Within this function we simply invoke the `callback()` function that will be passed into `getBounties()` as the second argument, passing it the data from the response.

Classified Intel

In this task we made use of the `done()` method to handle the successful response from the Stack Exchange API instead of the more familiar `success()` method. This is now the preferred way of handling successful responses (as of jQuery 1.8). The `error()` and `complete()` callback methods of the `jqXHR` object returned by any of jQuery's AJAX methods have been deprecated in favor of `fail()` and `always()`.

As of jQuery 1.5, the AJAX suite of methods have returned the `jqXHR` object as a promise, or deferred, object, so this change to the API brings the AJAX methods in line with other implementations of the promise API within jQuery.

Getting some bounties

In this task we need to get some bounties from stack overflow. We'll want to initialize a part of our script once the welcome page of our application has been initialized. Once this happens we can attach a handler for the `<button>` on the page to trigger an AJAX request using the `getBounties()` function that we add in the last part.

Engage Thrusters

Inside the outer function, but after the `getBounties()` function in `bounty-hunter.js`, add the following code:

```
$(document).on("pageinit", "#welcome", function () {

    $("#search").on("click", function () {

        $(this).closest(".ui-btn")
                .addClass("ui-disabled");

        tags = $("tags").val();

        getBounties(1, function(data) {

            data.currentPage = 1;

            localStorage.setItem("res", JSON.stringify(data));

            $.mobile.changePage("bounty-hunter-list.html", {
                transition: "slide"
            });
        });
    });
});
```

We can also add a handler for the `pageshow` event directly after the code we just added:

```
$(document).on("pageshow", "#welcome", function () {
    $("#search").closest(".ui-btn")
                        .removeClass("ui-disabled");
});
```

Objective Complete - Mini Debriefing

We use the `pageinit` event to execute code when the page is initialized for the first time. Due to the AJAX nature of how new pages are pulled into the DOM of the existing page and displayed, this event is more reliable than `document ready` when using jQuery Mobile.

We use jQuery's `on()` method to bind an event handler for this event to the document object, and set the first argument of the method to the `pageinit` event. Because our script will be used on every page, but the code we've added here is only relevant on the welcome page, we use the second argument of the method to ensure that the event handler (which we add as the third argument) is only executed when the event originates from the welcome page.

We then bind a handler for the `click` event to the search `<button>`, again using jQuery's `on()` method. Within the handler we first add the `ui-disabled` class to the outer `<button>` container to stop further requests being initiated. We then get any tags that may have been entered in the text field using jQuery's `val()` method. This will return the value of the text input, which we then store in our top-level `tags` variable.

Next we can call the `getBounties()` function that we added in the last task. As the request is being initiated by the welcome page we need to get the first page of the results, so we pass 1 to the function as the first argument.

We pass an anonymous function as the second argument to `getBounties()`. Remember, the handler we added for the `done()` method will execute the function and automatically pass the data from the response to it.

Within this function we first need to add a new property to our `data` object to store the current page number. We can then store the `data` object so that we can use it in the next page. We can do this using `localStorage`, but because only arrays and primitive types can be stored in `localStorage`, we need to convert the object to a JSON string using the browser's native `JSON.stringify()` method.

We then use the jQuery Mobile `changePage()` method to change the current page to the page on which we'll display the response. This method is passed the URL of the page to change to as the first argument, and a configuration object as the second argument.

We use this configuration object to set the transition to use when showing the new page with the `transition` option, which in this case we set to `slide`.

After the `pageinit` handler we also added an event handler for the `pageshow` event. This event is dispatched every time a page is shown, unlike the `pageinit` event which is dispatched only the first time a given page is initialized.

We bind the event to the `document` object again and filter the event by the `#welcome` selector once again to ensure that the code only runs when the welcome page is shown. Within the event handler we simply remove the `ui-disabled` class from the outer `<button>` container. If we've returned to the welcome page, it's probably because we want to perform a new search, maybe with a different tag.

Adding a JsRender template

At the end of the last task we used the `changePage()` method to call a new page, so now we need to create that page. We can add our JsRender template to the new page ready for when we build the list view in the next task.

Prepare for Lift Off

Create a new page using the starting template from jQuery Mobile once again. Call it `bounty-hunter-list.html` and save it in the root of our project folder. Change the `id` attribute of the `data-role="page"` wrapper to `list`.

The `<h1>` in the header `<div>` can be changed to something like `Active Bounties`, and we can add the home icon again as we did on the About page. The footer can stay the same as on the welcome page. The content `<div>` can be empty to begin with.

Engage Thrusters

Near the bottom of the new page we just created, inside the page container, add the following JsRender template:

```
<script id="listTemplate" type="text/x-jquery-tmpl">
    <ul data-role="listview">

        {{for items}}
            <li data-shadow="false" data-icon="arrow-r"
            data-iconpos="right">

                <a href="#" id="item-{{:#index}}">
                    <div class="bounty">
                        <span>+{{:bounty_amount}}</span>
```

```
                    <span class="expires">Expires on:
                        <span class="value">
                            {{:bounty_closes_date}}
                        </span>
                    </span>
                </div>
                <h1 class="title">{{:title}}</h1>
                <div class="meta">
                    <span>Answers:
                        <span class="value">
                            {{:answer_count}}
                        </span>
                    </span>
                    <span class="activity">
                        Last activity on:
                        <span class="value">
                            {{:last_activity_date}}
                        </span>
                    </span>
                </div>
            </a>
        </li>
    {{/for}}
</ul>
</script>
```

Objective Complete - Mini Debriefing

The `<script>` element that the template resides in is given a non-standard `type` attribute to stop the browser parsing the script. It's also given an `id` attribute so that we can easily select it from the page when we want to interpolate the template with data and render it to the page.

Inside the `<script>` element, we first create the `<ul>` element that will be turned into a Listview widget by jQuery Mobile. We give this element a `data-role` attribute of `listview`. We then use JsRender's loop construct `{{for}}`, which accepts the object or array to loop over. In this case we're interested in the `items` array that is part of the `data` object that is saved in localStorage at the end of the last task, and which will be passed to the template function that renders the template.

The code we add within the `{{for}}` loop will be repeated for each item in the `items` array, which will consist of a series of questions from stack overflow. The object the template will iterate will be passed into the loop when we call JsRender's `template()` method a little later on.

The first element we add is `<li>` as this should naturally be a child of the outer `<ul>` list. We give the `<li>` element several `data-` attributes including `data-shadow="false"` to disable shadows under each `<li>`, `data-icon="arrow-r"` to give each list item a right-pointing arrow icon, and `data-iconpos="right"` to position the icon at the right of the element.

> **Listitem icons**
>
> In order for the icons we've added to our list items to be displayed, each item should contain a link. If no `<a>` elements are found within the item when the widget is initialized, no icon will be added.

Inside the list item, we add an `<a>` element and a unique `id` for when we come to display the item view later on. We can create a unique `id` using the loop index of the template, which is available to us within the loop as `#index`.

Inside the `<a>` element we have several other elements. The first is a container for the bounty offered on the current question. Inside this container we have another JsRender token that will be replaced with the data from the object we are iterating. To access a property of the object within our template, we use `{{:` followed by the property name and ending with `}}`. The colon inside the opening double curly braces indicates that no HTML encoding should be carried out. The Stack Exchange API will sanitize the data for us so we can just use it as is.

We can also display some text and the date that the bounty expires using some nested `<span>` elements, one of which has a `class` for some specific styling, and another property from our data object.

We can output the title of the question using an `<h1>` element and another JsRender template tag that pulls out the `title` property from the current item from inside the `data` object.

Lastly we can display some meta-information about the question such as the number of answers it has and the last time there was activity on the question. This information is added in the same way as before, using a combination of `<span>` elements and JsRender template tags to display various properties from our data object.

Building the list view

Our application should now be at the point where it has received some data that needs to be formatted and displayed. We've also added a JsRender template ready to be used to build the Listitem elements for a Listview widget.

All we need to do now is render the template and display the results in our widget. We can also add some additional controls to the widget to let the visitor navigate through the paged results, although we won't make these functional just yet.

Engage Thrusters

First of all we can add some additional markup to the content container in our list page (bounty-hunter-list.html):

```
<div class="ui-bar ui-bar-c">
    <a href="#" data-role="button" data-icon="back"
    data-inline="true" data-mini="true" class="ui-disabled">
    Prev
    </a>

    <h2>Page
        <span class="num"></span> of <span class="of"></span>
    </h2>

    <a href="#" data-role="button" data-icon="forward"
        data-iconpos="right" data-inline="true"
        data-mini="true" class="ui-disabled">
        Next
    </a>
</div>

<div id="results"></div>

<div class="ui-bar ui-bar-c footer-bar">
    <a href="#" data-role="button" data-icon="back"
    data-inline="true" data-mini="true" class="ui-disabled">
    Prev
    </a>

  <h2>Page
    <span class="num"></span> of <span class="of"></span>
  </h2>

    <a href="#" data-role="button" data-icon="forward"
    data-iconpos="right" data-inline="true"
    data-mini="true" class="ui-disabled">
    Next
    </a>
</div>
```

Next we need to update our script in order to render the template and display the data. In `bounty-hunter.js`, add the following code directly after the event handler for the `pageshow` event:

```
$(document).on("pageinit", "#list", function () {

    var data = JSON.parse(localStorage.getItem("res")),
        total = parseInt(data.total, 10),
        size = parseInt(data.page_size, 10),
        totalPages = Math.ceil(total / size),
        months = [
            "Jan", "Feb", "Mar", "Apr", "May", "Jun", "Jul",
            "Aug", "Sep", "Oct", "Nov", "Dec"
    ];

    var createDate = function (date) {
        var cDate = new Date(date * 1000),
            fDate = [
                cDate.getDate(), months[cDate.getMonth()],
                cDate.getFullYear()
        ].join(" ");


        return fDate;
    }

    $.views.helpers({ CreateDate: createDate });


    $("#results").append($("#listTemplate")
                 .render(data))
                 .find("ul")
                 .listview();

    var setClasses = function () {
        if (data.currentPage > 1) {
            $("a[data-icon='back']").removeClass("ui-disabled");
        } else {
            $("a[data-icon='back']").addClass("ui-disabled");
        }

        if (data.currentPage < totalPages) {
            $("a[data-icon='forward']").removeClass("ui-disabled");
        } else {
```

```
        $("a[data-icon='forward']").addClass("ui-disabled");
    }
};

$("span.num").text(data.currentPage);
$("span.of").text(totalPages);

if (totalPages > 1) {
    $("a[data-icon='forward']").removeClass("ui-disabled");
}
});
```

We also need to change our template slightly. There are two places in our template where we show date properties; these both need to be changed so that they appear as follows:

```
{{:~CreateDate(bounty_closes_date)}}
```

And:

```
{{:~CreateDate(last_activity_date)}}
```

Lastly, we need to add some additional styling for our new elements, as well as the items that will be added to the Listview widget. Add the following styles to the bottom of `bounty-hunter.css`:

```css
.ui-bar { margin:0 -15px 14px -15px; text-align:center; }
.ui-bar a:first-child { margin-left:-5px; float:left; }
.ui-bar a:last-child { margin-right:-5px; float:right; }
.ui-bar h2 { margin-top:10px; font-size:14px; }
.footer-bar { margin-top:14px; }

.bounty {
    width:24%; border-radius:3px; margin-right:5%; float:left;
    text-align:center; font-size:90%; line-height:1.5em;
    font-weight:bold; color:#fff; background-color:#07d;
    text-shadow:none;
}
.bounty span { display:block; }
.expires {
    font-size:70%; font-weight:normal; line-height:1em;
}
.expires .value {
    display:block; font-size:110%; font-weight:bold;
    line-height:1.5em;
}
.title {
```

```
        width:70%; margin-top:-.25em; float:left;
        white-space:normal; font-size:80%; line-height:1.25em;
        color:#07d;
    }
    .meta { clear:both; }
    .meta span {
        width:24%; margin-right:5%; float:left; font-size:70%;
        font-weight:normal; color:#999;
    }
    .meta .value {
        width:70%; margin-right:0; float:none; font-size:90%;
        font-weight:bold;
    }
```

Objective Complete - Mini Debriefing

In the first step of this task we added some new HTML elements to the content container on the page.

The first element we added will be used as a toolbar that sits above the Listview widget. Within this toolbar are links for the visitor to navigate between different results pages. The toolbar will pick up a lot of styling from jQuery Mobile because we have given it the ui-bar and ui-theme class names.

The links are enhanced into Button widgets by jQuery Mobile because they have the data-role="button" attribute. We also add icons to them using the data-icon attribute, make them inline-block with the data-inline attribute, and make them smaller than standard buttons using the data-mini attribute.

Lastly, we give the buttons the ui-disabled class name initially. We can enable each button based on which page we are on and whether there are previous or next pages to navigate to.

Along with the buttons, the toolbar also contains an <h2> element that will tell the visitor which page they are on, and how many pages there are in total. The contents of the element are split into spans with id attributes so that we can easily update them later on.

We also add an empty container <div> to the page with an id of results. This container will be the element that we render our Listview widget into.

The second toolbar, which we added directly after the empty Listview container, is identical to the first toolbar in every respect except that it has an additional class of footer-bar. We use this to add a little CSS, which is only required by the bottom toolbar.

In our script we first added a new event handler for the `pageinit` event of the list page. This is bound in the same way as before using jQuery's `on()` method.

Within the event handler, we first set a series of variables. We store a reference to the data that was stored in localStorage in an earlier task, and store the `total` number of results and the `page_size` properties of the `data` object ready to use in various places in our code.

We also calculate the total number of pages based on the `total` and `size` variables that we just saved, and create an array containing shortened month names, which we'll use when we format the dates returned by Stack Exchange.

Next we need to add a new method that we can use as a helper function inside our template. We call the method `createDate` and specify that the method may accept a single argument, which will be a date string.

Inside the method, we first create a new date using the date string passed to the method. This will be in UNIX epoch format, so we need to multiply it by 1000 for it to work with JavaScript's `Date()` constructor.

The date string returned by the `Date()` constructor will be a full UTC date string, which is way too long for displaying in our little bounty box, so next we define a new array where each item in the array is part of the date string that we want to format the existing string into.

We can get the day of the month with the `getDay()` function. The `getMonth()` function will return a zero-based number so we can use this to extract the correct shortened month name from the array we created earlier. Lastly we get the four-digit year using the `getFullYear()` function. Once the array has been filled, we join it straight away using a space character as the join character and return the resulting string from the method.

Next we need to register our new method as a helper function so that the template we are using can access it. This is done using the `helpers()` method of the `views` object, which is created by JsRender and attached to jQuery. This method takes an object as its argument where each key in the object is the name of a helper method, and each value is the actual function we wish to use as the helper. In this example we map the `CreateDate` helper method to the `createDate` function we just defined.

We then select the Listview widget using its `id` and append to it the rendered template. The template is rendered using JsRender's `render()` method, which accepts the object containing the data to be rendered as an argument.

Next we define another simple function that will add or remove the `ui-disabled` class name for the buttons based on the `currentPage` property that we stored on the `data` object.

We can now update the headings to show the current page and the total number of pages. We can do that using jQuery's `text()` method and displaying `data.currentPage` and `totalPages` variables that we stored earlier.

As this will only be the first time the list page is loaded, we know that only the **Next** button needs to be enabled. We use an attribute selector to select just the two forward buttons based on their `data-icon` attribute. We'll add the functionality that will make this button work in the next and final task.

The last thing we do in our script is enable the forward buttons so that the next page can be viewed, but only if there are more pages to display, which we can determine by checking the `totalPages` variable again.

After adding the script we then updated our template to make use of the new date formatting helper method we created. To use a helper method inside a template we just need to use the ~ character followed by the registered name of the method. Any arguments that need to be passed, such as the `bounty_closes_date` and `last_activity_date` properties from each item in the array the template iterates, are passed using parentheses as would be used when calling a normal JavaScript function.

Once the template has been rendered, we need to initialize the Listview. We do this by first getting the new `<ul>` element inside the container and then using its widget method, `listview()` in this case, to enhance it into a Listview widget.

Lastly we added some additional CSS styling to tweak the styling applied by the default theme in jQuery Mobile. We need to make the toolbars full-width to match the Listview widget, which we can do in the same way as the Listview widget itself does – simply by using negative margin.

The Listview has negative margin for its `top` and `bottom` properties as well as its `left` and `right` properties, so we need to counteract this by adding some positive margin to the `bottom` of the top toolbar, and some positive `top` margin to the bottom toolbar.

We can also float the back and forward buttons left and right respectively and center the heading text. We also shrink down the size of the heading text by a couple of pixels to help ensure that it doesn't interfere with our buttons.

The styling for the elements inside the Listview is almost entirely for the visual appearance of the elements we added using the template. The Listview itself will inherit a lot of styling from the framework, so it's just the elements inside each Listitem we need to worry about.

Once the bounties button has been clicked and the results have been returned, the list view page should appear like the following screenshot:

Classified Intel

Like jQuery UI, jQuery Mobile widgets can be initialized completely from script, without using any hardcoded `data-` attributes in the underlying markup. We could just as easily have built the entire Listview widget from script instead of keeping the outer `<ul>` element in the markup.

To initialize a widget we can just call its widget method. If we are creating a Listview, the widget method is simply `listview()`. Other widgets can be initialized in the same way. Also like jQuery UI widgets, jQuery Mobile widgets can accept configuration options and event handlers, and have methods that can be called from script.

Building an item view

The Listview provides links for each list item containing a question. In this task we can add the page that is displayed when one of the questions is selected. This will be a much more detailed view of a single question so we can make use of some of the other properties returned to us by Stack Exchange. This time, instead of linking to an existing page, we'll create a new one dynamically and inject it into the app.

Engage Thrusters

We'll use another template to render the item view because it's so convenient; add the following code to `bounty-hunter-list.html` directly after the list template. We can start by adding the outer `<script>` wrapper, the outer page container, and the header:

```
<script id="itemTemplate" type="text/x-jquery-tmpl">
    <div data-role="page" id="{{:pageid}}" class="item-view">
        <div data-role="header" data-position="fixed">
            <a href="bounty-hunter-list.html"
            data-shadow="false" data-icon="arrow-l"
            data-transition="slide"
            data-direction="reverse"
            title="Back to list view">
            Back
            </a>

            <h1>{{:title}}</h1>

        </div>
    </div>
</script>
```

Next we can add the content area wrapper and the content header. This should go into the page container, directly after the header area:

```
<div data-role="content">
    <header class="ui-helper-clearfix">
        <div class="bounty">
            <span>+{{:bounty_amount}}</span>
        <span class="expires">
          Expires on:
          <span class="value">
            {{:~CreateDate(bounty_closes_date)}}
```

```
        </span>
    </span>
</div>

<div class="meta">
    <span>Asked on:
        <span class="value">
            {{:~CreateDate(creation_date)}}
        </span>
     </span>
    <span>Answers:
        <span class="value">
            {{:answer_count}}
        </span>
    </span>
    <span class="activity">Last activity on:
        <span class="value">
            {{:~CreateDate(last_activity_date)}}
        </span>
    </span>
</div>

<h1 class="title">{{:title}}</h1>
<ul class="tags">
    {{for tags}}
        <li>{{:#data}}</li>
        {{/for}}
</ul>

<div class="owner">
    <a href="{{:owner.link}}"
        title="{{:owner.display_name}}">
            <img src="{{:owner.profile_image}}"
                alt="{{:owner.display_name}}" />
        <div>
            <h3>{{:owner.display_name}}</h3>
            <span>
                {{:owner.accept_rate}}% accept rate
            </span>
        </div>
    </a>
</div>
```

```
        <a data-role="button" data-icon="gear"
        data-inline="true" href="{{:link}}"
        title="Answer on Stack Overflow">
        Answer on Stack Overflow
        </a>

    </header>

</div>
```

Next we can add the question and the list of answers. This should come directly after the header element (but still inside the content `<div>`) we just added:

```
<div class="question">{{:body}}</div>

<h2>Answers</h2>
<ul class="answer">
    {{for answers}}
        <li data-shadow="false">
            <h3>Answered by:
                <span class="answer-name">
                    {{:owner.display_name}}
                </span>, on
                <span class="answer-date">
                    {{:~CreateDate(creation_date)}}
                </span>
            </h3>

            <div>{{:body}}</div>
        </li>
    {{/for}}
</ul>
```

Lastly we can add the footer for the page. This should go directly after the content area, but still inside the outer page container:

```
<div data-role="footer" data-position="fixed"
    data-id="footer">

    <small>&copy; 2012 Some Company Inc.</small>
    <a href="bounty-hunter-about.html"
    data-icon="info" data-role="button"
    data-transition="slide">
    About
    </a>
</div>
```

We also need to add some script to render the template and handle the page change behavior. We can do this in the `pageinit` handler for the list page that we added in the last task:

```
$("#results").on("click", "li", function () {

    var index = $(this).find("a").attr("id").split("-")[1],
        question = data.items[index];

    question.pageid = "item-view-" + index;

    $("body").append($("#itemTemplate").render(question));

    var page = $("#item-view-" + index);

    page.attr("data-external-page", true).on
    ("pageinit", $.mobile._bindPageRemove);

    $.mobile.changePage(page, {
        transition: "slide"
    });
});
```

Lastly, we need some CSS for the new elements that are in the template we added. In `bounty-hunter.css`, add the following code to the end of the file:

```
header {
    padding:15px; border-bottom:1px solid #fff;
    margin:-15px -15px 0 -15px;
    box-shadow:0 1px 10px rgba(0,0,0,.3);
}
header:after {
    content:""; display:block; clear:both; visibility:hidden;
}
header .bounty { margin-bottom:.75em; }
header .meta { width:70%; float:left; clear:none; }
header .meta span { width:100%; }
header .title {
    width:auto; margin:0; float:none; clear:both;
    font-size:125%;
}
.tags { padding:0; }
.tags li {
    padding:.5%; border-right:1px solid #7f9fb6;
    border-bottom:1px solid #3e6d8e; margin-right:1%;
```

```
        margin-bottom:1%; float:left; list-style-type:none;
        font-size:90%; color:#4a6b82; background-color:#e0eaf1;
    }
    header a {
        margin-left:0; float:left; clear:both;
        text-decoration:none;
    }
    .owner {
        padding:2.5%; margin:15px 0; float:left; clear:both;
        font-size:70%; background-color:#e0eaf1;
    }
    .owner img { width:25%; margin-right:5%; float:left; }
    .owner div { width:70%; float:left; }
    .owner h3 { margin:-.25em 0 0; }
    .owner span { font-size:90%; color:#508850; }

    .question {
        padding:15px; border-bottom:1px solid #000;
        margin:-15px -15px 0 -15px;
    }
    .question img { max-width:100%; }

    .answer { padding:0; list-style-type:none; }
    .answer li { border-bottom:1px solid #000; font-size:80%; }
    .answer h1, .answer h2, .answer h4 { font-size:100%; }
    .item-view pre {
        max-width:95%; padding:2.5%; border:1px solid #aaa;
        background-color:#fff; white-space:pre-wrap;
    }
```

Objective Complete - Mini Debriefing

We started out by adding a new template for the page to display a single question. This template was considerably larger than the first one we added, for several reasons. Primarily, because we're using this template to build an entire page, but also because we're showing more stuff with this template. This is the detailed view of a question so we would naturally want to show more than the summary shown in the list view.

The outer page container that we specify is given an `id`, which we'll add in our script, so that we can easily select the correct page in order to show it. Aside from this we add some of the same elements to our template as we have been adding in our actual pages, such as the header, content, and footer containers.

Within the content container is where most of the action is, although we're using the template in exactly the same way as before – defining HTML elements and interpolating them with properties from the object passed to the `render()` method.

The only new technique in this template is the creation of the tags list. We use the `for` construct to iterate the list of tags, but this time the property we are iterating is a flat string array instead of an object. As there isn't a key for us to use in the template tags to get the value, we can instead use the special value `#data`, which will give us the current item in the array being iterated.

All of the code we added to our script was contained within a click handling function that we bind to the list of results display on the page, because we want to react to an individual list item being clicked.

Within the handler function, we first set the variable which will contain the numerical part of the `id` attribute of the list item that was clicked. We can easily get the numerical portion by using JavaScript's `split()` function and specifying a hyphen as the character to split on.

When we render the template, we only want to show a single item, so we don't need to pass in the entire object received from the AJAX request. Instead we use the `index` variable that we just set to pull just the object representing the question we are interested in from the `items` array within the `data` object.

Once we stored the object we'll be passing to our template to render, we need to add a new property to it that is added as the `id` attribute for the page container in the template. This is the `pageid` property that we set on the `question` object.

Next we render our template using JsRender's `render()` method once more. We pass it the `question` object that we just prepared and this time the template is rendered to the body of the page. Because it gets rendered outside of the page container it won't be visible immediately.

Once the template has been rendered to the page, we select the outer page container and store a reference to it in the `page` variable. When a new page is created dynamically and appended to the page, jQuery Mobile will keep its markup in the page, even if we navigate away from it.

To stop this from happening, we need to do two things; first of all we need to set the `data-external-page` attribute of the page to `true`. Secondly we need to set a handler for the `pageinit` event of the dynamic page. Once the new page has been initialized, we mark it for deletion when the visitor navigates away from it using the internal jQuery Mobile `_bindPageRemove` method.

Once this is done, we can transition to the new page using the `changePage()` method. We pass the method the page element that we stored earlier, and use the configuration object to set the transition.

Because we've passed the `changePage()` method a DOM element and not specified a URL, the address bar of the browser will not be updated and an entry will not be left in the browser's history.

At this point we should be able to run the page on a smartphone or tablet, click on one of the list items on the list view page and see the item view, as shown in the following screenshot:

Handling paging

For our last task we'll look at wiring up the paging elements we added earlier. The Stack Exchange API makes it easy to get results in a paged format, so we can leverage that to our advantage.

The trade-off for requesting all available data from Stack Exchange, saving ourselves that massive one-off hit, is that we make much smaller requests in response to the user initiating a request for more data.

Engage Thrusters

Directly after the `click` handler we added for the `<li>` elements inside the Listview, add the following code:

```
$("a[data-icon='forward'], a[data-icon='back']").on("click", function
() {

    var button = $(this),
        dir = button.attr("data-icon"),
        page = parseInt($("span.num").eq(0).text(), 10);

    if (dir === "forward") {
        page++;
    } else {
        page--;
    }

    getBounties(page, function (newData) {

        data = newData;
        data.currentPage = page;
        localStorage.setItem("res", JSON.stringify(newData));

        $.mobile.hidePageLoadingMsg();

        $("#results").empty()
                    .append($("#listTemplate")
                    .render(newData))
                    .find("ul")
                    .listview();

        $("span.num").text(page);

        setClasses();
    });
});
```

Objective Complete - Mini Debriefing

We attach a listener for all four buttons using the `data-icon` attribute once more to select them from the page. Don't forget that this will only be done once, the first time the list page loads.

We then store a reference to the button that was clicked, the value of the data-icon attribute of the clicked button, and the current page. We then check the value of the `dir` attribute and if it is equal to `forward` we increment the current page, otherwise we decrement it.

We can then call our `getBounties()` method once more, passing it the updated `page` variable and the handler function to execute after the request.

Within this handler function, we first update the stored data by updating the `data` variable with the new object returned by the most recent call to `getBounties()`. We add a `currentpage` property to the `data` object once more and update the copy we have in localStorage.

We can then hide the spinner manually using the `hidePageLoadingMsg()` jQuery Mobile method and then re-render the list template using the new data. Once this is done we can update the display showing the current page, and call our `setClasses()` utility function to enable or disable the forward and back buttons respectively.

Mission Accomplished

At this point we should have a fully working jQuery Mobile app than runs on both desktop and mobile devices. It's a simple app, but we've gotten to explore a reasonable amount of the framework. There is much more to learn, but seeing the bits that we've used in this project should be more than enough to inspire you to delve deeper into the framework and what it offers.

You Ready To Go Gung HO?
A Hotshot Challenge

One thing that we haven't looked at in this project so far is the theming capabilities of jQuery Mobile. Like jQuery UI, jQuery Mobile benefits from the advanced theming capabilities of Themeroller.

Your challenge for this project is to head on over to Themeroller at `http://jquerymobile.com/themeroller/` and build yourself a custom theme for the finished application.

Project 5

jQuery File Uploader

It's now possible to create a fully featured file upload widget with nothing but a few of the latest HTML5 APIs and jQuery. We can easily add support for advanced features such as multiple uploads, and a drag-and-drop interface, and with just a little help from jQuery UI we can also add engaging UI features such as detailed file information and progress feedback.

Mission Briefing

In this project we'll build an advanced multifile upload widget using the HTML5 file API to provide the core behavior, and using jQuery and jQuery UI to build an attractive and engaging interface that visitors will find a pleasure to use.

We'll build the widget as a jQuery plugin because it's the kind of thing that we'd probably like to be encapsulated so that we can drop it into numerous pages and have it work with just a little configuration, instead of having to build a custom solution every time we require this functionality.

Why Is It Awesome?

jQuery provides some great features that make writing reusable plugins a breeze. Over the course of this project we'll see just how easy it is to package up specific functionality and a mechanism for generating all of the necessary mark-up and adding all of the required types of behaviors.

Handling file uploads on the client side gives us a lot of opportunity for adding experience enhancing features, including information about each file selected for upload, and a rich progress indicator that keeps the visitor informed about how long the upload is likely to take.

We can also allow the visitor to cancel the upload while it is in progress, or remove previously selected files before the upload begins. These kinds of features just aren't available using purely server-side techniques for handling file uploads.

At the end of this project we'll have produced the following widget:

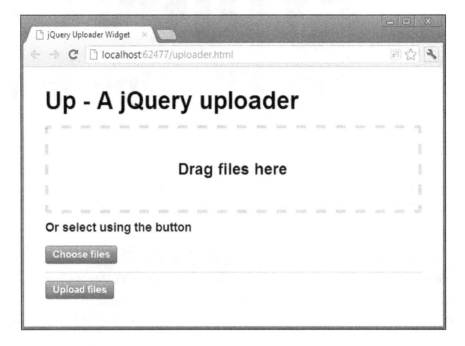

Your Hotshot Objectives

To arrive at the completed project, we'll need to complete the following tasks:

- ▸ Creating the page and plugin wrapper
- ▸ Generating the underlying markup
- ▸ Adding event handlers for receiving files to upload
- ▸ Displaying the list of selected files
- ▸ Removing files from the upload list
- ▸ Adding a jQuery UI progress indicator
- ▸ Uploading the selected files
- ▸ Reporting success and tidying up

Mission Checklist

Like in some of our previous projects, as well as using jQuery, we'll also be using jQuery UI in this project. The copy of jQuery UI we downloaded at the start of the book should already contain all of the widgets we require.

Like in the previous project, we'll also need to use a web server for this project, which means running the page using a proper `http://` URL and not a `file:///` URL. See the previous project for information on compatible web servers.

Creating the page and plugin wrapper

In this task we'll create the page that links to the required resources, as well as add the wrapper that our plugin will live within.

Prepare for Lift Off

At this point we should create the different files we'll need for this project. First, save a new copy of our template file in the main project folder and call it `uploader.html`. We'll also need a new style sheet, which should be saved in the `css` folder as `uploader.css`, and a new JavaScript file, which should be saved in the `js` folder as `uploader.js`.

The new page should link to the jQuery UI style sheet so that we get the styling required by the Progressbar widget, and also the style sheet for this project in the `<head>` of the page, directly after the existing link to `common.css`:

```
<link rel="stylesheet" href="css/ui-lightness/jquery-ui-1.10.0.custom.
min.css" />

<link rel="stylesheet" href="css/uploader.css" />
```

We'll also need to link to jQuery UI and the JavaScript file for this example. We should add both of these script files directly after the existing `<script>` element for jQuery:

```
<script src="js/jquery-ui-1.10.0.custom.min.js"></script>
<script src="js/uploader.js"></script>
```

Engage Thrusters

All our plugin will require is a container that the widget can render the required markup into. In the <body> of the page, before the <script> elements linking to the different JavaScript resources, add the following code:

```
<div id="uploader"></div>
```

As well as linking to the script file that contains the code for our plugin, we'll also need to call the plugin in order to initialize it. Directly after the existing <script> elements, add the following code:

```
<script>
    $("#uploader").up();
</script>
```

The plugin's wrapper is a simple construct that we'll use to initialize the widget. In uploader.js, add the following code:

```
;(function ($) {

    var defaults = {
        strings: {
            title: "Up - A jQuery uploader",
            dropText: "Drag files here",
            altText: "Or select using the button",
            buttons: {
                choose: "Choose files",
                upload: "Upload files"
            },
            tableHeadings: [
                "Type", "Name", "Size", "Remove all x"
            ]
        }
    }

    function Up(el, opts) {

        this.config = $.extend(true, {}, defaults, opts);
        this.el = el;
        this.fileList = [];
        this.allXHR = [];
    }

    $.fn.up = function(options) {
        new Up(this, options);
```

```
        return this;
    };

}(jQuery));
```

Objective Complete - Mini Debriefing

When building jQuery plugins, the best thing we can do is make our plugins easy to use. Depending on what the plugin is for, it is best to have as few prerequisites as possible so if a complex markup structure is required by the plugin, it is usually best to have the plugin render the markup it needs, rather than making the users of the plugin try to add all of the required elements.

In light of this, we'll write our plugin so that all it requires on the page is a simple container that the plugin can render the markup into. We added this container to the page and gave it an `id` attribute for easy selecting.

Developers using our plugin will need a way to invoke it. jQuery plugins extend the `jQuery` object with additional methods and our plugin will add a new method to jQuery called `up()`, which is called like any other jQuery method name – on a set of elements that have been selected by jQuery.

The extra `<script>` element we add to the bottom of the `<body>` element calls our plugin method in order to invoke the plugin, which is how someone using our plugin would invoke it.

In our script file, we start out with a semicolon and an immediately-invoked anonymous function. The semi-colon supports the modular nature of jQuery plugins and protects our plugin from other plugins that don't stop execution correctly.

If another plugin in use on the page didn't end its final statement or expression with a semi-colon, and we didn't start our plugin with a semi-colon, it could produce script errors that prevented our plugin working.

We use an anonymous function as a wrapper for our plugin and invoke it immediately with an extra set of parentheses after the function body. We can also ensure that our plugin works with jQuery's `noConflict()` method by locally scoping the `$` character within our plugin and passing the `jQuery` object into the anonymous function as an argument.

Within the anonymous function we first define an object literal called `defaults` that will be used as a configuration object for our plugin. This object contains another object called `strings`, which is where we store all of the different bits of text that are displayed in various elements.

The reason for using a configuration object for text strings is to make our plugin easy to localize, making it easier for non-English speaking developers to use. Making plugins as flexible as possible is a good way of making the plugin more appealing.

After the `defaults` object we define a constructor function that will generate instances of our widget. The plugin is called Up and we capitalize the first letter of its name because this is the general convention for functions that should be invoked using the `new` keyword.

The constructor function can accept two arguments; the first is a jQuery element or collection of elements and the second a configuration object defined by the developer using our plugin.

Within the constructor function we first attach some members to the instance. The first is called `config` and will contain the object returned by jQuery's `extend()` method, which is used to merge two objects together, and unlike most jQuery methods, it's called on the `jQuery` object itself rather that a collection of HTML elements.

It takes four arguments; the first argument instructs the `extend()` method to deep-copy the object being merged into the jQuery object, which we need to do because the `defaults` object contains other objects.

The second argument is an empty object; any other objects will be merged together and their own properties added to this object. This is the object that the method will return. If we didn't pass in an empty object, the first object passed into the method would be returned instead.

The next two arguments are the objects we are going to merge. These are the `defaults` object that we defined a moment ago, and the `opts` object that may be passed to the constructor when it is invoked.

This means that if a developer wishes to pass in a configuration object, they can overwrite the values that we've defined in the `defaults` object. The properties not overwritten with this configuration object will be set to the default values instead.

We also store a reference to the element, or collection of elements, as a member of the instance as well so that we can easily operate on the elements in other parts of our code.

Lastly we add a couple of empty arrays that will be used to store the list of files to upload and the XHR requests in progress. We'll see how these properties are used later in the project, so don't worry too much about them now.

jQuery provides the `fn` object as a shortcut to its prototype, which is how we extend jQuery with our plugin method. In this case the method is called `up()` and is the method we invoked using the `<script>` element at the bottom of `uploader.html`. We specify that the method may accept a single argument, which is an object containing the configuration options that someone using our plugin may wish to provide.

Within the method, we first create a new instance of the uploader using the `new` keyword in conjunction with our constructor function. We pass the constructor function the element (or collection of elements) that the method is called on, and the `options` object.

Lastly we returned `this` from the method. Inside a method added to jQuery's prototype, the `this` object refers to the jQuery collection. It's very important to return the collection of elements that the method was called on in order to preserve chaining.

Classified Intel

Chaining is an inherent feature of jQuery that developers using it have come to expect. It is important that developers' expectations are met with regard to the style of programming they use. People using our plugin will expect to be able to add additional jQuery methods after calling our plugin's method.

Now that we are returning the collection of elements by returning the `this` object, developers can do things like this:

```
$("#an-element").up().addClass("test");
```

So that's a simple example of what's possible, but it should illustrate why it is important to always return `this` from a plugin.

Generating the underlying markup

In this task, we'll add an initialization method to our plugin which will generate the required markup that the widget requires.

Engage Thrusters

First of all we should add the following code directly after the `Up()` constructor function in `uploader.js`:

```
Up.prototype.init = function() {
    var widget = this,
        strings = widget.config.strings,
        container = $("<article/>", {
          "class": "up"
        }),
    heading = $("<header/>").appendTo(container),
    title = $("<h1/>", {
        text: strings.title
    }).appendTo(heading),
    drop = $("<div/>", {
```

```
            "class": "up-drop-target",
            html: $("<h2/>", {
                text: strings.dropText
            })
        }).appendTo(container),
        alt = $("<h3/>", {
            text: strings.altText
        }).appendTo(container),
        upload = $("<input/>", {
            type: "file"
        }).prop("multiple", true).appendTo(container),
        select = $("<a/>", {
            href: "#",
            "class": "button up-choose",
            text: strings.buttons.choose
        }).appendTo(container),
        selected = $("<div/>", {
            "class": "up-selected"
        }).appendTo(container),
        upload = $("<a/>", {
            href: "#",
            "class": "button up-upload",
            text: strings.buttons.upload
        }).appendTo(container);

        widget.el.append(container);


    }
```

We also need to call this new `init()` method. Change the method added to jQuery's `fn` object so that it appears as follows:

```
$.fn.up = function(options) {
    new Up(this, options).init();
    return this;
};
```

We can also add the CSS for the markup generated by the plugin. In `uploader.css`, add the following styling:

```
article.up { width:90%; padding:5%; }
article.up input { display:none; }
.up-drop-target {
    height:10em; border:5px dashed #ccc; border-radius:5px;
    margin-bottom:1em; text-align:center;
```

```
}
.up-drop-target h2 {
    margin-top:-.5em; position:relative; top:50%;
}
.up-selected { margin:1em 0; border-bottom:1px solid #ccc; }
```

Objective Complete - Mini Debriefing

We can add an `init()` method that takes care of creating and injecting the markup that the widget is built from by adding it to our constructor's `prototype`. All objects created by the constructor will inherit the method.

We first store the `this` object, which inside our `init()` method still refers to the jQuery collection of elements, so that we can easily refer to it inside event handlers, which we'll add in the next task.

We also locally scope the `strings` property to make resolution slightly faster, as we refer to this property frequently in order to add the visible text strings to the widget's visible UI.

Next we create the new HTML elements and store each of them in variables. This means that we can create the container and append all of the required elements to it while it's still in memory, and then inject the entire widget into the page's DOM in one go, instead of repeatedly modifying the DOM and adding the elements one by one.

The outer container for the widget is an `<article>` element which has a class name for easy styling. The HTML5 specification describes an `<article>` as a self-contained interactive widget, so I feel this is the perfect container for our widget. Although equally as relevant, the `<article>` is not restricted to what we would traditionally describe as an "article" – for example, a blog/news post or an editorial style piece.

We have a `<header>` element to contain the main heading for the widget, within which we use a standard `<h1>`. We also use two `<h2>` elements inside the widget to show the different sections (the drag-and-drop area, and the more traditional file `<input>`).

The `<input>` element has a `type` attribute of `file` and is also given the `multiple` attribute, using jQuery's `prop()` method, so that multiple files can be uploaded in supporting browsers. Current versions of IE (9 and below) do not support this attribute.

We also add an `<a>` element directly after the `<input>`, which we'll use to open the Open dialog used to select the files to upload. The problem with the standard `file` type `<input>`, is that there is no standard!

Almost every browser implements the `file` type `<input>` differently, with some browsers showing an `<input>` as well as a `<button>` and some browsers just showing a `<button>` and some text. It's also impossible to style the `<input>` or `<button>` generated by the control as these are part of the **shadow DOM**.

 For more information on what the shadow DOM is, see `http://glazkov.com/2011/01/14/what-the-heck-is-shadow-dom/`.

To get around these cross-browser differences, we'll hide the `<input>` with CSS and use the `<a>` element, styled to appear like an attractive button, to open the dialog.

We also add an empty `<div>` element that we'll use to list the selected files and display some information about each one, followed by another `<a>` element that will be styled like a button. This button will be used to initiate the upload.

We used the standard jQuery 1.4+ syntax for creating new HTML elements and supplied a configuration object for most of the elements we created. Most elements are given a class name and some also get text or HTML content. The class names we use are all scoped with a sensible prefix so as to avoid potential conflicts with existing styles already used on the page.

The CSS we added is mostly just for presentation. The important aspects are that we hide the standard file `<input>`, and give the drop target a fixed size so that files can easily be dropped on it.

At this point we should be able to run the page in a browser (via a web server) and see the basic elements and layout of the plugin. The page should appear as in the first screenshot of this project.

Adding event handlers for receiving files to upload

We can use the `init()` method that we added in the last task to attach the event handlers that our widget will need to handle files being selected for upload. This may happen either when files are dropped onto the drop target, or when they are selected using the button.

Engage Thrusters

Directly after appending the new HTML elements to the container at the end of the `init()` method in `uploader.js` (but still within the `init()` method), add the following code:

```
widget.el.on("click", "a.up-choose", function(e) {
    e.preventDefault();

    widget.el.find("input[type='file']").click();
});

widget.el.on("drop change dragover", "article.up", function(e) {

    if (e.type === "dragover") {
        e.preventDefault();
        e.stopPropagation();
        return false;
    } else if (e.type === "drop") {
        e.preventDefault();
        e.stopPropagation();
        widget.files = e.originalEvent.dataTransfer.files;
    } else {
        widget.files = widget.el
        .find("input[type='file']")[0]
        .files;
    }

    widget.handleFiles();
});
```

Objective Complete - Mini Debriefing

We first use jQuery's `on()` method, in event-delegation mode, to attach an event handler to the outer container of the widget. We specify the `click` event as the first argument, and a selector that matches our button with the class name `up-choose` as the second argument.

Within the handler function passed to `on()` as the third argument, we first prevent the default behavior of the browser using JavaScript's `preventDefault()`, and then trigger a `click` event for the hidden `<input>` element used to select the files to upload. This will cause the File dialog to open in the browser and allow files to be selected.

We then attached another event handler. This time we are looking for either the `drop`, `dragover`, or `change` events. The `drop` event will be triggered when files are dropped onto the drop zone, the `dragover` event will be triggered while files are held over the drop zone, and the `change` event will be triggered if files are removed.

All of these events will bubble up from either the drop zone (the `<article>` with the class name up) or the hidden `<input>` and will pass through the outer container of the widget, to which the event handler is bound.

Within this handler function we first check whether it's the `dragover` event; if it is, we again prevent the default behavior of the browser using `preventDefault()` and `stopPropagation()`. We also need to `return false` from this branch of the conditional.

The next branch of the `if` checks whether the event that triggered the handler was the `drop` event. If it was we still need to use `preventDefault()` and `stopPropagation()`, but this time we can also get the list of selected files using the event object that jQuery creates and passes to the handler function, and store them in a property on the widget instance.

If neither of these conditions is `true`, we get the list of files from the `<input>` element instead.

The property we need is part of the `originalEvent` object that jQuery packages into its own event object. We can then get the `files` property from the `dataTransfer` object. If the event was the `change` event instead, we can just get the `files` property of the hidden `<input>`.

Whichever method is used, the collection of files selected for upload is stored on the instance of the widget under the `files` property. This is just a temporary property, which will get overwritten each time new files are selected, unlike the widget's `filelist` array, which will store all the files for an upload.

Lastly we call the `handleFiles()` method. We'll add this method to the widget's `prototype` in the next task so once this has been done, we'll be able to call the method here without running into problems.

Combining the two events and detecting which event occurred in this way is much better than attaching to separate event handlers. It means that we don't need two separate handler functions that both do essentially the same thing, and regardless of whether files are selected with the button and standard dialog, or by dropping files onto the drop target, we can still get the list of files.

As this point we should be able to either drop files onto the drop zone, or click the button and select files using the dialog. However, a script error will be thrown because we haven't yet added the `handleFiles()` method of our plugin.

Displaying the list of selected files

In this task we can populate the `<div>` we created in order to display the list of files that have been selected for upload. We'll build a table where each row in the table lists a single file with information such as the filename and type.

Engage Thrusters

Directly after the `init()` method in `uploader.js`, add the following code:

```
Up.prototype.handleFiles = function() {

    var widget = this,
        container = widget.el.find("div.up-selected"),
        row = $("<tr/>"),
        cell = $("<td/>"),
        remove = $("<a/>", {
            href: "#"
        }),
    table;

    if (!container.find("table").length) {
        table = $("<table/>");

        var header = row.clone().appendTo(table),
            strings = widget.config.strings.tableHeadings;

        $.each(strings, function(i, string) {
            var cs = string.toLowerCase().replace(/\s/g, "_"),
                newCell = cell.clone()
                                            .addClass("up-table-head "
    + cs)
                                            .appendTo(header);

            if (i === strings.length - 1) {
                var clear = remove.clone()
                                            .text(string)
                                            .addClass("up-remove-
    all");

                newCell.html(clear).attr("colspan", 2);
            } else {
                newCell.text(string);
            }
        });
    } else {
        table = container.find("table");
```

```
        }

                $.each(widget.files, function(i, file) {
                var fileRow = row.clone(),
                        filename = file.name.split("."),
                        ext = filename[filename.length - 1],
                        del = remove.clone()
                                        .text("x")
                                        .addClass("up-remove");

                cell.clone()
                        .addClass("icon " + ext)
                        .appendTo(fileRow);

                cell.clone()
                        .text(file.name).appendTo(fileRow);
                cell.clone()
                        .text((Math.round(file.size / 1024)) + " kb")
                        .appendTo(fileRow);

                cell.clone()
                        .html(del).appendTo(fileRow);
                cell.clone()
                        .html("<div class='up-progress'/>")
                        .appendTo(fileRow);


                fileRow.appendTo(table);

                widget.fileList.push(file);
        });

        if (!container.find("table").length) {
                table.appendTo(container);
        }
}
```

We can also add some additional CSS for the new markup we've created. Add the following code to the bottom of upload.css:

```
.up-selected table {
    width:100%; border-spacing:0; margin-bottom:1em;
}
.up-selected td {
    padding:1em 1% 1em 0; border-bottom:1px dashed #ccc;
    font-size:1.2em;
}
.up-selected td.type { width:60px; }
```

```css
.up-selected td.name { width:45%; }
.up-selected td.size { width:25%; }
.up-selected td.remove_all_x { width:20%; }

.up-selected tr:last-child td { border-bottom:none; }
.up-selected a {
    font-weight:bold; text-decoration:none;
}
.up-table-head { font-weight:bold; }
.up-remove-all { color:#ff0000; }
.up-remove {
    display:block; width:17px; height:17px;
    border-radius:500px; text-align:center;
    color:#fff; background-color:#ff0000;
}
.icon {
    background:url(../img/page_white.png) no-repeat 0 50%;
}
.doc, .docx {
    background:url(../img/doc.png) no-repeat 0 50%;
}
.exe { background:url(../img/exe.png) no-repeat 0 50%; }
.html { background:url(../img/html.png) no-repeat 0 50%; }
.pdf { background:url(../img/pdf.png) no-repeat 0 50%; }
.png { background:url(../img/png.png) no-repeat 0 50%; }
.ppt, .pptx {
    background:url(../img/pps.png) no-repeat 0 50%;
}
.txt { background:url(../img/txt.png) no-repeat 0 50%; }
.zip { background:url(../img/zip.png) no-repeat 0 50%; }
```

Objective Complete - Mini Debriefing

We started out by adding the handleFiles() method to the widget's prototype, making the method call widget.handleFiles() that we added at the end of the last task work. It was added in exactly the same way as the init() method earlier, and just like inside init(), the this object points to the instance of the widget inside handleFiles(). This makes the element on the page, the configuration options, and the selected file list easy to access.

Inside the method, we first created a series of variables. Like in the init() method we create a local variable called widget that stores the this object. We won't be adding any event handlers to this method so we don't absolutely have to do this, but we do access the object several times so it makes sense to cache it in a variable.

We also cache the selected files container using `widget.el` – don't forget that `el` already refers to the jQuery-wrapped instance of the outer widget container, so we can call jQuery methods, such as `find()` directly on it without rewrapping it.

Next we create a series of new DOM elements ready for them to be cloned inside loops. This is a much better way of creating elements, especially inside loops, and avoids having to continually create new jQuery objects.

We also define a variable called `table`, but we don't initialize it straight away. Instead we use the `if` conditional to check whether the container already contains a `<table>` element by checking if jQuery's `find("table")` returns a collection that has `length`.

If `length` is equal to `false`, we know that no `<table>` elements were selected so we initialize the `table` variable with a new `<table>` element created with jQuery. We then create a header row for the `<table>` which we'll use to add headings for each of the columns in the new table.

At this point the `<table>` element only exists in memory, so we can add the new row to it without modifying the DOM of the page. We also cache a reference to the `tableHeadings` property of the `strings` object used in our configuration object.

We then use jQuery's `each()` utility to create all of the `<td>` elements used as the table headings. As well as being able to call `each()` on a collection of elements selected from the page, we can also call `each()` on the jQuery object in order to iterate a pure JavaScript array or object.

The `each()` method accepts the array or object to iterate. In this case it's an array, so the iteration function called for each item in the array receives the index of the current item and the value of the current item as arguments.

Inside the iterator, we first create a new string that we can use as a class name. The word `class` is a **reserved word** in JavaScript, so we call our variable `cs` instead. To create the class name, we just convert the current string to lowercase using JavaScript's `toLowerCase()` function, and then remove any empty spaces using JavaScript's `replace()` function.

 For a complete list of the reserved words in JavaScript, see the MDN documentation at `https://developer.mozilla.org/en-US/docs/JavaScript/Reference/Reserved_Words`.

The `replace()` function takes the regular expression to match as the first argument, and the replacement string as the second argument. We could use the string " " as the first argument instead, but then only the first blank space would be removed, whereas using a regular expression with the `g` flag allows us to remove all spaces.

We then create a new `<td>` element by cloning one of the elements we created and stored in a variable at the start of the task. We give it a general class name for styling purposes, and the unique class name that we just created so that each column can be styled independently if required, and then append it straight to the header row that we created a moment ago.

We then check whether we're iterating the last item in the array by testing whether the current index is equal to the `length` of the array minus 1. If it is the last item, we add a clear all link by cloning the `<a>` element we created and cached at the start of the task.

We set the text of the new `<td>` element to the value of the current array item and add the `up-remove-all` class for styling purposes so that we can filter events dispatched by it. We can also use jQuery's `attr()` method to set a `colspan` attribute of 2 to this `<td>`. The new `<a>` element is then added as the HTML content of the new `<td>` element.

If it's not the last item in the array we simply set the text content of the new `<td>` element to the value of the current array item.

This is all done in the first branch of the outer `if` statement which occurs when the table does not exist. If the container does already contain a `<table>` element, we still initialize the table variable by selecting the `<table>` from the page.

Don't forget that the `handleFiles()` method we're inside will be invoked once files have been selected, so now we need to build a new row in the table for each of the files that were selected.

Again we use jQuery's `each()` method, this time to iterate the collection of stored files in the widget's `files` property. For each file that was selected (either by dropping onto the drop zone, or using the button) we first create a new `<tr>` by cloning our `row` variable.

We then split the `name` property of the current file on the . character. We store the extension of the file by getting the last item in the array created by the `split()` function.

At this point we also create a delete link, which can be used to remove an individual file from the list of files to upload, by cloning the `<a>` element we created at the start of the task. It is given the text `x` and the class name `up-remove`.

Next we create a series of new `<td>` elements by cloning the cached `<td>` in the `cell` variable again. The first `<td>` is given a generic class name of `icon`, and the extension for the current file so that we can add an icon for the different file types that can be uploaded, and append it to the new row.

The second `<td>` element displays the name of the file. The third `<td>` element shows the size of the file in kilobytes. If we knew that large files were likely to be uploaded, we could instead convert to megabytes, but for the purpose of this project, kilobytes will be sufficient.

The fourth `<td>` element has the new delete link added to it using jQuery's `html()` method and the last `<td>` element has an empty `<div>` element added to it which we'll use for the jQuery UI Progressbar widget.

Once the new cells have been created and appended to the new row, the new row itself is appended to the table. We can also add the current file to our `fileList` array ready to be uploaded.

Lastly we need to check once more whether the selected files container already has a `<table>` element inside it. It if doesn't, we append the new `<table>` we have just built to the container. If it does contain the `<table>` already, the new rows will already have been added to it.

The CSS we added in this part was purely presentational. One thing I've done is to add some classes so that an icon can be shown for different file types that might be selected for upload. I've only added a few as an example; the ones you actually require would depend on the type of files that you expected your users to upload. A generic icon is also created for types that do not match the selectors we've added.

> The icons used in this example are part of the Farm Fresh icon pack. I've renamed the files for conciseness and can be found in the code download accompanying this book. The icons are available at Fat Cow web hosting at (`http://www.fatcow.com/free-icons`).

At this point we should be able to run the page in a browser, select some files to upload, and see the new `<table>` we have just created:

Classified Intel

We manually created the elements needed to display the list of selected files in this example. Another way to do it would be to use a templating engine, such as jsRender or Dust.js, instead. This would have the benefit of being faster and more efficient than our manual creation, would keep our plugin code simpler and more concise, and the file smaller.

Of course, it would add another dependency to our plugin because we'd have to include the templating engine itself, as well as a precompiled template stored in a JavaScript file. We aren't creating that many elements in this example, so it's probably not worth adding another dependency. When many elements need to be created, the cost of adding a dependency is outweighed by the efficiency it adds.

This is the kind of thing that needs to be considered on a case-by-case basis when writing a jQuery plugin.

Removing files from the upload list

In this task we'll add the event handlers that will make the **Remove** and **Remove all** links in the new file list work. We can attach the event handlers in the same place that we added other event handlers earlier to keep things organized.

Engage Thrusters

In `upload.js`, within the widget's `init()` method and directly after the existing calls to jQuery's `on()` method, add the following new code:

```
widget.el.on("click", "td a", function(e) {

    var removeAll = function() {
        widget.el.find("table").remove();
        widget.el.find("input[type='file']").val("");
        widget.fileList = [];
    }

    if (e.originalEvent.target.className == "up-remove-all") {
        removeAll();
    } else {
        var link = $(this),
            removed,
            filename = link.closest("tr")
                                .children()
                                .eq(1)
```

```
                                              .text();

        link.closest("tr").remove();

        $.each(widget.fileList, function(i, item) {
        if (item.name === filename) {
            removed = i;
        }
    });
    widget.fileList.splice(removed, 1);

    if (widget.el.find("tr").length === 1) {
        removeAll();
    }
  }
}
});
```

Objective Complete - Mini Debriefing

We use jQuery's on() method to add a click event again. We attach it to the outer container of the widget as we have our other events, and this time we filter the events based on the selector td a as the event will only originate from <a> elements inside <td> elements.

Inside the event handler we first prevent the default behavior of the browser because we don't want the link to be followed. We then define a simple helper function that removes the <table> element from the widget, removes the value of the file <input>, and clears the fileList array.

We need to clear the <input> because otherwise if we selected some files and then removed them from the list of files, we wouldn't be able to then reselect the same group of files. It's a bit of a fringe case, but this simple little trick allows it to work so we may as well include it.

Next we check what the className property of the element that triggered the event is. We can see this property using the target property of the originalEvent object that is included in the jQuery event object which is passed to our handler function. We could also use the srcElement property of the jQuery event object, but this does not work in current versions of Firefox.

When the className property matches up-remove-all, we simply call our removeAll() helper function to remove the <table> element and clear the <input> and fileList array.

If the `className` property doesn't match the **Remove all** link, we have to remove just the row of the `<table>` element that contains the `<a>` that was clicked. We first cache a reference to the `<a>` that triggered the event, which is set to `this` inside our handler function.

We also define a variable called `removed`, which we'll initialize with a value shortly. Lastly we store the `filename` of the file that the row we are about to remove represents.

Once we've set our variables, the first thing we do is remove the row that we can get using jQuery's `closest()` method, which finds the first parent element that matches the selector passed to the method.

We then use jQuery's `each()` method to iterate the `fileList` array. For each item in the array, we compare the item's `name` property with the `filename` variable we just initialized. If the two match, we set the `index` number, which is passed automatically to the iterator function by jQuery, to our `removed` variable.

Once the `each()` method has finished, we can use JavaScript's `splice()` function to remove the file the current `<tr>` represented. The `splice()` function takes two arguments (it can take more but we don't need them here), where the first argument is the index of the item to begin removing at, and the second argument is the number of items to remove.

Lastly, we check whether the `<table>` element has more than one row left in it. If it only has one row left, this will be the header row so we know that all files have been removed. We can therefore call our `removeAll()` helper function to tidy up and reset everything.

Now when we've added files to the upload list, we should then be able to remove individual files using the inline **x** buttons, or clear the list using the **Remove all** link.

Adding a jQuery UI progress indicator

In this task we'll add the elements and initialization code required by the jQuery UI Progressbar widget. The widget won't actually do anything yet because we won't be actually uploading anything until the next task, but we need to wire everything up ready.

Engage Thrusters

We'll add an `initProgress()` method to our widget's prototype to select the `<div>` elements that we added to the `<table>` element and convert them into Progressbar widgets. We can also add the method that will be used to update the Progressbars.

Directly after the `handleFiles()` method, add the following code:

```
Up.prototype.initProgress = function() {

    this.el.find("div.up-progress").each(function() {
        var el = $(this);

        if (!el.hasClass("ui-progressbar")) {
            el.progressbar();
        }
    });
}
```

Next, we'll need to call this method after new rows have been added to `<table>`. Add the following call to our new method right at the end of the `handleFiles()` method:

```
widget.initProgress();
```

Now we can add the code that updates the Progressbar. Add the following code directly after the `initProgress()` method we just added:

```
Up.prototype.handleProgress = function(e, progress) {

    var complete = Math.round((e.loaded / e.total) * 100);

    progress.progressbar("value", complete);
}
```

We also need a tiny bit of CSS for the new progress bars. Add the following code to the end of `uploader.css`:

```
.up-progress {
    height:1em; width:100px; position:relative; top:4px;
}
```

Objective Complete - Mini Debriefing

This was a shorter task than some of those we've covered in this project so far, but no less important. We added the new method in the same way that we've added most of the functionality for our plugin.

Inside the method we first select all `<div>` elements with the class name `up-progress`. Don't forget that we can access the widget's container element using `this.el` and as it's a jQuery object already we can call jQuery methods, such as `find()` on it.

We then iterate each element in the selection using jQuery's `each()` method. We're using the standard `each()` method in this task, where the current element in the collection is set to `this` inside the iterator function.

In the iterator function we first cache the current element. We then check whether it has the jQuery UI class name `ui-progressbar` and if it doesn't, we convert the element into a Progressbar using the jQuery UI method `progressbar()`.

Doing it this way means that the progress bar will always be created, whether it is the initial set of files being selected for uploading, or additional files that are being added to an existing `<table>`.

We also added a call to the new `initProgress()` method at the end of the `handleFiles()` method, which is called whenever new files are selected for upload.

Next we added the `handleProgress()` method, which we'll bind to an event in the next task. This method will be passed two arguments, the first is the event object and the second is an already-wrapped jQuery object representing an individual Progressbar.

Within the method, we first calculate how much of the file has been uploaded. We can determine this by dividing the loaded property of the event object by the total property, and then dividing by 100 to give us the percentage of the file that has been uploaded so far.

The `loaded` and `total` properties are special properties that are added to the event object when the progress event is fired by the browser.

Once we have the percentage, we can call the `value` method of the Progressbar widget in order to set the value to the percentage. This is a jQuery UI method and so is called in a special way. Rather than calling `value()` directly, we instead call the `progressbar()` method, and pass the name of the method to invoke, `value`, as the first argument. All jQuery UI methods are called in this way.

Lastly, we added a little presentational CSS just to tweak the default styling provided by the default jQuery UI theme in use. When we add files to be uploaded now, we should see an empty Progressbar after each file in the `<table>`.

Uploading the selected files

We now have a list of files attached to the instance of our plugin ready to be uploaded. In this task we'll do just that and upload the files asynchronously using jQuery. This behavior will be tied to the **Upload files** button that we added to the markup generated by the plugin.

We can also use this task to update our Progressbars with the current progress of each file being uploaded.

Engage Thrusters

As this is another event handler, we'll add it in the `init()` method along with all of the other event handlers so that they're all kept in one place. Add the following code at the end of the `init()` method, after the existing event handlers:

```javascript
widget.el.on("click", "a.up-upload", function(e) {
    e.preventDefault();

    widget.uploadFiles();
});
```

Next add the new `uploadFiles()` method. This can go after the progress-related methods that we added in the last task:

```javascript
Up.prototype.uploadFiles = function() {
    var widget = this,
    a = widget.el.find("a.up-upload");

    if (!a.hasClass("disabled")) {

        a.addClass("disabled");

        $.each(widget.fileList, function(i, file) {
            var fd = new FormData(),
                prog = widget.el
                                        .find("div.up-progress")
                                        .eq(i);

            fd.append("file-" + i, file);

            widget.allXHR.push($.ajax({
                type: "POST",
                url: "/upload.asmx/uploadFile",
                data: fd,
                contentType: false,
                processData: false,
                xhr: function() {

                    var xhr = jQuery.ajaxSettings.xhr();

                    if (xhr.upload) {
```

```
                    xhr.upload.onprogress = function(e) {
                        widget.handleProgress(e, prog);
                    }
                }

                return xhr;
            }
        }));
    });
}
}
```

Objective Complete - Mini Debriefing

Within our uploadFiles() method, we first store a reference to the widget as we have in some of the other methods we've added. We also store a reference to the **Upload files** button.

The next thing to do is to check that the button doesn't have class name of disabled. If it does have this class name, it means that an upload has already been initiated for the selected files so we want to avoid making a duplicate request. If the button doesn't have the disabled class, it means that this is the first time the button has been clicked. So to prevent duplicate requests we then add the class disabled.

Next we iterate over the list of files that we've collected and which is stored in the widget instance's fileList property. For each file in the array we first create a new FormData object.

FormData is a part of the new XMLHttpRequest (XHR) level 2 specification which allows us to dynamically create a <form> element and submit that form asynchronously using XHR.

Once we've created a new FormData object, we also store a reference to the Progressbar widget associated with the current file. We then use the FormData's append() method to append the current file to the new FormData object so that the file is encoded and sent to the server.

Next we post the current FormData object to the server using jQuery's ajax() method. The ajax() method will return the jqXHR object for the request. This is a special version of the XHR object that jQuery enhances with additional methods and properties. We need to store this jqXHR object so that we can use it a little later on.

We'll look at exactly how it's used in the next task, but for now just understand that the jqXHR object returned by the ajax() method is pushed into the allXHR array that we stored as a member on the widget instance right at the start of the project.

The `ajax()` method accepts a configuration object as an argument which allows us to control how the request is made. We set the request to POST using the `type` option, and specify the URL to post to using the `url` option. We add the `FormData` object as the payload of the request using the data option and set the `contentType` and `processData` options to `false`.

If we don't set the `contentType` option to `false`, jQuery will try to guess which content type should be used for the request, which it may or may not do correctly, meaning some uploads will work and some will fail, seemingly for no apparent reason. The `content-type` of the request will be set to `multipart/form-data` by default as we are using `FormData` which have files appended to them.

Setting the `processData` option to `false` will ensure that jQuery doesn't try to transform the file into a URL-encoded query string.

We need to modify the underlying XHR object used to make the request, so that we can attach our handler function to the progress event. The handler must be bound to the event before the request is made and the only way to do that currently is using the `xhr` option.

The option takes a callback function which we can use to modify the original XHR object and then return it for the request to be made. Inside the callback, we first store the original XHR object, which we can get from jQuery's `ajaxSettings` object.

We then check whether the object has an `upload` property, and if it does we set an anonymous function as the value of `onprogress`. Within this function, we simply call the `handleProgress()` method of our widget that we added in the last task, passing it the progress event object and the Progressbar widget that we stored at the start of this task.

Reporting success and tidying up

In this task we need to show when each file has finished uploading. We also need to clear the `<table>` from the widget and re-enable the upload button once all of the uploads have completed.

Engage Thrusters

We can show when each individual file has completed uploading using jQuery's `done()` method, which we can chain after the `ajax()` method that we added in the last task:

```
.done(function() {

    var parent = prog.parent(),
```

```
    prev = parent.prev();

    prev.add(parent).empty();
    prev.text("File uploaded!");
});
```

In order to tidy up following the uploads, we can make use of jQuery's `when()` method. We should add the following code directly after the `each()` method in `uploadFiles()`:

```
$.when.apply($, widget.allXHR).done(function() {
    widget.el.find("table").remove();
    widget.el.find("a.up-upload").removeClass("disabled");
});
```

Objective Complete - Mini Debriefing

Because jQuery's `ajax()` method returns a `jqXHR` object, and because this object is a special object called a **promise object**, we can call certain jQuery methods on it. The `done()` method is used to execute code when the request completes successfully.

 You may be more used to using jQuery's `success()` method to handle successful AJAX requests, or the `error()` or `complete()` methods. These methods have been removed from the library in version 1.9, so we should use their replacements `done()`, `fail()`, and `always()` instead.

Within this function all we need to do is remove the clear button and the Progressbar widget for the file that has just finished uploading. We can find the elements that need to be removed easily by navigating to them from the current Progressbar widget.

We stored a reference to each individual Progressbar in the last task and because the `done()` method is chained to the `ajax()` method, we can still access this element using the variable after the request has completed.

Notice that there appears to be an extra closing bracket at the end of the `done()` method. The reason for this is because it's still within the `push()` method that we added in an earlier task. It's critical that the `done()` method is added to the correct place – it must be chained to the `ajax()` method inside the `push()` method.

Once these elements have been removed, we add a simple message that says the file has finished uploading.

We also need to remove the `<table>` element from the page once all the requests have been completed. It was for this reason that we stored all of the `jqXHR` objects generated when uploading the files in the last task. We can use jQuery's `when()` method to do this.

The `when()` method can accept a series of promise objects and returns when they have all been resolved. However, this method doesn't accept an array, which is why we call it using JavaScript's `apply()` method instead of calling it normally.

We can again use the `done()` method to add a callback function to be invoked once the `when()` method has returned. Within this callback, all we do is remove the `<table>` element showing the files that were uploaded and re-enable the upload button by removing the `disabled` class.

This is all we need to do to actually upload the file or files that were selected and receive progress feedback on each file individually, as shown in the following screenshot:

Viewing the example file

To see this project in action you'll need to view the page we've created using a web server (using `http://localhost` on your own computer). It won't work if you open the file by double-clicking on it in Explorer or Finder.

Mission Accomplished

We've made it to the end of the project. At this point we should have an uploader plugin that is easy to use and provides rich features in supporting browsers such as multiple files, file information, an editable upload list, and upload progress reports.

 Not all browsers are able to use the features that this widget is built to exploit. The Opera browser for example, sees programmatically triggering the file dialog box as a security risk and so does not allow it.

Also, legacy versions of Internet Explorer (anything prior to version 10) will not be able to handle this code at all.

Supporting incompatible or legacy browsers is beyond the scope of this example, but it would be relatively straight forward to add a fallback that made use of some other technology, such as Flash, in order to provide support for some of the behavior our plugin demonstrates.

Or there are a range of older jQuery plugins that make use of `<iframe>` elements to simulate uploading files via AJAX. Instead of focusing on what isn't supported, I've chosen to focus on what *can* be done in supporting browsers.

You Ready To Go Gung HO?
A Hotshot Challenge

By uploading the files individually, we were able to add an event handler to monitor the progress of the files being uploaded. This also opens up of the possibility of aborting the upload of individual files.

For this challenge why not see if you can add a mechanism for canceling the upload of a file. We already have the remove button which is used to remove files before they are uploaded. These could easily be updated so that they cancelled the upload if the upload is in progress.

A handler for the abort event can be added to the XHR object in the same way as the progress event handler was attached, so it should be easily achievable.

Project 6

Extending Chrome with jQuery

Building an extension for Chrome (or any other browser that can be extended with plugins and extensions) is an easy way to create custom behavior or additional tools to enhance our browsing experience.

Chrome allows us to leverage our web development skills to extend its browser interface, using technologies we're already familiar with such as HTML, CSS, and JavaScript, and where you can use JavaScript you can usually use jQuery.

Mission Briefing

In this project we'll build a Chrome extension that highlights elements on the page that are marked up with `Schema.org` **microdata**. Microdata is a way of specifying descriptive information about a variety of different entities, such as businesses, locations, or people using standard HTML attributes, and is rumored to become an important factor in Google's ranking algorithms.

Whenever we visit a page containing elements described as contact details, we can grab them from the page and store them in our extension, allowing us to slowly build up a directory of contact information for people that are using or making stuff we love.

We can also use templating in this project to make creating a repeated group of elements much more efficient, as well as easier to maintain. We used JsRender in the previous project, so we can use it again, but this time we'll need to use it slightly differently than before. Once completed, our extension will look something like that shown in the following screenshot:

Why Is It Awesome?

Microdata is used to describe the information contained within web pages in order to promote better interoperability between autonomous systems, such as search engine spiders and HTML documents.

When different elements on the page are described as being a company, a person, a product, or a movie, it allows things such as search engines to better understand the information contained on the page.

Microdata is rapidly becoming more commonplace on the Web and is set to take an ever increasingly important role in the results generated by Google for search results, so there has never been a better time to exploit it.

Your Hotshot Objectives

The tasks this project is broken down into are as follows:

- ▸ Setting up the basic extension structure
- ▸ Adding a manifest and installing the extension
- ▸ Adding a sandboxed JsRender template
- ▸ Posting a message to the sandbox
- ▸ Adding a content script
- ▸ Scraping the page for microdata
- ▸ Adding a mechanism for saving the microdata

Setting up the basic extension structure

In this task we'll create the underlying files required by the extension. All files used by an extension need to reside in the same directory, so we'll set that up and make sure it contains all the files we need.

Prepare for Lift Off

One thing I should point out, although hopefully you'll already have realized – we're going to require the Chrome browser for the duration of this project. If you don't have it installed, which as a web developer you really ought to, if only for testing purposes, get it and install it immediately.

 The latest version of Chrome can be downloaded from `https://www.google.com/intl/en/chrome/browser/`.

We'll keep all of the files for this project in a single directory, so set one up in the project folder now and call it `chrome-extension`. The extension will be built from the same base code files as most of the other projects that we've created have been built from; the only difference is that all files will need to be local to the extension.

We're going to need a copy of JsRender, so we should also download a copy of that and place it in the `chrome-extension` directory. Last time we used JsRender we linked to the live hosted version. This time we'll download it.

The latest version of JsRender can be downloaded from
`https://github.com/BorisMoore/jsrender/`.

We can use the template file that we've started the other projects with, but we should make sure the paths to jQuery, the JavaScript file, and the style sheets all point to files in the same directory. All of the files used by a Chrome extension must be in the same folder, which is why we download the scripts instead of linking to online versions.

We should place copies of jQuery, JsRender, and the `common.css` style sheet into the new directory. We also need to create a new JavaScript file called `popup.js` and a new style sheet called `popup.css` and save these files into the new directory also.

Lastly, we can create a new HTML page called `popup.html`. This file should also be saved in the `chrome-extension` directory, and should contain the following code:

```
<!DOCTYPE html>
<html lang="en">
    <head>
        <meta charset="utf-8" />
        <title>jQuery-Powered Chrome Extension</title>
        <link rel="stylesheet" href="common.css" />
        <link rel="stylesheet" href="popup.css" />
    </head>
    <body>
        <script src="jquery-1.8.0.min.js"></script>
        <script src="jsrender.js"></script>
        <script src="popup.js"></script>
    </body>
</html>
```

Engage Thrusters

The HTML file we just created will be used as the extension's popup. This is the page that is displayed as a popup when the extension's icon is clicked in the toolbar. In this project we'll be creating a type of extension known as a **browser action**, which automatically adds a button to Chrome's toolbar which is used to open the popup.

The popup will display a button used to trigger a scan of the current page for microdata and display any previously saved contacts. Any previously stored contacts will be retrieved using the localStorage API, and we can use a template to render them.

First we can add the general markup to the page; in `popup.html` add the following code to the `<body>` of the page:

```
<section role="main">
    <header>
        <h1>Web Contacts</h1>
    </header>
    <ul id="contacts"></ul>
</section>
<iframe id="poster" src="template.html"></iframe>
```

We can also add some basic styling for these elements. In `popup.css`, add the following code:

```
body { width:32em; padding:0 2em; }
header { padding-top:2em; }
ul { padding:0 0 1em; font-size:1.5em; }
iframe { display:none; }
```

Objective Complete - Mini Debriefing

Chrome extensions are built using the same files that as web developers we're used to working with – HTML, CSS, and JavaScript. The extension will add a button to the toolbar and when this button is clicked, it will display a popup. The HTML page that we added in this task is the basis of this popup.

We create the page like we would create any other standard HTML5 page. We linked to the CSS and JavaScript files as usual, and then added a small `<section>` container which will be used as a container for any previously saved contacts. Initially there won't be any, and when there are, we'll render them using a template.

We've added a `<header>` containing a `<h1>` to give the saved contacts a title, and have added an empty `<ul>` element that we'll populate shortly with a script.

Lastly we added an `<iframe>` to the page, which will be hidden from view. We'll use this to communicate with another part of the extension a little later on. The `src` attribute of the element is set to the page we want to send messages to.

The CSS we added was purely for presentation and just laid out the initial elements in a simple layout. We're also linking to the common CSS file that each of the other projects have also used, but don't forget, all files used by the extension must be in the extension's directory.

Classified Intel

As we are creating a browser action we'll get a new button added to Chrome's toolbar which will be visible as long as the unpacked extension is loaded. By default it will have the standard extension icon – a puzzle piece, but we can replace this with an icon of our own creation.

We can also create other types of extension which don't add a button to the toolbar. We could create a page action instead of a browser action, which adds an icon to the address bar instead of the toolbar.

Whether this icon is visible on all pages or not will depend on how the extension behaves. For example, if we wanted to run our extension every time a page was loaded in the browser, but only display the icon if it found Schema.org microdata on the page, we could use a page action.

A browser action, such as we'll create here, is accessible all of the time, regardless of the page being viewed. We're using a browser action instead of a page action because the users of our extension will probably want to be able to see contacts they have previously found and saved, so a browser action is perfect for facilitating an always-available button to display any data stored by the extension.

Adding a manifest and installing the extension

In order to actually install our extension and see the fruits of our labor so far, we'll need to create a manifest file. This special file, saved in JSON format, controls certain aspects of the extension such as the pages it uses, and the content scripts it can run.

Prepare for Lift Off

In a new file add the following code:

```
{
    "name": "Web Contacts",
    "version": "1.0",
    "manifest_version": 2,
    "description": "Scrape web pages for Schema.org micro-data",
    "browser_action": {
        "default_popup": "popup.html"
    }
}
```

Save this file in the chrome-extension directory that we created at the start of the task within our main project directory as manifest.json.

If the text editor you're using doesn't show **.json** in the **Save as type:** (or equivalent) drop-down, select the **All types (*)** option and type the full filename `manifest.json` in the **File name:** input field.

Engage Thrusters

In order to view the extension as it currently exists, it will need to be loaded in Chrome as an extension. To do this, you should go to **Settings | Tools | Extensions**.

 In recent versions of Chrome, the **Settings** menu is accessed by clicking on the button that has three stripes as its icon, which is situated at the top-right of the browser window.

When the extensions page loads, there should be a button to **Load unpacked extension....** If there isn't, tick the **Developer mode** checkbox and the button will appear.

Hit the button and select the `chrome-extension` folder as the extension directory. This should install the extension and add the browser action button to the toolbar for us.

Objective Complete - Mini Debriefing

The simple manifest file is required by the extension before it can be loaded in the browser. Only manifests of at least Version 2 are allowed by the current version of Chrome. The manifest is required and the extension will not run without it. It is a simple text file, in JSON format, that is used to tell the browser some of the basic information about the extension, such as its name, who authored it, and the current version.

We can specify that our extension is a browser action, which adds a button for the extension to Chrome's toolbar. We can also specify the page that will be displayed in the popup using the manifest.

When the new button for our extension is clicked, the HTML page (`popup.html`) we added in the previous task will be displayed in the extension popup, as shown in the following screenshot:

Adding a sandboxed JsRender template

In this task we can add the template that JsRender will use to display the saved contacts. At this point we don't have any saved, but we can still wire it up ready, and then when we do have some contacts, they'll be rendered into the popup without any fuss.

Prepare for Lift Off

Chrome uses a **Content Security Policy (CSP)** in order to prevent a large number of common **cross-site scripting (XSS)** attacks, and because of this we are not allowed to execute any scripts that use either `eval()` or `new Function()`.

The JsRender templating library, like many other popular libraries and frameworks, uses `new Function()` when compiling templates and therefore is not allowed to run directly inside the extension. There are two ways we can overcome this problem:

▶ We could switch to a templating library that offers a pre-compilation of templates, such as the popular `Dust.js`. We could then compile our template outside of the extension in a browser and link to a JavaScript file containing the function that the template is compiled into from within the extension. The function that would be created with `new Function()` would then already have been created prior to the extension even being installed, and the template could then be rendered inside the extension, interpolated with any data made available within the extension.

▶ Or, Chrome's extension system allows us to use certain files inside a specified sandbox. Unsafe string-to-function features such as `eval()` or `new Function()` are allowed to run in the sandbox because the code is insulated from the extension's data and API access within the browser.

We'll use the sandboxing feature in this example, so that we can continue using JsRender.

Engage Thrusters

First of all we have to set up the sandbox, which is done by specifying which pages to sandbox using the manifest file that we created earlier. Add the following code to `manifest.json`, directly before the final closing curly bracket:

```
"sandbox": {
    "pages": ["template.html"]
}
```

Don't forget to add a comma directly after the closing curly bracket of the `browser_action` property.

We've specified `template.html` as the page to sandbox. Create a new file called `template.html` and save it in the `chrome-extension` directory. It should contain the following code:

```html
<!DOCTYPE html>

<html lang="en">
    <head>
        <meta charset="utf-8" />
        <script id="contactTemplate" type="text/x-jsrender">
            {{for contacts}}
                <li>
                    <article>
                        <div class="details">
                            <h1>{{:name}}</h1>
                            {{if url}}
                                <span>website: {{url}}</span>
                            {{/if}}
                            {{if jobTitle}}
                                <h2>{{:jobTitle}}</h2>
                            {{/if}}
                            {{if companyName}}
                                <span class="company">
                                    {{:companyName}}
                                </span>
                            {{/if}}
                            {{if address}}
                                <p>{{:address}}</p>
                            {{/if}}
                            {{if contactMethods}}
                                <dl>
                                    {{for
                                    ~getMembers(contactMethods)}}
                                        <dd>{{:key}}</dd>
                                        <dt>{{:val}}</dt>
                                    {{/for}}
                                </dl>
                            {{/if}}
                        </div>
                    </article>
```

```
                    </li>
                {{/for}}
            </script>
            <script src="jquery-1.9.0.min.js"></script>
            <script src="jsrender.js"></script>
            <script src="template.js"></script>
        </head>
    </html>
```

The template page also references the `template.js` script file. We should create this file in the `chrome-extension` directory and add the following code to it:

```
(function () {
    $.views.helpers({
        getMembers: function (obj) {
            var prop,
                arr = [];

            for (prop in obj) {
                if (obj.hasOwnProperty(prop)) {
                    var newObj = {
                        key: prop,
                        val: obj[prop]
                    }

                    arr.push(newObj);
                }
            }

            return arr;
        }
    });
} ());
```

Objective Complete - Mini Debriefing

We started out by adding a new HTML page to the extension. The page called `template.html` is like a regular web page except that it doesn't have a `<body>`, just a `<head>` that links to some JavaScript resources, and a `<script>` element containing the template we'll be using.

Usually in a Chrome extension, the CSP prevents us from running any inline scripts – all scripts should reside within external files. Using a non-standard `type` attribute on the `<script>` element allows us to circumvent this so that we can store our template inside the page instead of having another external file.

The bulk of the new page is the template itself. `Schema.org` microdata allows people to add a lot of additional information to describe the elements on the page, so there are a range of different bits of information that may be stored in the extension.

Our template therefore makes use of a lot of conditionals to display things if they are present. The extension should always display the name, but aside from that it may display an image, a job title and company, an address, or various contact methods, or any combination thereof.

The most complex part of the template is the `getMembers()` helper function. We'll call this helper function for each object in the `contactMethods` object using JsRender's `{{for}}` tag, which calls the helper function using the tilde (~) character. Inside the loop we'll have access to the values returned by the helper and can insert these into the relevant elements.

Next we added the `template.js` script file. At this point all we need to add to this script file is the helper method used by the template to render any contact methods. These will be in the format `{ email: me@me.com }`.

The helper is registered using JsRender's `helpers()` method. This method is passed an object where the name of the helper is specified as the key and the function that should be invoked is the value.

The function receives an object. We first create an empty array and then iterate the object using a standard `for in` loop. We first check that the property being iterated belongs to the object and is not inherited from the prototype using JavaScript's `hasOwnProperty()` function.

We then just create a new object and set the key as a property called `key`, and the value as a property called `val`. These are the template variables that we use in the `<dl>` in our template.

This new object is then pushed into the array we created, and once the object passed to the helper has been iterated, we return the array to the template for the `{{for}}` loop to iterate.

Posting a message to the sandbox

In this task we'll set up the communication between our popup and the sandboxed template page to see how we can get the template to render when the popup is opened.

Engage Thrusters

First of all we can add the code that sends the message to the sandboxed page requesting the template to render. In `popup.js`, add the following code:

```
var iframe = $("#poster"),
    message = {
        command: "issueTemplate",
        context: JSON.parse(localStorage.getItem("webContacts"))
    };
    iframe.on("load", function () {
        if (message.context) {
            iframe[0].contentWindow.postMessage(message, "*");
        } else {
            $("<li>", {
                text: "No contacts added yet"
            }).appendTo($("#contacts"));
        }
    });

window.addEventListener("message", function (e) {
    $("#contacts").append((e.data.markup));
});
```

Next we need to add the code that will respond to the initial message. Add the following code to `template.js` directly after the helper method we added in the last task:

```
var template = $.templates($("#contactTemplate").html());

window.addEventListener("message", function (e) {
    if (e.data.command === "issueTemplate") {

        var message = {
            markup: template.render(e.data.context)
        };

        e.source.postMessage(message, event.origin);
    }
});
```

Objective Complete - Mini Debriefing

First of all we set up the initial messaging in `popup.js`. We cached the `<iframe>` element from the popup in a variable and then composed a message. The message is in the form of an object literal with a `command` property and a `context` property.

The `command` property tells the code running in the `<iframe>` what to do, while the `context` contains the data to be rendered into a template. The data that we'll render will be stored in localStorage under the `webContacts` key, and the data will be in JSON format so we need to convert it back to a JavaScript object using `JSON.parse()`.

We then add a load handler to the `<iframe>` element using jQuery's `on()` method. The code contained in the anonymous function passed to `on()` will be executed when the contents of the `<iframe>` have loaded.

Once this occurs, we check whether the `context` property of the `message` object has a truthy value. If it does, we post the `message` object to the `<iframe>` using the `postMessage()` function of the iframe's `contentWindow` property.

The `postMessage()` function takes two arguments – the first is what to post, which in this case is our `message` object, and the second argument specifies which files can receive the message. We set this to a wildcard * so that any files can subscribe to our message.

If there aren't any stored contacts, the `context` property of our `message` object will have the falsey value `null`. In this case we simply create a new `<li>` element with a text message advising that there are no saved contacts and append this directly to the empty `<ul>` hardcoded into `popup.html`.

Our script file `popup.js` will also need to receive messages. We use the standard JavaScript `addEventListener()` function to attach a listener for `message` events to the `window`. By default jQuery does not handle `message` events.

The messages received by `popup.js` will be the response from the sandboxed page containing the HTML markup to render. The markup will be contained in a property called `markup`, which will be contained in the `data` property of the event object. We simply select the `<ul>` element in `popup.html` and append the markup we receive.

We also added some code to `template.js`, the script file referenced by the page inside our `<iframe>`. We used the `addEventListener()` function here to subscribe to message events again.

This time we first check whether the `command` property of the object sent as the message is equal to `issueTemplate`. If it is, we then create and render the data into our JsRender template and compose a new `message` object containing the rendered template markup.

Once the message object has been created we post it back to popup.js. We can get the window object to send the message using the source property of the event object, and we can specify which files can receive the message using the origin property of the event object.

These two properties are very similar except that source contains a window object and origin contains a filename. The filename will be a special chrome extension name. At this point we should be able to launch the popup and see the **No contacts** message as we don't have any saved contacts yet.

Adding a content script

We're now at the stage where everything is in place to display stored contacts, so we can focus on actually getting some contacts. In order to interact with pages that the user navigates to in their browser, we need to add a content script.

A content script is just like a regular script, except that it interacts with the page being displayed in the browser instead of with the files that make up the extension. We'll see that we can post messages between these different areas (the page in the browser and the extension) in a similar way that we posted a message to our sandbox.

Engage Thrusters

First we'll need to add some new files to the chrome-extension directory. We'll need a JavaScript file called content.js and a style sheet called content.css. We need to tell our extension to use these files, so we should also add a new section to the manifest file (manifest.json) we created earlier in the project:

```
"content_scripts": [{
    "matches": ["*://*/*"],
    "css": ["content.css"],
    "js": ["jquery-1.9.0.min.js", "content.js"]
}]
```

This new section should be added directly after the sandbox section that we added earlier (as before, don't forget to add the trailing comma after the sandbox property).

Next we can add the required behavior to `content.js`:

```
(function () {

    var people = $("[itemtype*='schema.org/Person']"),
        peopleData = [];

    if (people.length) {

        people.each(function (i) {

            var person = microdata.eq(i),
                data = {},
                contactMethods = {};

            person.addClass("app-person");

        });
    }
} ());
```

We can also add some basic styling that highlights any elements that contain microdata attributes using the `content.css` style sheet. Update this file now so that it contains the following code:

```
.app-person {
    position:relative; box-shadow:0 0 3px rgba(0,0,0, .5);
    background-color:#fff;
}
```

Objective Complete - Mini Debriefing

First of all we updated our manifest file to include a content script. As I mentioned, content scripts are used to interact with the visible page being displayed in the browser instead of any files used by the extension.

We can enable a content script using the `content_script` rule in the manifest. We need to specify which pages the content script should be loaded into. We use a wildcard (*) for the `protocol`, `host`, and `path` portions of URLs so that the script is loaded when any page is visited.

When using `Schema.org` microdata to describe people, the different bits of information that are present are placed within a container (usually a `<div>` element although any element can be used) that has the special attribute `itemtype`.

The value of this attribute is a URL that specifies what the data the elements it contains describe. So to describe a person, this container would have the URL `http://schema.org/Person`. This means that the elements the container has in it may have additional attributes that describe a specific piece of data, such as a name, or a job title. These additional attributes on the elements within the container will be `itemprop`.

In this case we're using a jQuery attribute-contains selector (`*=`) to attempt to select elements containing this attribute from the page. If the array the attribute selector returns has length (and is therefore not empty), we know that at least one of these elements exists on the page and so can process the element further.

The collection of elements with this attribute are stored in a variable called `people`. We also create an empty array in the variable `peopleData` ready to store all of the information about all of the people found on the page.

We then use jQuery's `each()` method to iterate the elements selected from the page. Instead of using `$(this)` inside our `each()` loop, we can use the collection of elements that we've already selected from the page, in conjunction with jQuery's `eq()` method along with the current index of the loop in order to reference each element, which we store in a variable called `person`.

We also create an empty object and store it in a variable called `data` ready to store the microdata for each person, and an empty object called `contactMethods` as any microdata for a telephone number or e-mail address needs to be added to a subobject for our template to consume.

All we do at this point is add a new class name to the container element. We can then use the `content.css` style sheet to add some very basic styling to the element so that it is brought to the user's attention.

Scraping the page for microdata

Now that we've got our content script in place, we can interact with any web page that the user of the extension visits and check whether it has any microdata attributes.

At this point, any element containing microdata is highlighted to the user, so we need to add the functionality that will allow the user to view the microdata and save it if he/she wishes, which is what we'll be covering in this task.

Engage Thrusters

Directly after where we add a class name to each element that has an itemtype attribute in content.js, add the following code:

```js
person.children().each(function (j) {

    var child = person.children().eq(j),
        iProp = child.attr("itemprop");

    if (iProp) {

        if (child.attr("itemscope") !== "") {

            if (iProp === "email" || iProp === "telephone") {
                contactMethods[iProp] = child.text();
            } else {
                data[iProp] = child.text();
            }
        } else {

            var content = [];

            child.children().each(function (x) {
                content.push(child.children().eq(x).text());
            });

            data[iProp] = content.join(", ");
        }
    }
});

var hasProps = function (obj) {
    var prop,
    hasData = false;

    for (prop in obj) {
        if (obj.hasOwnProperty(prop)) {
            hasData = true;
            break;

        }
    }

    return hasData;
```

```
};

if (hasProps(contactMethods)) {
    data.contactMethods = contactMethods;
}

peopleData.push(data);
```

Objective Complete - Mini Debriefing

In the last task we added a class name to each container of elements marked up with microdata. In this task we're still in the context of the each() loop that processed each container.

So in the code we added in this task we first call each() again, this time on the direct children of the container element; we can get these easily using jQuery's children() method.

Inside this each() loop we first get the current item from the existing cached person variable using the loop counter passed to our iteration function (j) as an argument for jQuery's eq() method. This avoids creating a brand new jQuery object inside our loop.

We also store the value of the current element's itemprop attribute in a variable called iProp because we'll need to refer to it a number of times and using a nice short variable means less typing for us.

At this point we don't know whether we're dealing with a regular element, or an element containing microdata, so we use an if statement that checks whether the iProp variable we just set has a truthy value. If the element doesn't have an itemprop attribute this variable will hold an empty string, which is falsey and stops the code progressing further if the element is just a regular element.

Inside this conditional we know we're dealing with an element containing microdata, but there are different formats that the data may take. If the element contains an address for example, it won't have any content directly, but will have child elements of its own containing the data instead. In this case, the element will have an itemscope attribute. First we want to process the elements that don't contain an itemscope attribute so the first branch of our nested conditional checks the value returned by selecting the itemscope attribute is not an empty string.

If you remember our template, we set up a helper function that displayed contact information using an object. In order to create this new object instead of creating a new property of the data object, we use another nested if statement to check whether the iProp variable contains an e-mail or telephone number.

If it does, we add the value of the `iProp` variable as the key of the `contactMethods` object, and the text of the element as the value. If the `iProp` variable doesn't contain an e-mail address or a telephone number, we set the `iProp` variable as a key of the `data` object, and its value as the element's content.

The next branch of the second nested `if` statement is for elements that do have an `itemscope` attribute. In this case, we first define an empty array and store it in a variable called `content`. We then iterate over the child elements using jQuery's `each()` method and push the text content of each element into the `content` array.

Once we have iterated over the child elements and populated the array, we can then add the current `iProp` variable and the data in the `content` array to our `data` object. Any element that has an `itemscope` attribute should still have an `itemprop` attribute, so this should still work.

So at this point our data object should be an accurate representation of the microdata set on elements inside our main container. Before we do anything with them however, we need to check whether the `contentMethods` object has been populated, and if so add it to our `data` object.

We can use the `hasProps()` function to check whether an object has its own properties. The function will receive the object to test as an argument. Inside the function we first define the `hasData` variable, which we set to `false`.

We then use a `for in` loop to iterate over each property of the object. For each property we check whether the property actually exists on the object and was not inherited using JavaScript's `hasOwnProperty()` function. If the property does belong to the object, we set the `hasData` to `true` and then break out of the loop using `break`.

We then check whether the `contactMethods` object has any properties by passing it to our `hasProps()` function, and if it does we add it to the `data` object. Finally, once all this processing has been done, we add the `data` object to the `peopleData` array we defined at the start of our code.

Adding a mechanism for saving the microdata

At this point, if the page being displayed in Chrome contains any person microdata, we'll have an array containing one or more objects that contain the microdata and the text it describes. In this task we'll allow the user to store that data if he/she wishes.

Because our content script runs in the context of a web page and not our extension, we'll need to use messaging once again to pass any gathered data back to the extension for storage.

Prepare for Lift Off

In order to set up messaging between our content script and the extension, we'll need to add a background page. A background page runs continuously while the extension is installed and enabled and will allow us to set up handlers to listen and respond to messages sent from the content script.

Background pages may be HTML or JavaScript. In this project we'll use the JavaScript version. Create a new file now and save it in the `chrome-extension` directory as `background.js`. We also need to register this file as a background script by adding a new `background` section to the `manifest.json` file:

```
"background": {
    "scripts": ["jquery-1.9.0.min.js", "background.js"]
}
```

This code should come directly after the array listing the `content_scripts`. Again, don't forget the trailing comma after the array.

Engage Thrusters

First we'll add the required behavior to our background page. In `background.js`, add the following code:

```
chrome.extension.onConnect.addListener(function (port) {

    port.onMessage.addListener(function (msg) {

        if (msg.command === "getData") {

            var contacts = localStorage.getItem("webContacts")
|| '{ "message": "no contacts" }',
                jsonContacts = JSON.parse(contacts);

            port.postMessage(jsonContacts);

        } else if (msg.command === "setData") {

            localStorage.setItem("webContacts",
JSON.stringify({
                contacts: msg.contacts
            }));

            port.postMessage({ message: "success" });
        }
    });
});
```

Next, in `content.js`, directly after where we pushed a `data` object into the `peopleData` array, add the following code:

```
$("<a/>", {
    href: "#",
    "class": "app-save",
    text: "Save"
}).on("click", function (e) {
    e.preventDefault();

    var el = $(this),
        port = chrome.extension.connect(),
        contacts;

    if (!el.hasClass("app-saved")) {

        port.postMessage({ command: "getData" });
        port.onMessage.addListener(function (msg) {

            if (msg.message === "no contacts") {

                contacts = [peopleData[i]];

                port.postMessage({
                    command:"setData",
                    contacts:contacts
                });
            } else if (msg.contacts) {

                contacts = msg.contacts;
                contacts.push(peopleData[i]);

                port.postMessage({
                    command: "setData",
                    contacts: contacts
                });

            } else if (msg.message === "success") {

                el.addClass("app-saved")
                    .text("Contact information saved");

            port.disconnect();

            }
        });
    }
}).appendTo(person);
```

Finally, we can add a little styling for the new save link that we just added. In `content.css`, add the following code at the bottom of the file:

```
.app-save { position:absolute; top:5px; right:5px; }
.app-saved { opacity:.5; cursor:default; }
```

Objective Complete - Mini Debriefing

We added quite a lot of code in this task as there were a number of different files that we updated in order to get the different parts of the extension communicating.

Adding the communication module

First of all we updated the behavior page that we added at the start of the task. We'll be using localStorage to store saved contacts gathered by the extension, but the content script that runs in the context of web pages viewed by the user of the extension only has access to the localStorage area for any given page, but we need access to the localStorage area for the extension itself.

To achieve this, our `background.js` file will act as a mediator that will access the extension's localStorage area and pass data back and forth between the content script and the extension.

First we added a listener to the `onConnect` event, which we can access via Chrome's `extension` utility module. When a content script makes a connection to the extension, a port will be opened automatically by the browser. An object representing this port will be passed to our handler function automatically.

We can use the port to add an event handler for message events. As with our simple `<iframe>` messaging from earlier in the project, this handler function will automatically be passed the message that triggers the event.

Inside the message handler, we check whether the message's `command` property is equal to `getData`. If it is, we first create a `contacts` object, which will consist of either the contacts obtained from the localStorage `getItem()` method, or a very simple JSON object that simply contains the message `no contacts`, which we can create manually.

Once we have either of these JSON objects, we can then parse it into a proper JavaScript object using Chrome's native JSON `parse()` method. We can then pass this object back to the port using the `postMessage()` method. A new port will be opened whenever a new connection is made, so messages will automatically be passed back to the correct port without additional configuration by us.

If the `command` property of the `msg` object does not equal `getData`, it may equal `setData` instead. If it does, we want to store one or more new contacts to localStorage. In this case we'll pass the contacts to store as an object contained in the `contacts` property of the `msg` object, so we can simply use the `stringify()` method on the object in this property as the second argument to the `setItem()` method.

We can then pass back a short message confirming that saving the data has been a success using the `port` object's `postMessage()` method once more.

Updating the content script

Secondly we updated the `content.js` file in order to harvest and store any contact information found on the web page being viewed by the visitor.

We started out by adding a new `<a>` element that will be used as a button to save contact information and which will be added to any element containing microdata. We added a simple `# href` attribute to the new element, a class name for styling purposes, and the text `Save`.

Most of the new functionality is contained in a click event handler attached directly to each new `<a>` element when it is created using jQuery's `on()` method.

Within this event handler we first stop the default behavior of the browser using `preventDefault()`, as we usually do when attaching event handlers to `<a>` elements. We then cache a reference to the current `<a>` element by storing `$(this)` in a variable called `el`. We also open up a new port to handle our communication needs using the `extension` module's `connect()` method. A `contacts` variable is declared but not defined straight away.

The rest of the code resides within an `if` conditional that checks the element does not already have the class name `app-saved`, which will help prevent duplicate entries for the same person on a single page being saved to localStorage.

In the conditional we first need to get any previously stored contacts, so we request the saved contacts from the behavior page by posting a message to the port we opened a moment ago. We send an object as the message which has a `command` property set to `getData`.

We then add a handler for the response to this message using the `addListener()` method on the `onMessage` event. The rest of our code is within this handler, which consists of another conditional that reacts differently depending on the response message.

The first branch of the conditional deals with when the `message` property of the response `msg` contains the string `no contacts`. In this case we create a new array which contains the contact information harvested from the person for whichever save link was clicked. We already have this information in the `peopleData` array and as we're still inside the loop that updates each person, we can use the `i` variable to store the correct person.

We can then send this array to the behavior page for permanent storage in the extension's localStorage area.

If the `msg` object doesn't have a `message` property it may have a `contacts` property instead. This property will contain the array of previously stored contacts so we can save the array to a variable, and add the new contact to this array before posting the updated array back to the behavior page for permanent storage.

The final branch of the conditional deals with a successful save of the contact. In this case the `message` property of the `msg` object will contain the `success` string. In this case we add the class name `app-saved` to the `<a>` element and change the text to `Contact information saved`. As the port is no longer required we can close it using the `disconnect()` method of the `port` object.

Adding the simple styling

Lastly we added some very simple styling for the save links. It's important to show feedback once the operation that the user initiates has completed.

In this example, we do that by changing the text of the link simply making it more opaque using CSS to make it look as if it is no longer clickable, which is the case because of the `if` statement we used in the script.

At this point we should now be able to browse to a page that contains microdata and save contact information. When the browser action button is clicked, we'll see the popup, which should display the saved contact, as shown in the screenshot at the start of the project.

Classified Intel

When testing content scripts, it's important to realize that whenever any of the content files change, which in this case means either the JavaScript file or the style sheet, the extension must be reloaded.

To reload the extension, there's a **Reload** (*Ctrl + R*) link below the extension listed on Chrome's **Extensions** page. We'll need to click on this link to apply changes made to any of the content files. Other parts of the extension, such as the popup files for example, do not require that the extension be reloaded.

Another useful tool for extension programmers is the developer tool, which can be opened specifically to monitor the code in the background page. This can be useful for troubleshooting errors and script debugging when using a background page.

Mission Accomplished

In this project we've covered most of the basics of building a Chrome extension. We covered creating a browser action that triggers a popup when it is clicked in order to display saved contacts.

We also saw how we can safely sandbox pages that need to run dangerous code such as `eval()` or `new Function` in order to protect our extension from XSS attacks, and how we can use the simple messaging API to send messages and receive responses to an `<iframe>` element containing the sandboxed page.

We saw that as well as defining scripts that run in the context of the extension, we can also add content scripts that run in the context of the web page being displayed in the browser. We also learned how to use the `manifest.json` file to specify these different areas of our extension.

We also saw that we can use a much more advanced messaging system that allows us to open ports that allow for more than simple one-way messages. Communicating via ports allows us to send as many messages back and forth from different areas of our extension as we need to in order to complete a given task such as saving data to the extension's localStorage area.

We also learned about the type of data that can be described using `Schema.org` microdata, and the HTML attributes that can be added to elements in order to do the describing. As well as being able to describe people, there are also `Schema.org` formats for describing places, companies, movies, and much more.

We've learned a lot about creating extensions in Chrome, but we've also used a ton of jQuery methods in order to simplify the scripts that we've written to power the extension.

You Ready To Go Gung HO?
A Hotshot Challenge

When our extension saves new contacts, the highlighted elements representing the elements containing microdata are given a new CSS class name and have some very minimal additional styling added to them.

This is ok, but a better way of confirming success would be to make use of Chrome's desktop notification system to generate growl-style pop-up notifications that confirm success instead.

Check out the notification documentation at `http://developer.chrome.com/extensions/notifications.html` and see if you can update the extension to include this feature.

Project 7
Build Your Own jQuery

With the 1.8 release of jQuery, something new was introduced that the development community as a whole had been wanting for a while – the ability to build custom versions of jQuery that contained only the functionality that was required for a given task.

Mission Briefing

In this project we'll set up the environment we need in order to use jQuery's build tool. We'll see what other software we need to use, how to run the build tool itself, and what we can expect as output of the build tool.

Why Is It Awesome?

While it's fairly common for someone to say that they use jQuery in every site they build (this is usually the case for me), I would expect it much rarer for someone to say that they use the exact same jQuery methods in every project, or that they use a very large selection of the available methods and functionality that it offers.

The need to reduce file size as aggressively as possible to cater for the mobile space, and the rise of micro-frameworks such as **Zepto** for example, which delivers a lot of jQuery functionality at a much-reduced size, have pushed jQuery to provide a way of slimming down.

As of jQuery 1.8, we can now use the official jQuery build tool to build our own custom version of the library, allowing us to minimize the size of the library by choosing only the functionality we require.

 For more information on Zepto, see `http://zeptojs.com/`.

Your Hotshot Objectives

To successfully conclude this project we'll need to complete the following tasks:

- ▸ Installing Git and Make
- ▸ Installing Node.js
- ▸ Installing Grunt.js
- ▸ Configuring the environment
- ▸ Building a custom jQuery
- ▸ Running unit tests with QUnit

Mission Checklist

We'll be using Node.js to run the build tool, so you should download a copy of this now. The Node website (`http://nodejs.org/download/`) has an installer for both 64 and 32-bit versions of Windows, as well as a Mac OS X installer. It also features binaries for Mac OS X, Linux, and SunOS. Download and install the appropriate version for your operating system.

The official build tool for jQuery (although it can do much more besides build jQuery) is **Grunt.js,** written by *Ben Alman*. We don't need to download this as it's installed via the **Node Package Manager** (**NPM**). We'll look at this process in detail later in the project.

 For more information on Grunt.js, visit the official site at `http://gruntjs.com`.

First of all we need to set up a local working area. We can create a folder in our root project folder called `jquery-source`. This is where we'll store the jQuery source when we clone the jQuery Github repository, and also where Grunt will build the final version of jQuery.

Installing Git and Make

The first thing we need to install is Git, which we'll need in order to clone the jQuery source from the Github repository to our own computer so that we can work with the source files. We also need something called Make, but we only need to actually install this on Mac platforms because it gets installed automatically on Windows when Git is installed.

 As the file we'll create will be for our own use only and we don't want to contribute to jQuery by pushing code back to the repository, we don't need to worry about having an account set up on Github.

Prepare for Lift Off

First we'll need to download the relevant installers for both Git and Make. Different applications are required depending on whether you are developing on Mac or Windows platforms.

Mac developers

Mac users can visit `http://git-scm.com/download/mac` for Git.

Next we can install Make. Mac developers can get this by installing XCode. This can be downloaded from `https://developer.apple.com/xcode/`.

Windows developers

Windows users can install **msysgit**, which can be obtained by visiting `https://code.google.com/p/msysgit/downloads/detail?name=msysGit-fullinstall-1.8.0-preview20121022.exe`.

Engage Thrusters

Once the installers have downloaded, run them to install the applications. The defaults selected by the installers should be fine for the purposes of this mission. First we should install Git (or msysgit on Windows).

Mac developers

Mac developers simply need to run the installer for Git to install it to the system. Once this is complete we can then install XCode. All we need to do is run the installer and Make, along with some other tools, will be installed and ready.

Windows developers

Once the full installer for msysgit has finished, you should be left with a Command Line Interface (CLI) window (entitled MINGW32) indicating that everything is ready for you to hack. However, before we can hack, we need to compile Git.

To do this we need to run a file called `initialize.sh`. In the MINGW32 window, `cd` into the `msysgit` directory. If you allowed this to install to the default location, you can use the following command:

```
cd C:\\msysgit\\msysgit\\share\\msysGit
```

Once we are in the correct directory, we can then run `initialize.sh` in the CLI. Like the installation, this process can take some time, so be patient and wait for the CLI to return a flashing cursor at the `$` character.

An Internet connection is required to compile Git in this way.

Windows developers will need to ensure that the Git.exe and MINGW resources can be reached via the system's PATH variable. This can be updated by going to **Control Panel | System | Advanced system settings | Environment variables**.

In the bottom section of the dialog box, double-click on **Path** and add the following two paths to the git.exe file in the bin folder, which is itself in a directory inside the msysgit folder wherever you chose to install it:

- ;C:\msysgit\msysgit\bin;
- C:\msysgit\msysgit\mingw\bin;

Update the path with caution!

You must ensure that the path to Git.exe is separated from the rest of the Path variables with a semicolon. If the path does not end with a semicolon before adding the path to Git.exe, make sure you add one. Incorrectly updating your path variables can result in system instability and/or loss of data. I have shown a semicolon at the start of the previous code sample to illustrate this.

Once the path has been updated, we should then be able to use a regular command prompt to run Git commands.

Post-installation tasks

In a terminal or Windows Command Prompt (I'll refer to both simply as the CLI from this point on for conciseness) window, we should first cd into the jquery-source folder we created at the start of the project. Depending on where your local development folder is, this command will look something like the following:

```
cd c:\jquery-hotshots\jquery-source
```

To clone the jQuery repository, enter the following command in the CLI:

```
git clone git://github.com/jquery/jquery.git
```

Again, we should see some activity on the CLI before it returns to a flashing cursor to indicate that the process is complete.

Depending on the platform you are developing on, you should see something like the following screenshot:

```
Administrator: Windows Command Processor                        _ □ ×
Microsoft Windows [Version 6.1.7601]
Copyright (c) 2009 Microsoft Corporation.  All rights reserved.

C:\Windows\System32>cd C:\Sites\jquery-hotshots\jquery-source

C:\Sites\jquery-hotshots\jquery-source>git clone git://github.com/jquery/jquery.
git
Cloning into 'jquery'...
remote: Counting objects: 27452, done.
remote: Compressing objects: 100% (7270/7270), done.
remote: Total 27452 (delta 20183), reused 26691 (delta 19584)
Receiving objects: 100% (27452/27452), 14.21 MiB | 112 KiB/s, done.
Resolving deltas: 100% (20183/20183), done.

C:\Sites\jquery-hotshots\jquery-source>
```

Objective Complete - Mini Debriefing

We installed Git and then used it to clone the jQuery Github repository in to this directory in order to get a fresh version of the jQuery source. If you're used to SVN, cloning a repository is conceptually the same as checking out a repository.

Again, the syntax of these commands is very similar on Mac and Windows systems, but notice how we need to escape the backslashes in the path when using Windows. Once this is complete, we should end up with a new directory inside our jquery-source directory called jquery.

If we go into this directory, there are some more directories including:

▶ build: This directory is used by the build tool to build jQuery

▶ speed: This directory contains benchmarking tests

▶ src: This directory contains all of the individual source files that are compiled together to make jQuery

▶ Test: This directory contains all of the unit tests for jQuery

It also has a range of various files, including:

▶ Licensing and documentation, including jQuery's authors and a guide to contributing to the project

▶ Git-specific files such as .gitignore and .gitmodules

▶ Grunt-specific files such as Gruntfile.js

▶ JSHint for testing and code-quality purposes

Make is not something we need to use directly, but Grunt will use it when we build the jQuery source, so it needs to be present on our system.

Installing Node.js

Node.js is a platform for running server-side applications built with JavaScript. It is trivial to create a web-server instance, for example, that receives and responds to HTTP requests using callback functions.

Server-side JS isn't exactly the same as its more familiar client-side counterpart, but you'll find a lot of similarities in the same comfortable syntax that you know and love. We won't actually be writing any server-side JavaScript in this project – all we need Node for is to run the Grunt.js build tool.

Prepare for Lift Off

To get the appropriate installer for your platform, visit the Node.js website at `http://nodejs.org` and hit the download button. The correct installer for your platform, if supported, should be auto-detected.

Engage Thrusters

Installing Node is a straightforward procedure on either the Windows or Mac platforms as there are installers for both. This task will include running the installer, which is obviously simple, and testing the installation using a CLI.

On Windows or Mac platforms, run the installer and it will guide you through the installation process. I have found that the default options are fine in most cases. As before, we also need to update the `Path` variable to include Node and Node's package manager NPM. The paths to these directories will differ between platforms.

Mac

Mac developers should check that the `$PATH` variable contains a reference to `usr/local/bin`. I found that this was already in my `$PATH`, but if you do find that it's not present, you should add it.

 For more information on updating your `$PATH` variable, see `http://www.tech-recipes.com/rx/2621/os_x_change_path_environment_variable/`.

Windows

Windows developers will need to update the `Path` variable, in the same way as before, with the following paths:

- ▸   `C:\Program Files\nodejs\;`
- ▸   `C:\Users\Desktop\AppData\Roaming\npm;`

 Windows developers may find that the `Path` variable already contains an entry for Node so may just need to add the path to NPM.

Objective Complete - Mini Debriefing

Once Node is installed, we will need to use a CLI to interact with it. To verify Node has installed correctly, type the following command into the CLI:

`node -v`

The CLI should report the version in use, as follows:

```
Administrator: Windows Command Processor                        _ □ ×
Microsoft Windows [Version 6.1.7601]
Copyright (c) 2009 Microsoft Corporation.   All rights reserved.

C:\Windows\System32>node -v
v0.8.16

C:\Windows\System32>
```

We can test NPM in the same way by running the following command:

`npm -v`

Installing Grunt.js

In this task we need to install Grunt.js, which is extremely quick and easy to do, just like the Node installation. We don't even need to download anything manually and as before the same commands should work on either Mac or Windows systems, with only very minor adjustments.

Engage Thrusters

We need to use **Node Package Manager NPM** to install it, and can do this by running the following command (note that Node itself must not be running):

```
npm install -g grunt-cli
```

 Mac users may need to use `superuser` do at the start of the command:

```
sudo -s npm install -g grunt
```

Be prepared to wait a few minutes. Again, we should see a lot of activity as the resources Grunt needs are downloaded and installed. The prompt will return to a flashing cursor once the installation is complete. The CLI should appear like the following screenshot, depending on which platform you are developing on:

```
Administrator: Windows Command Processor                               _ □ ✕
npm http 304 https://registry.npmjs.org/underscore.string
npm http 304 https://registry.npmjs.org/underscore
grunt@0.4.0 C:\Users\Desktop\AppData\Roaming\npm\node_modules\grunt
├── dateformat@1.0.2-1.2.3
├── which@1.0.5
├── colors@0.6.0-1
├── findup-sync@0.1.1
├── hooker@0.2.3
├── async@0.1.22
├── eventemitter2@0.4.11
├── coffee-script@1.3.3
├── iconv-lite@0.2.7
├── underscore.string@2.2.0rc
├── lodash@0.9.2
├── nopt@1.0.10 (abbrev@1.0.4)
├── rimraf@2.0.3 (graceful-fs@1.1.14)
├── minimatch@0.2.11 (sigmund@1.0.0, lru-cache@2.2.2)
├── glob@3.1.21 (inherits@1.0.0, graceful-fs@1.2.0)
├── js-yaml@1.0.3 (argparse@0.1.12)
```

Objective Complete - Mini Debriefing

If all goes according to plan (which, unless you have problems with your system, it generally should), you should see a lot of activity in the CLI while Grunt and its dependencies are downloaded and installed globally via NPM, and once that finishes Grunt will be installed and ready to use.

 An Internet connection is required for packages to be downloaded and installed automatically using NPM.

To verify that Grunt has installed correctly, we can type the following command into the CLI:

```
grunt -version
```

This will output the current version of Grunt and should work from any directory as Grunt was installed globally.

Classified Intel

As well as building custom versions of jQuery, Grunt can also be used to create a few different common projects. We start by choosing one of the following project types:

- `gruntfile`
- `commonjs`
- `jquery`
- `node`

We can run the built-in `init` task and specify one of these projects, and Grunt will go ahead and set up a skeleton project containing resources commonly used with that project.

For example, running the `jquery init` task will set up a working directory for creating a jQuery plugin. Inside the directory, Grunt will create folders for the source script files and the unit tests, as well as create a range of files including a `package.json` file.

It is likely that at some point all new jQuery plugins will need to be structured in the way that Grunt structures the working directory when creating this project type, so Grunt will become an invaluable, time-saving tool for any jQuery plugin developer.

Configuring the environment

There're just a couple of things left we need to do before we're ready to build our own version of jQuery. We can also test our installation and configuration by building the full version of jQuery in order to test that everything is working as it should.

Prepare for Lift Off

We'll need to install some additional Grunt dependencies so that we can create the jQuery Script files using the source files that we cloned from Github. There are also a range of NPM modules that the project uses, which also need to be installed. Fortunately the NPM can install everything for us automatically.

Engage Thrusters

Before we can build the jQuery source, we need to install some additional Grunt dependencies in the `jquery` source folder. We can do this using NPM and so can enter the following command into the CLI:

```
npm install
```

 Make sure you have already used the `cd` command to navigate to the `jquery` directory before running the `install` command.

There should be a lot of activity in the CLI after running the `install` command, and by the end of the process, the CLI should appear something like the following screenshot:

```
Administrator: Windows Command Processor                          _ □ ✕
npm http GET https://registry.npmjs.org/uglify-js
npm http 304 https://registry.npmjs.org/traverse
npm http 304 https://registry.npmjs.org/uglify-js
grunt-update-submodules@0.2.0 node_modules\grunt-update-submodules

grunt-compare-size@0.3.1 node_modules\grunt-compare-size
└── gzip-js@0.3.1 (crc32@0.2.2, deflate-js@0.2.2)

testswarm@0.2.2 node_modules\testswarm
└── request@2.14.0

grunt-contrib-watch@0.1.4 node_modules\grunt-contrib-watch
└── gaze@0.2.2 (async@0.1.22, lodash@0.10.0, minimatch@0.2.11, glob@3.1.21)

grunt-contrib-jshint@0.1.1rc6 node_modules\grunt-contrib-jshint
└── jshint@0.9.1 (minimatch@0.0.5, cli@0.4.3)

grunt-contrib-uglify@0.1.1rc6 node_modules\grunt-contrib-uglify
├── gzip-js@0.3.1 (crc32@0.2.2, deflate-js@0.2.2)
└── uglify-js@2.2.5 (optimist@0.3.5, source-map@0.1.8)

grunt@0.4.0rc5 node_modules\grunt
├── dateformat@1.0.2-1.2.3
├── which@1.0.5
├── colors@0.6.0-1
├── findup-sync@0.1.1
├── hooker@0.2.3
├── async@0.1.22
├── eventemitter2@0.4.11
├── iconv-lite@0.2.7
├── coffee-script@1.3.3
├── underscore.string@2.2.0rc
├── lodash@0.9.2
├── nopt@1.0.10 (abbrev@1.0.4)
├── rimraf@2.0.3 (graceful-fs@1.1.14)
├── minimatch@0.2.11 (sigmund@1.0.0, lru-cache@2.2.2)
├── glob@3.1.21 (inherits@1.0.0, graceful-fs@1.2.0)
└── js-yaml@1.0.3 (argparse@0.1.12)

grunt-git-authors@1.0.0 node_modules\grunt-git-authors
└── grunt@0.3.17 (dateformat@1.0.2-1.2.3, colors@0.6.0-1, semver@1.0.14, async@
.1.22, hooker@0.2.3, underscore@1.2.4, underscore.string@2.1.1, uglify-js@1.3.4
 nopt@1.0.10, gzip-js@0.3.1, temporary@0.0.5, glob-whatev@0.1.8, jshint@0.9.1,
rompt@0.1.12, connect@2.4.6, nodeunit@0.7.4)

C:\Sites\jquery-hotshots\jquery-source\jquery>
```

To test that everything is working together as it should, we can build the full version of jQuery. Simply run the `grunt` command in the CLI:

grunt

> If you get any errors or warnings at this point, something has not been installed or configured correctly. There could be any number of reasons why the process has failed, so the best thing to do is to uninstall everything we have installed, and start the process again, ensuring that all steps are followed to the letter.

Again, we should see a lot of activity on the CLI to indicate that things are happening:

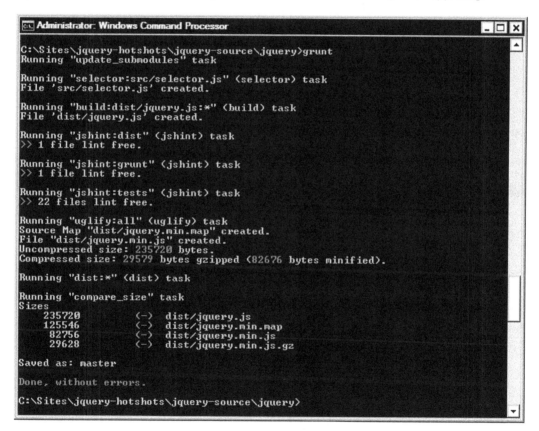

Objective Complete - Mini Debriefing

Once the install process has completed, we should find that the Node dependencies have been installed into a directory within the `jquery` directory called `node_modules`. Within this folder are any additional files that Grunt needs for this specific project.

To test everything, we then ran the default build task for jQuery using the `grunt` command. This task will do the following things:

- ▸ Read all of the jQuery source files
- ▸ Create a `/dist` directory for the output of the task
- ▸ Build the `jquery.js` distribution file
- ▸ Lint the distribution file with `jshint`
- ▸ Run the units tests
- ▸ Build a source map of the distribution file
- ▸ Build the `jquery.min.js` distribution file

The script files should be 230 KB for the full file and 81 KB for the `.min` file, although these figures may differ as the jQuery version number increases.

Building a custom jQuery

In this task we'll build a custom version of jQuery, which will not consist of all of the different modules that make up the "full" version of jQuery combined into the single file which we would normally download from the jQuery site, just like the files we built at the end of the last task, instead it will contain only the core modules.

Engage Thrusters

Now we can build a custom version of jQuery. To build a barebones version of jQuery, omitting all of the non-core components, we can enter the following command into the CLI:

```
grunt custom:-ajax,-css,-deprecated,-dimensions,-effects,-offset
```

Objective Complete - Mini Debriefing

Once we have the source and have configured our local environment, we are able to build a custom version of jQuery containing only the core components and omitting all of the optional components.

In this case we've excluded all of the optional components, but we could exclude any one of them, or any combination of them to produce a script file that is only as large as it needs to be.

If we check the /dist directory at this point, we should find now that the full-fat script file is now 159 KB, while the .min version is just 57 KB, saving us approximately 30 percent of the file size; not bad for a few minutes work!

 Changes in the functionality or scope of your project may necessitate that the source file be rebuilt and previously excluded modules included. Once excluded, optional modules cannot be added to the built files without rebuilding.

Classified Intel

As jQuery evolves, especially once the 2.0 milestone is passed, more and more of jQuery's components will be exposed to the build tool as optional components, so that it will become possible to exclude a wider portion of the library.

While at the time of writing the savings we make in file size may well be offset by the fact that the majority of our visitors won't have our custom version of jQuery in their cache and will therefore have to download it, there may come a time when we are able to shrink the size of the file so much that it will still be more efficient to download our super-light script file than it is to load the full source from the cache.

Running unit tests with QUnit

QUnit is the official test suite for jQuery and is included in the source that we cloned from Git earlier in the project. If we take a look in the test folder inside the jquery folder, we should find that there are a lot of unit tests written to test the different components that make jQuery.

We can run these tests against the individual components of jQuery in order to look at the environment that QUnit needs, and to see how easy testing JavaScript files using it can be. For this task we'll need to install a web server and PHP.

 For more information on QUnit, see the documentation at http://qunitjs.com.

Prepare for Lift Off

Mac developers should already have everything required in order to run QUnit through a web server, because Mac computers come with Apache and PHP already installed. Windows developers will probably have some setup to do however.

There are two options for the web server in this case, Apache or IIS. Both support PHP. Those developers wishing to use Apache can install something like **WAMP** (**Windows Apache Mysql PHP**) to have Apache installed and configured, and MySQL and PHP installed as modules.

To download and install WAMP, visit the **Download** section of the Wamp Server website (`http://www.wampserver.com/en/`).

Pick the appropriate installer for your platform and run it. This should install and configure everything necessary.

Those wishing to use IIS can install it via the **Add/Remove Windows Components** area of the **Programs and Features** page in the control panel (the Windows installation CD will be required in this case), or using the **Web Platform Installer** (**WPI**), which can be downloaded from `http://www.microsoft.com/web/downloads/platform.aspx`.

Download and run the installer. Once it has launched, search for IIS and let the application install it. Once this has installed, search for PHP and install that through the WPI also.

To run QUnit using a web server and PHP, you'll need to either copy the source files from the `jquery` directory inside our project folder into the folder used by the web server to serve files from, or configure the web server to serve files from the `jquery` directory.

On Apache, we can configure the default directory (the directory from which pages are served when requested by the browser) by editing the `httpd.conf` file (there should be an entry for this in the Start menu). Read down through the configuration file until you find the line for the default directory and change it so that it points to the `jquery` directory in your project folder.

On IIS, we can add a new website using the IIS Manager. Right-click on **Sites** in the **Connections** pane at the left and choose **Add Web Site...**. Fill out the details in the dialog that opens and we should be good to go.

Engage Thrusters

To run the tests, all we need to do is visit the `/test` directory using `localhost:8080` (or whichever hostname/port is configured) in a browser:

```
localhost:8080/test
```

The tests should appear as shown in the following screenshot:

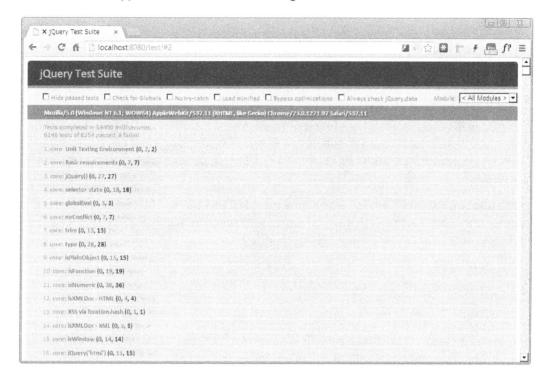

Objective Complete - Mini Debriefing

When the URL for the test suite is visited in a browser, QUnit will run all of the unit tests that have been written for jQuery. There are currently over 6000 tests for the full build of jQuery, and around 4000 tests for a custom build with all optional modules excluded.

You may find that some of the tests fail. Don't worry, this is normal and the reason for it is because the default version of jQuery we get from Git will be the latest development version. As I write this, the current version of jQuery is 1.8.3, but the version cloned from Git is 2.0.0pre.

To fix this, we could switch to the current stable branch and do a build from there instead. So if I wanted to get version 1.8.3, I could use the following command in the CLI:

```
git checkout 1.8.3
```

We could then build the source again, run QUnit, and all the tests should pass.

 After checking out another version of the jQuery source, we'll need to run `npm install` in the `jquery` directory to reinstall the node dependencies.

Classified Intel

Unit testing is a process not always followed religiously by front-end developers, but once your applications cross a rough threshold in size and complexity, or when working in a team environment, unit testing becomes essential for maintenance, so it is best to at least learn the basics.

QUnit makes writing unit test for JavaScript easy. It features a simple API based around the concept of making assertions that we can prove with simple functions. QUnit's API includes methods we can use to make these assertions including:

- `equal()`
- `notEqual()`
- `ok()`

This makes it easy to check that a variable is equal to a particular value, or the return value of a function does not equal a particular value, and so on.

A test in QUnit is built using the global `test()` method, which accepts two arguments; a string describing the test and a function which is invoked to perform the test:

```
test("Test the return value of myCustomMethod()", function() {
    //test code here
});
```

Within the function we can then use one or more of the assertions to check the result of some operation performed by the method or function we're testing:

```
var value = myCustomMethod();
equal(value, true, "This method should return true");
```

The `equal()` method checks that the first and second arguments are equal and the final argument is a string which describes what we expect to happen.

 If you open up some of the script files in the `jquery/test/unit` directory, it is easy to see how the tests can be structured.

The documentation on the QUnit site is excellent. It not only describes the API clearly and concisely, but it also has a lot of information about the concepts of unit testing, and so is a great place to start for those new to unit testing.

On the site you can also find the source files required to run QUnit outside of Grunt and a HTML template page you can use to run the test suite in a browser.

Mission Accomplished

In this mission we've learned not just how to build a custom version of jQuery by excluding components that we don't require, and how to run jQuery's unit test suite, but also, perhaps more importantly, we've learned how to set up a decent build environment for writing clean, lint and error free, application-grade JavaScript.

You Ready To Go Gung HO?
A Hotshot Challenge

We've learned how to build our own jQuery, and excluded the maximum number of components, so at the time of writing, there isn't much more we can do.

If you're reading this after version 1.9 of jQuery has been released, there may be more components that you can exclude, or other techniques for building jQuery, so to really cement your understanding of the build process, build a new custom build that also excludes any new optional components.

If there aren't any new optional components, I'd recommend you to spend some time writing QUnit tests for any custom scripts that you've written. The idea is to write a test that replicates a bug. Then you can fix the bug and watch the test pass.

Project 8

Infinite Scrolling with jQuery

Infinite scrolling is a technique employed by a lot of popular sites that minimizes the amount of data loaded on a page initially, and then incrementally loads more data when the user has scrolled to the bottom of the page. You can see this effect on the Facebook or Twitter timelines among others.

Mission Briefing

In this project we'll build an infinite scrolling system using jQuery that mimics the effect seen on sites such as those mentioned earlier. We'll make a request for some data and display it on the page. Once the user has scrolled to the bottom of the page, we'll make another request for the next page of data, and so on and so forth as the user continues scrolling.

Once we've built our infinite scrolling system, we should end up with something similar to the following screenshot:

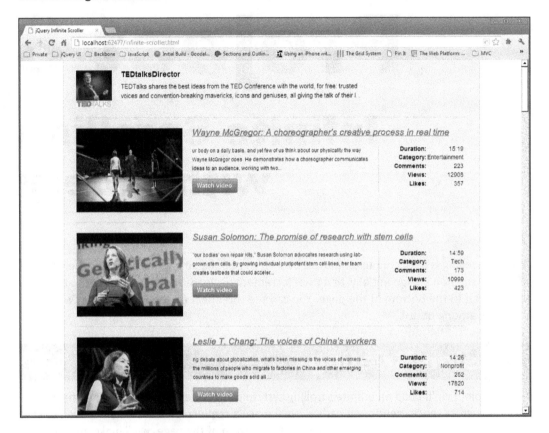

Why Is It Awesome?

If you have a lot of data to display and it can easily be arranged in reverse-chronological order, using the infinite scrolling technique is an easy way to maximize the user experience of the page with progressive disclosure – showing incrementally more to the user.

A small subset of the data, which will make the page load quicker, as well as prevent your visitor being overwhelmed with data, can be displayed at first, which gradually increases following user interaction.

The data that we'll consume in this project will be a list of videos uploaded to the TEDTalks channel on YouTube, in JSON format.

Remember, JSON is a lightweight, text-based data format perfect for
transportation across networks. For more information on JSON, see
`http://www.json.org/`.

There are thousands of videos that can be found on this channel, so it makes a good test bed
for our project. Data that can be sorted into a time-based order makes a great basis for an
infinite scroller.

The TEDTalks channel can be viewed directly on the YouTube website at
`http://www.youtube.com/user/tedtalksdirector`.

Your Hotshot Objectives

This project will be broken down into the following tasks:

- Preparing the underlying page
- Getting the initial feeds
- Displaying the initial set of results
- Handling scrolling to the bottom of the page

Mission Checklist

We can link to the hosted version of JsRender like we did in some of our previous examples,
but in this project we're going to make use of a handy little jQuery plugin called imagesLoaded,
which allows us to fire a callback function when all the images with a selected container have
finished loading.

The imagesLoaded plugin can be downloaded from `https://github.com/desandro/`
`imagesloaded` and should be saved in our project's `js` directory.

Preparing the underlying page

In this task we'll set up the files that we're going to use throughout this project and prepare
the underlying page that our infinite scroller will reside on.

Prepare for Lift Off

As usual we'll be using a custom style sheet for this project and a custom script file, so let's add them first. Create a new JavaScript file called `infinite-scroller.js` and save it in the `js` directory. Then create a new style sheet called `infinite-scoller.css` and save it in the `css` directory. Lastly, save a copy of the `template.html` file in the root project folder and call it `infinite-scroller.html`.

Engage Thrusters

The underlying markup used by the example page will be minimal – a lot of the elements that we'll be working with will be generated dynamically by our template, which we can also add in this task.

First of all we should add references to our new files to the HTML page. Start by adding a `<link>` element for the style sheet to the `<head>` of `infinite-scroller.html`, directly after the link to `common.css`:

```
<link rel="stylesheet" href="css/infinite-scroller.css" />
```

Next we can link to the two new JavaScript files. Add the following `<script>` elements directly after jQuery:

```
<script src="http://borismoore.github.com/jsrender/jsrender.js">
</script>
<scriptsrc="js/jquery.imagesloaded.min.js"></script>
<scriptsrc="js/infinite-scroller.js"></script>
```

We also need to add a simple container to render our data into. Add the following code to the `<body>` of the page:

```
<div id="videoList"></div>
```

Now we can add the templates we'll use. In this project we'll use two templates – one to render the outer container and user data, which will be rendered once, and one to render the list of videos, which we can use repeatedly as required.

As before, they will sit inside the `<script>` elements in the `<body>` of the page. Before the existing `<script>` elements, add following new templates:

```
<script id="containerTemplate" type="text/x-jsrender">
    <section>
        <header class="clearfix">
            <imgsrc="{{>avatar}}" alt="{{>name}}" />
            <hgroup>
                <h1>{{>name}}</h1>
```

```
                <h2>{{>summary.substring(19, 220)}}</h2>
            </hgroup>
        </header>
        <ul id="videos"></ul>
    </section>
</script>
```

Now for the video template:

```
<script id="videoTemplate" type="text/x-jsrender">
    <li>
        <article class="clearfix">
            <header>
                <a href="{{>content[5]}}" title="Watch video">
                    <imgsrc="{{>thumbnail.hqDefault}}"
                    alt="{{>title}}" />
                </a>
                <cite>
                    <a href="{{>content[5]}}"
                    title="Watch video">{{>title}}</a>
                </cite>
            </header>
            <p>
                {{>~Truncate(12, description)}}
                    <a class="button" href="{{>content[5]}}"
                    title="Watch video">Watch video</a>
            </p>
            <div class="meta">
                <dl>
                    <dt>Duration:</dt>
                    <dd>{{>~FormatTime(duration)}}</dd>
                    <dt>Category:</dt>
                    <dd>{{>category}}</dd>
                    <dt>Comments:</dt>
                    <dd>{{>commentCount}}</dd>
                    <dt>Views:</dt>
                    <dd>{{>viewCount}}</dd>
                    <dt>Likes:</dt>
                    <dd>{{>likeCount}}</dd>
                </dl>
            </div>
        </article>
    </li>
</script>
```

We can also add the styling for these elements now as well. In `infinite-scroller.css`, add the following selectors and rules:

```css
section { width:960px; padding-top:20px; margin:auto; }
section {
    width:960px; padding:2em 2.5em 0;
    border-left:1px solid #ccc; border-right:1px solid #ccc;
    margin:auto; background-color:#eee;
}
section> header {
    padding-bottom:2em; border-bottom:1px solid #ccc;
}
img, hgroup, hgroup h1, hgroup h2 { float:left; }
hgroup { width:80%; }
headerimg { margin-right:2em; }
hgroup h1 { font-size:1.5em; }
hgroup h1, hgroup h2 { width:80%; }
hgroup h2 {
    font-weight:normal; margin-bottom:0; font-size:1.25em;
    line-height:1.5em;
}
ul { padding:0; }
li {
    padding:2em 0; border-top:1px solid #fff;
    border-bottom:1px solid #ccc; margin-bottom:0;
    list-style-type:none;
}
article header a {
    display:block; width:27.5%; margin-right:2.5%; float:left; }
aimg { max-width:100%; }
article cite {
    width:70%; margin-bottom:10px; float:left;
    font-size:1.75em;
}
article cite a { width:auto; margin-bottom:.5em; }
article p {
    width:45%; padding-right:2.5%;
    border-right:1px solid #ccc; margin:0 2.5% 2em 0;
    float:left; line-height:1.75em;
}
article .button { display:block; width:90px; margin-top:1em; }
article dl { width:19%; float:left; }
article dt, article dd {
    width:50%; float:left; font-size:1.15em; text-align:right;
```

```
}
article dt { margin:0 0 .5em; clear:both; font-weight:bold; }

li.loading{ height:100px; position:relative; }
li.loading span {
    display:block; padding-top:3em; margin:-3em 0 0 -1em;
    position:absolute; top:50%; left:50%; text-align:center;
    background:url(../img/ajax-loader.gif) no-repeat 50% 0;
}
```

 The `ajax-loader.gif` image used in this project can be found in the accompanying code download for this book.

Objective Complete - Mini Debriefing

So practically the entire page is built from the templates we added to the `<body>` of the page, except for an empty `<div>` that will give us a container to render the data into. The template contains the markup used not just for the list of videos, but also information about the user whose videos we're displaying.

In the first template, the outer container for the data is a `<section>` element. Within this is a `<header>` which displays information about the user, including his/her profile picture, name, and bio.

The actual bio returned by YouTube for a specified user can be quite long, so we'll use the JavaScript `substring()` function to return a shortened version of this summary. This function is passed two arguments; the first is the character to start copying from and the second is the character to end on.

In the second template the actual list of videos will be displayed in the `<ul>` element added in the first template, with each video occupying an `<li>`. Within each `<li>`, we have an `<article>` element, which is an appropriate container for an independent unit of content.

Within the `<article>`, we have a `<header>` containing some of the key information about the video such as its title and a thumbnail. Following the `<header>` we display a short summary of the video in a `<p>`, element. We also use our shortening helper function `Truncate()`, starting at character 12.

Lastly we display some meta-information about the video such as the number of plays, the number of likes, and the video's duration, using a `<dl>`.

We use another helper function to display the duration in the video, `FormatTime()`. YouTube returns the length of the video in seconds, so we can convert this into a nicely formatted time string instead.

We used the > character to HTML-encode any data we insert into the page. It's always best to do this as a security measure.

The CSS that was added was purely presentational; merely used to lay out the page in a list format, and make it look slightly interesting and presentable. Feel free to change any aspect of how the layout is styled, or the elements are themed.

Classified Intel

The SEO-conscious among you will realize that a page that is built almost entirely from AJAX delivered content is unlikely to be well placed in search results. Traditionally, this would almost certainly have been true, but now we can use the awesome pushState() method of the HTML History API to deliver a dynamic website that is completely indexable by search engines.

A complete description of pushState() is beyond the scope of this book, but there are plenty of great examples and tutorials out there. Considered by many to be the definitive guide to the History API is the documentation on Mozilla's Developer Network, which includes a section on pushState(). You can see the documentation at https://
developer.mozilla.org/en-US/docs/DOM/Manipulating_the_browser_history.

Getting the initial feeds

In this task we'll focus on getting the initial set of data in order to create the page when it first loads. We need to write our code so that the function for getting the first page of data is reusable for any page of data so that we can make use of it later on in the project.

Prepare for Lift Off

We can use the standard document ready shortcut provided by jQuery, just like we have in a number of previous projects. We can get ready by adding the following code to the infinite-scroller.js file that we create earlier:

```
$(function () {

    //rest of our code will go here...

});
```

Engage Thrusters

First of all we can add the code that retrieves the data from YouTube. Replace the comment in the preceding snippet of code with the following:

```
var data = {},
    startIndex = 1;

var getUser = function () {
    return $.getJSON("http://gdata.youtube.com/
    feeds/api/users/tedtalksdirector?callback=?", {
        v: 2,
        alt: "json"
    }, function (user) {
        data.userdata = user.entry;
    });
};

var getData = function () {
    return $.getJSON("https://gdata.youtube.com/
    feeds/api/videos?callback=?", {
        author: "tedtalksdirector",
        v: 2,
        alt: "jsonc",
        "start-index": startIndex
    }, function (videos) {
        data.videodata = videos.data.items;
    });
};
```

Next we need to process the response a little. We can use the following code to execute a callback function once both of the AJAX requests have completed, which should be added directly after the code we added a moment ago:

```
$.when(getUser(), getData()).done(function () {
    startIndex+=25;

    var ud = data.userdata,
        clean = {};

    clean.name = ud.yt$username.display;
    clean.avatar = ud.media$thumbnail.url;
    clean.summary = ud.summary.$t;
    data.userdata = clean;
});
```

Objective Complete - Mini Debriefing

We started out by defining a couple of variables. The first is an empty object that we'll populate with the results of our AJAX requests. The second is an integer that represents the index number of the first video we wish to get. YouTube videos are not zero-based like regular JavaScript arrays, so we initially define the variable with a value of 1.

Next we added our two functions that we'll use to get our data. The first is the request to get the profile data of the user whose feed we're going to be displaying. We're only going to be using this function once, when the page initially loads, but you'll see why it's important that we define the function as a variable in this way in just a moment.

The second function will be reused, so storing it in a variable is a great way to store it ready to be invoked whenever we wish to get a new page of video data. It's important that these functions both return the `jqXHR` objects returned by the `getJSON()` method.

Both of the requests use jQuery's `getJSON()` method to make the requests. In the user request we only need to set the `v` and `alt` query parameters, which are set in the object passed to `getJSON()` as the second argument. The user whose profile data we want actually forms part of the URL we are making the request to.

The callback function for this request simply adds the contents of the `user.entry` object received from the request to the `userdata` property of our `data` object.

The second request requires slightly more configuration. We still set the API version we want to use with the `v` parameter, but this time we set the format of the response to be `jsonc` instead of `json`. In the callback function for this request we store the array of videos in the `videodata` property of our `data` object.

JSON-C stands for json-in-script and is a format that Google can respond with for some requests. Data returned in JSON-C format is generally more lightweight and more efficient to process than the same response in JSON due to how Google's API has been engineered.

The properties that we need to use are only returned when this format is used. The only reason we don't use it when requesting the user data is because there is not a JSON-C response for that particular query.

 For more information on JSON-C responses from Google's APIs, see the documentation at `https://developers.google.com/youtube/2.0/developers_guide_jsonc`.

Next we make use of jQuery's `when()` method to initiate both of our requests, and then use the `done()` method to execute a callback function once both of the `jqXHR` objects have been resolved. This is why it was important that the single-use `getUser()` function is structured in the same way as the reusable `getData()` function.

Inside the callback function for `done()`, we first increment the `startIndex` variable by 25 so that when we make another request we get the next "page" of 25 videos. As we have the first page of data now, when we use the `getData()` function later on, we'll automatically get the "next" page of results.

 The `when()` and `done()` methods are the preferred way of handling asynchronous operations since jQuery 1.5.

At this point we just need to do a little processing of our `userdata` object. There's a whole bunch of data we don't need to use, and some of the data we do need to use is buried within nested objects, so we simply create a new object called `clean` and set just the data we need on this object directly.

Once this has been done we can save our clean object back to our `data` object, overwriting the original `userdata` object. This should make the object easier to process in our template.

Displaying the initial set of results

Now that we have data being returned by YouTube's API, we can render our template. However, in order to render our template, we need to add helper functions used to format some of the data. In this task we can add those helper functions and then render the template.

Engage Thrusters

The template helpers don't need to reside within the `$.done()` callback function. We can add them directly before this code in `infinite-scroller.js`:

```
var truncate = function (start, summary) {
      return summary.substring(start,200) + "...";
    },
    formatTime = function (time) {
        var timeArr = [],
            hours = Math.floor(time / 3600),
            mins = Math.floor((time % 3600) / 60),
            secs= Math.floor(time % 60);

        if (hours> 0) {
            timeArr.push(hours);
        }

        if (mins< 10) {
            timeArr.push("0" + mins);
```

```
        } else {
            timeArr.push(mins);
        }

        if (secs< 10) {
            timeArr.push("0" + secs);
        } else {
            timeArr.push(secs);
        }

        return timeArr.join(":");
    };
```

Next we just need to register the helper functions. Directly after the previous code add the following:

```
$.views.helpers({
    Truncate: truncate,
    FormatTime: formatTime
});
```

Lastly we can render our template. We want a function that we can call from anywhere in our code, ready for when we make further requests later on. Add the following code after registering the helper functions:

```
var renderer = function (renderOuter) {

    var vidList = $("#videoList");

    if (renderOuter) {
        vidList.append(
$("#containerTemplate").render(data.userdata));
    }
    vidList.find("#videos")
            .append($("#videoTemplate").render(data.videodata));
}
```

Now we just need to call this function at the end of our $.done() callback function:

```
renderer(true);
```

Objective Complete - Mini Debriefing

Our first helper function, `truncate()` is ultra-simple. We simply return a shortened version of the string that the function receives as an argument. The `substring()` function takes two arguments; the first is the position in the string to begin copying at, and the second argument is the number of characters to copy, which we fix at `200`.

To show that the string has been shortened, we also append an ellipsis to the end of the returned string, which is why we use a helper function here, instead of using a substring in the template directly as we did earlier.

The `formatTime()` helper function is a little more complex, but still relatively straightforward. This function will receive a time in seconds, which we want to format into a slightly nicer string that shows the hours, if there are any, the minutes, and seconds.

We first create an empty array to store the different components of the string. We then create a number of variables to hold the hours, minutes, and seconds portions of the time string we're going to create.

The hours are calculated by dividing the total number of seconds by 3600 (the number of seconds in an hour). We use `Math.floor()` on it so that we only get a whole number result. We need to calculate the minutes slightly differently because we need to take into account the hours if there are any.

We use the modulus operator (`%`) here to remove any hours first and then divide the remainder by `60`, which will tell us either the total number of minutes or the remaining minutes after the hours have been accounted for. To work out the number of seconds, we just need to use the modulus operator again and the value `60`.

We then use a series of conditionals to determine which of the variables to add to the array. If there are any hours (which is unlikely given the nature of the videos) we push them into the array.

If there are less than `10` minutes, we add `0` to the minutes figure and then push it into the array. If there are more than `10` minutes we just push the `mins` variable into the array. The same logic is applied to the `secs` variable before it is pushed into the array.

This function returns a nicely formatted time by joining the items in our array and using a colon as the separator. The string will be in the format `H:MM:SS` or `MM:SS` depending on the length of the video. Then we registered the helper functions with the template using JsRender's `helpers` object, which is itself nested within the `views` object, which is added to jQuery by the templating library. The helper functions we wish to add are set as the values in an object literal, where the keys match the function calls in our template.

Next we added a function that we can call in order to render our template. The `renderer()` function takes a single argument, which is a Boolean specifying whether to render both the container template and video template, or just the video template. Inside the function we first cache a reference to the outer container of the video list.

If the `renderOuter` argument has a truthy value (that is if it specifically holds the value `true`), we render the `containerTemplate` and append it to the empty `<div>` we added to the `<body>` of the page. We then render the `videoTemplate`, appending the rendered HTML to the `<ul>` that is added by the `containerTemplate`.

Lastly we called our `renderer()` function for the first time, passing `true` as the argument to render both the containers and the initial list of videos.

Handling scrolling to the bottom of the page

Now that we've got the first page of videos, we want to add a handler that monitors the window for scroll events and detects when the page has been scrolled right to the bottom.

Engage Thrusters

First of all we need to add a couple of new variables. Change the very first set of variables near the top of the file so that they appear as follows:

```
var data = {},
    startIndex = 1,
    listHeight = 0,
    win = $(window),
    winHeight = win.height();
```

Now we need to update our `renderer()` function so that when the templates have been rendered we update the new `listHeight` variable. Add the following code after where we render the `videoTemplate`:

```
vidList.imagesLoaded(function () {
    listHeight = $("#videoList").height();
});
```

Next we can add a handler for the scroll event. Directly after the `when()` method in `infinite-scroller.js`, add the following code:

```
win.on("scroll", function () {

    if (win.scrollTop() + winHeight >= listHeight) {
        $("<li/>", {
            "class": "loading",
            html: "<span>Loading older videos...</span>"
        }).appendTo("#videos");

        $.when(getData()).done(function () {
            startIndex += 25;

            renderer();

            $("li.loading").remove();

        });
    }
}).on("resize", function() {
    winHeight = win.height();
});
```

We're using a spinner to show the user that more data is being retrieved. We need a few extra styles to handle the position of the spinner, so we can also add the following code to the bottom of our `infinite-scroller.css` style sheet:

```
li.loading{ height:100px; position:relative; }
li.loading span {
    display:block; padding-top:38px; margin:-25px 0 0 -16px;
    position:absolute; top:50%; left:50%; text-align:center;
    background:url(../img/ajax-loader.gif) no-repeat 50% 0;
}
```

Objective Complete - Mini Debriefing

We attach a handler to the window using our cached `win` object and the `on()` method. The event type is specified as `scroll`. Inside the callback function we first check whether the current `scrollTop` property of the `window`, plus the `height` of the viewport is greater than or equal to the `height` of our `videolist` container. We need to do this to know when the page has been scrolled to the bottom.

If the heights are equal, we create a temporary loader to provide visual feedback to the user that something is happening. We append a new `<li>` element to the `<ul>` containing the videos and give it a class name of `loading` so that we can easily target it with some CSS. We set a `<span>` element as the content of the new list item.

We can get the current value of the `scrollTop` property using jQuery's `scrollTop()` method. We're using a cached value for the window's `height`. Our scroll handler will be fairly intensive as it will be invoked every time the user scrolls, so using a cached value for the window `height` makes this process slightly more efficient.

It does mean however that if the window is resized, this value will no longer be accurate. We fix this by adding a resize handler for the window which recalculates this value every time the window is resized. This is done by chaining another call to the `on()` method after the scroll handler, which looks for the resize event of the `window` object and updates the `winHeight` variable accordingly.

We then use jQuery's `when()` method once again, which invokes our `getData()` function to retrieve the next 25 videos. We also use the `done()` method again to execute a callback function once the request has completed.

Within this callback function we increment our `startIndex` variable by 25 again, ready to request the next set of videos. The `getData()` function will populate our `data` object with the new video data so all we need to do is call our `renderer()` function to display the new videos, and then remove the temporary loader.

At this point we should have a fully functional infinite loader that loads more videos when the user scrolls to the bottom of the page. We should be able to run the page and see something like the following when we scroll to the bottom:

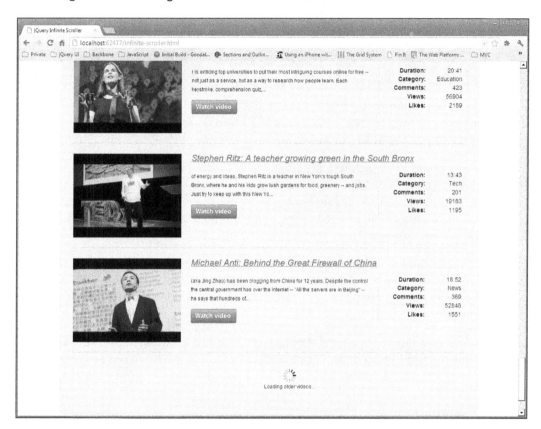

Mission Accomplished

A lot of the code we've written in this project has been concerned with getting the data we want to display. Actually adding the infinite scroll feature itself requires only a minimal amount of code – a single handler that watches for the scroll event and triggers a new request for more data when the document is scrolled to the bottom.

As you can see this is a feature that would be easy to retrofit to existing functionality as an additional layer. This technique is best suited to data that can easily be arranged in reverse-chronological order, with new items appearing at the top and older items appearing at the bottom.

It's not necessarily a complete replacement for paged data, but certainly makes sense when dealing with things such as news stories, blog posts, tweets, or status updates. It works very well with social data.

You Ready To Go Gung HO?
A Hotshot Challenge

In this project we're simply providing links back to a full-screen video player for each video on the YouTube site. So when the visitor clicks on a video thumbnail or title, they'll be sent off to YouTube to actually watch the video.

While there's nothing inherently wrong in doing this, a much cooler thing to do would be to open up a lightbox containing a video player embedded in an `<iframe>`. This would let the visitor view the video without ever leaving your site. The response from YouTube for the videos contains a link that can be used as the `src` attribute of an `<iframe>`, so why not see if you can hook this up yourself?

You'll notice that if you scroll to the bottom of the page, but then carry on scrolling down immediately, the same set of videos are requested multiple times. As an alternative task, see if you can prevent this from happening by only requesting more data if there is not currently a request in progress.

This should be very easy to set up and simply involves setting a flag when the request begins, and removing the flag when it ends. We can then only make requests if the flag is not set.

Project 9

A jQuery Heat Map

A heat map can tell you a lot about how your website is used. It's a valuable tool in the world of analytics that can tell you which features of your website are the most used, and which areas might need some improvement in order to truly engage visitors.

Mission Briefing

In this project we're going to build our own heat map to record which areas of any page are clicked the most. We'll need to build a way of actually recording where every click occurs and a way of transmitting that information somewhere so that it can be stored.

We'll actually be building two different bits of the overall heat map – the client-side part that is executed in visitors' browsers to capture the clicks, and an admin console that displays the heat map to the owner of the site.

We'll need to account for different resolutions and devices in order to capture the maximum amount of information and ensure that our script is efficient enough to run in the background unnoticed.

Nothing visible will happen at the client side of course (all that part will do is record and store the clicks) but at the end of the project we'll be able to display detailed information in the admin console on the number and positions of all clicks on a page, as shown in the following screenshot:

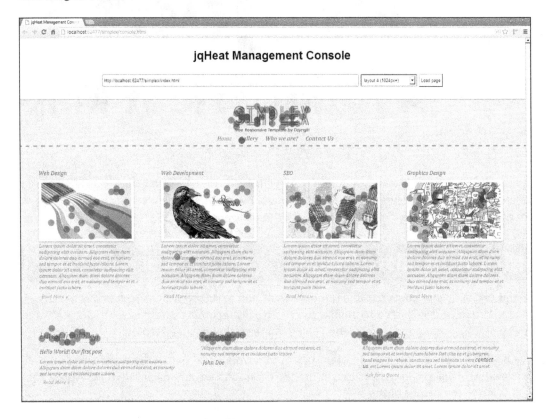

Why Is It Awesome?

All analytics are useful to the owner of a website and can give detailed information about the people visiting the site, including things such as their computing environment, which pages they enter the site on, which pages they leave from, and how many pages they visit.

A heat map can be just as informative, but from a developer's point of view instead of an owner's. Which bits of your pages are clicked most frequently? A heat map can tell you.

The heat map that we'll build will be for responsive websites that are able to change their layout to suit the screen width of the device being used to view the site. A single project is not nearly enough to cover all aspects of responsive design, and because we're focusing mainly on the script itself, we won't be covering it in much detail.

If you've used responsive techniques already then you won't need the additional information. If you haven't worked with responsive principles before, this should be a gentle introduction to the subject that should act as a primer for the subject.

Your Hotshot Objectives

In this project we'll cover the following tasks:

- Determining and saving the environment
- Capturing visitor clicks
- Saving the click data
- Adding the management console
- Requesting click data
- Displaying a heat map
- Allowing different layouts to be selected
- Showing heat maps for each layout

Mission Checklist

This is the only project where we aren't going to build the HTML and CSS that we need ourselves. We want our heat map to work with a variety of layouts and the best way to test that is with a responsive layout. Were we to code this ourselves, it would take us most of this project to code and discuss just the layout, before we even got to the heat map.

We'll use a prebuilt responsive template for this project then, so that we can jump straight into the fun part without getting distracted. The template that we'll use is called Simplex, but unfortunately it's no longer available online. You'll need to use the template files found in the accompanying download for this book. Simply copy the `simplex` folder from the downloaded archive in to the main `jquery-hotshots` project directory. All we need to do is add a few script references to each of the HTML pages in the template. The files that should be updated are:

- `contact.html`
- `gallery.html`
- `index.html`
- `who-we-are.html`

The new `<script>` elements can go at the bottom of the `<body>` in each of the four pages. First we need jQuery obviously:

```
<script src="../js/jquery-1.9.0.min.js"></script>
```

We'll also be making use of the imagesLoaded plugin that we used in the last project:

```
<script src="../js/jquery.imagesloaded.min.js"></script>
```

In this project we'll create two scripts, one to run on the client and one for the admin console. Initially we'll be working with the client script, so we should add the following to each page:

```
<script src="../js/heat-map-client.js"></script>
```

This file doesn't exist yet of course, so while we're getting set up we can go ahead and create this now. It should be saved in the js directory along with our other scripts.

Determining and saving the environment

In our first task we'll store some information about the current browsing environment, such as the URL of the current page. We'll also parse any attached style sheets looking for media queries.

Prepare for Lift Off

We'll start with our document ready shortcut, as we have in most of our other projects. In the heat-map-client.js file, add the following code:

```
$(function () {

});
```

All the additional code we add to this file will go into this callback function.

Engage Thrusters

We'll first set a series of variables that will be used throughout the script. We'll also need to parse any attached style sheets and look for **media queries** so that we can determine which breakpoints are defined for the different layouts.

 Media queries are a way to specify in CSS that a group of styles should only be applied if certain conditions are met, such as the width of the screen. For more information see http://en.wikipedia.org/wiki/Media_queries.

Add the following code inside the callback function we just added:

```
var doc = $(document),
    clickStats = {
        url: document.location.href,
        clicks: []
    },
    layouts = [];

$.ajaxSetup({
    type: "POST",
    contentType: "application/json",
    dataType: "json"
});

$.each(doc[0].styleSheets, function (x, ss) {

  $.each(ss.rules, function (y, rule) {

    if (rule.media&&rule.media.length) {

      var jq = $,
          current = rule.media[0],
          mq = {
            min: (current.indexOf("min") !== -1) ?
            jq.trim(current.split("min-width:")[1]
            .split("px")[0]) : 0,

            max: (current.indexOf("max") !== -1) ?
            jq.trim(current.split("max-width:")[1]
            .split("px")[0]) : "none"
          };

      layouts.push(mq);
    }
  });
});

layouts.sort(function (a, b) {
    return a.min - b.min;
});

$.ajax({
    url: "/heat-map.asmx/saveLayouts",
    data: JSON.stringify({ url: url, layouts: layouts })
});
```

Objective Complete - Mini Debriefing

We start out by defining a series of variables. We cache a reference to the document object and wrap it with jQuery functionality. We then create an object called clickStats which we'll use as a general storage container for the session.

Within the object we store the URL of the page and define an empty array called clicks which will be used to store each click that occurs. Lastly we create another array, this time outside of our clickStats object, which we'll use to store objects representing each layout for the document.

We also set some defaults for any AJAX requests using jQuery's ajaxSetup() method, which accepts an object containing the options to set. We'll be making a couple of requests, so it makes sense to set defaults for any options that we set in both requests. In this example we'll need to set the type to POST, the contentType to application/json, and the dataType to json.

Our next block of code is concerned with parsing any style sheets attached to the document via <link> elements and extracting any media queries defined in them.

We start by using jQuery's each() method to iterate the style sheet objects stored in the StyleSheets collection of the document object. For each style sheet, there will be an object in the collection that contains all of its selectors and rules, including any media queries.

The collection that we're iterating consists of objects, so the callback function we pass to the each() method will receive the index of the current object, which we set to x, and the current object itself, which we set to ss as arguments.

Within our callback function we again use jQuery's each() method. This time we're iterating the rules collection of the ss object passed into the callback function. This collection will contain a series of objects. The callback function we pass to this incantation of the method will receive the index once again, this time set to y, and the current object, this time set to rule.

The type of object will differ depending on what it is. It may be a CSSImportRule for @ import statements, a CSSFontFaceRule for @font-face rules, a CSSStyleRule for any selectors defined by the style sheet, or a CSSMediaRule for any media queries.

We are only interested in the CSSMediaRule objects, so within the callback in the nested each() we first check whether the rule object has a media property and if the media property has a length.

Only CSSMediaRule objects will have a media property, but this property may be empty, so we can check for the presence of this property and check that it has length using an if conditional within the nested callback.

If both of these conditions are `true` (or truthy) we know we've found a media query. We first set a couple of new variables. The first variable is the first item of the `media` collection, which will contain the text string defining the media query, and the second is an object called `mq` that we'll use to store the breakpoints of the media query.

We set two properties of this object – the `min` and `max` values of the media query. We set the `min` property by checking whether the text string contains the word `min`. If it does we first split the string on the term `min-width:` and take the second item in the array that the `split()` function will return, and then split this resulting string on the term `px` and take the first item. We can chain `split()` like this because the function returns an array, which is also what it is called on.

If the string does not contain the word `min` we set the value to `0`. We do the same to extract the `max-width` if there is one. If there isn't a `max-width`, we set it to the string `none`. Once we've created our `layout` object we push it into the `layouts` array.

Lastly we sort our breakpoints array so that it is in ascending order. We can do this by passing a sorting function to JavaScript's `sort()` method, which is called on an array. The function we pass in will receive two items from the array we are sorting.

If the `min` property of first object is less than the `min` property of the second b object, the function will return a negative number, which puts the smaller number before the larger number in the array – exactly what we want.

So we'll end up with an array where each item is a specific breakpoint, which increases throughout the array, making checking against it later on to detect which breakpoint is being applied much easier.

Lastly we need to send this data to the server, potentially so that it can be saved. The only options we need to set for this request are the URL to make the request to, and the `data` option which we use to post the URL of the page and the array of media queries to the server. The AJAX defaults we set earlier will also be used of course.

Classified Intel

If you're familiar with media queries already, feel free to skip to the start of the next task; if not we'll just look at them briefly here so that we all know what our script is trying to do.

A media query is like an `if` conditional, but expressed in CSS. A media query in a CSS file will look something like the following code snippet:

```
@media screen and (max-width:320px) {
    css-selector { property: style; }
}
```

The statement begins with @media to signify a media query. The query specifies a medium, such as screen, and optionally additional conditions, such as max-width or min-width. The styles contained within the query will only be applied if the query is satisfied.

Media queries are one of the staples of responsive web design, the other being relative dimensions. Typically, a responsively built web page will have one or more media queries that allow us to specify different layouts for a range of screen sizes.

Each media query we include will set a breakpoint between layouts. When a breakpoint is exceeded, such as when the maximum width of the device is less than 320px in the previous media query, the layout changes as directed by the media query.

Capturing visitor clicks

In this task we need to build the part that captures any clicks that occur on the page. While the page is open we want to record information about the layout and the click itself.

Engage Thrusters

We can capture clicks and record the other information we want to store using the following code, which should be added directly after the ajax() method that we added to heat-map-client.js in the last task:

```
$.imagesLoaded(function() {

    doc.on("click.jqHeat", function (e) {

        var x = e.pageX,
            y = e.pageY,
            docWidth = doc.outerWidth(),
            docHeight = doc.outerHeight(),
            layout,
            click = {
                url: url,
                x: Math.ceil((x / docWidth) * 100),
                y: Math.ceil((y / docHeight) * 100)
            };

        $.each(layouts, function (i, item) {

            var min = item.min || 0,
                max = item.max || docWidth,
```

```
            bp = i + 1;

        if (docWidth>= min &&docWidth<= max) {
            click.layout = bp;
        } else if (docWidth> max) {
            click.layout = bp + 1;
        }
    });

    clickStats.clicks.push(click);
    });
});
```

Objective Complete - Mini Debriefing

We can listen for clicks on the page by adding a handler using jQuery's on() method, and we'll also want to ensure that any images in the page have loaded fully before we start capturing clicks, because images will affect the height of the document, and that in turn will affect our calculations. Therefore we need to attach our event handler inside the callback function for the imagesLoaded() method.

We specify click as the event to listen for as the first argument, but also namespace the event with jqHeat. We'll probably want to use this on a range of pages, each of which may have its own event handling code that we don't want to interfere with this code.

Within the event handler we first need to set up some variables. The function receives the event object as an argument and we use this to set our first two variables, which store the x and y positions of the click. This figure will represent pixel points on the page.

We then store the width and height of the document. The reason we store this on every click is because the width, and therefore the height of the document, may change while the page is open.

People say that only developers resize their browsers while they are testing responsive builds, but this is not always the case. Depending on the breakpoints defined by any media queries in use, a change in device orientation could affect the width and height of the document, which could happen at any time after the page has loaded.

We define the layout variable next but we don't assign a value to this for now. We also create a new object to represent the click. Within this object we initially store the click coordinates as percentages.

Converting the pixel coordinates into percentage coordinates is a trivial operation that simply involves dividing the pixel coordinate by the width (or height) of the document and then multiplying the figure by `100`. We use JavaScript's `Math.ceil()` function so that the number is rounded up to the next integer.

Next we need to determine which layout we are in. We can iterate our `layouts` array using jQuery's `each()` method again. The callback function receives the index of the current item in the `layouts` array as the first argument and the second is the actual object.

Inside the callback function we first set our variables. This time the variables we need are the minimum width of the layout, which we set to either the `min` property of the object, or zero if there is no `min` defined. We also set the `max` variable to either the `max` property of the current item, or the `width` of the document if there is no `max` property.

Our last variable simply adds `1` to the current index. The index will be zero-based but it makes more sense for our layouts to be labeled `1` to the number of layouts instead of `0` to the number of layouts.

We then use an `if` conditional to figure out which layout is currently being applied. We first check whether the current document width is greater or equal to the minimum value for the media query and less than or equal to the maximum. If it is, we know we're inside the current layout and so save the converted layout index to our `click` object.

If we haven't matched any of our layouts, the browser must be larger than the highest `max-width` value defined by a media query, so we set the layout to the converted layout plus one again. Lastly we add the `click` object that we've created to the `clicks` array in our `clickStats` object.

Saving the click data

Someone has visited a page on which our heat map client script is running, they've clicked around, and our script so far has recorded each of those clicks. Now what? Now we need a way of transmitting that information to the server for permanent storage and display in the management console. This is what we'll look at in this task.

Engage Thrusters

We can ensure that any captured clicks are sent to the server for permanent storage using the following code, which should be added after the `imagesLoaded()` callback function:

```
window.onbeforeunload = function () {

    $.ajax({
        async: false,
```

```
        type: "POST",
        contentType: "application/json",
        url: "/heat-map.asmx/saveClicks",
        dataType: "json",
        data: JSON.stringify({ clicks: clicks })
    });
}
```

Objective Complete - Mini Debriefing

We attached a handler for the `beforeunload` event to the `window` object in order to post the data to the server before leaving the page. Unfortunately, this event isn't handled 100 percent of the time – there may be occasions when it doesn't fire.

In order to minimize this as much as possible we've attached the event handler directly to the native `window` object, not the jQuery wrapped one, which we can access via the first item in the array that is the jQuery object.

Using any jQuery method, including `on()`, adds overhead in that jQuery method, and as the underlying JavaScript functions are invoked. To reduce this overhead as much as possible we avoid using jQuery here and revert back to the old-school way of attaching event handlers by prefixing the event name with `on` and assigning a function as their value.

All we need to do inside this function is post the data to the server so that it can be inserted into a database. We use jQuery's `ajax()` method to make the request, and set the `async` option to `false` to make the request synchronous.

This is important and will ensure the request is made in Chrome. We're not interested in a response from the server anyway – we just need to ensure the request is made before the page unloads.

We also set the `type` to `POST` as we're sending data to the server, and set the `contentType` to `application/json`, which will set the appropriate headers for the request to ensure that the data is handled correctly on the server.

The `url` is clearly the URL for the web service that we're sending the data to, and we set the `dataType` to `json`, which again can help to make consuming the data on the server easier.

Lastly we stringify the `clicks` array and wrap it in an object using the browser's native JSON engine. We send the stringified data to the server using the `data` option.

At this point, when a page that this script is attached to is opened, the script will run quietly in the background recording the coordinates of any points on the page that are clicked. When the user leaves the page, the click data they've generated is dispatched to the server for storage.

Classified Intel

Browsers that do not have a JSON engine, such as Version 7 of Internet Explorer and below, will not be able to run the code we added in this task, although there are polyfill scripts that can be used in these situations.

For more information see the JSON repository at Github (`https://github.com/douglascrockford/JSON-js`).

Adding the management console

I said at the start of this project that we wouldn't need to write any HTML or CSS. That was a minor exaggeration; we'll have to build the management console page ourselves, but don't worry, we won't have to write much – most of what we'll display on the page will be created dynamically.

Prepare for Lift Off

Create a new HTML page based on our standard template file called `console.html` and save it in the `simplex` directory that we've been working in for this project. Next create a new script file called `console.js` and save it in the same folder. Lastly, create a new style sheet called `console.css` and save it in the `css` folder inside the `simplex` directory.

We should link to the new style sheet from the `<head>` of our new HTML page:

```
<link rel="stylesheet" href="css/console.css" />
```

We should also link to jQuery and our new script file at the bottom of the `<body>`:

```
<script src="../js/jquery-1.9.0.min.js"></script>
<script src="console.js"></script>
```

Lastly, we should add the class name `jqheat` to the `<body>` element:

```
<body class="jqheat">
```

Engage Thrusters

The page will need to display an interface that can be used to select a page to view the click stats for. Add the following code to the `<body>` of `console.html`:

```
<header>
    <h1>jqHeat Management Console</h1>
    <fieldset>
        <legend>jqHeat page loader</legend>
        <input placeholder="Enter URL" id="url" />
```

```
        <button id="load" type="button">Load page</button>
    </fieldset>
</header>
<section role="main">
    <iframe scrolling="no" id="page" />
</section>
```

We can also add some very basic CSS for these elements. Add the following code to
`console.css`:

```
.jqheat{ overflow-y:scroll; }
.jqheat header {
    border-bottom:1px solid #707070; text-align:center;
}
.jqheat h1 { display:inline-block; width:100%; margin:1em 0; }
.jqheat fieldset {
    display:inline-block; width:100%; margin-bottom:3em;
}
.jqheat legend { display:none; }
.jqheat input {
    width:50%; height:34px; padding:0 5px;
    border:1px solid #707070; border-radius:3px;
}
.jqheat input.empty{ border-color:#ff0000; }
.jqheat button { padding:9px5px; }
.jqheat section {
    width:100%;margin:auto;
    position:relative;
}
.jqheat iframe, .jqheat canvas {
    Width:100%; height:100%; position:absolute; left:0; top:0;
}
.jqheat canvas { z-index:999; }
```

In this task we won't add any real functionality, but we can prepare our script file with the
usual `document ready` handler in preparation for the next task. In `console.js`, add the
following code:

```
$(function () {

});
```

Objective Complete - Mini Debriefing

Our page starts out with a `<header>` element that contains a heading for the page in `<h1>` and `<fieldset>`. Inside the `<fieldset>` is the mandatory `<legend>` and a very simple UI for the page, which consists of a single `<input>` and a `<button>` element. Both the `<input>` and the `<button>` elements have `id` attributes so that we can easily select them from the page in our script.

The main content area of the page consists of a `<section>` element, which is given a `role` attribute of `main`. It's standard practice to markup the main content area of the page using this attribute, which helps clarify the intent of the area to assistive technologies.

Inside the `<section>` is an `<iframe>`. We'll use the `<iframe>` to display the page the user wants to view click statistics for. For now it just has an `id` attribute, again so that we can select it easily, and the non-standard `scrolling` attribute set to `no`. I'm not a huge fan of using non-standard attributes, but in this case it is the simplest way to prevent the `<iframe>` having a pointless scrollbar when the content document is loaded into it.

There is a high chance of the page causing a scrollbar, and rather than have the movement that occurs when the scrollbar appears, we may as well set the `<body>` of our page to have a vertical scrollbar permanently, which we do in the CSS. Other than this, the CSS is mostly just positional stuff which we won't look at too deeply.

Classified Intel

We used the HTML5 `placeholder` attribute on our `<input>` element, which in supporting browsers displays the text added as the value of the attribute inside the `<input>`, acting as an inline label.

This is useful because it means we don't have to add a whole new element just to display a `<label>`, but support, while good at the time of writing, is not 100 percent. Luckily there are some excellent `polyfills` that handle providing a sensible fallback in un-supporting browsers.

There are a whole range of `placeholder` polyfills (and many more besides) recommended by the Modernizr team. You can see the list in full by visiting `https://github.com/Modernizr/Modernizr/wiki/HTML5-Cross-Browser-Polyfills`.

Requesting click data

The console page starts out almost empty, containing mostly a form for loading the page that we want to view click data for. In this task we'll look at how we can load that page and request its data from the server.

Engage Thrusters

Start out by adding the following code to the empty function in `console.js`:

```
var doc = $(document),
    input = doc.find("#url"),
    button = doc.find("#load"),
    iframe = doc.find("#page"),
    canvas = document.createElement("canvas");

$.ajaxSetup({
    type: "POST",
    contentType: "application/json",
    dataType: "json",
    converters: {
        "textjson": function (data) {
            var parsed = JSON.parse(data);

            return parsed.d || parsed;
        }
    }
});
```

We can then add a click handler for the `<button>` element:

```
doc.on("click", "#load", function (e) {
    e.preventDefault();

    var url = input.val(),
        len;

    if (url) {
        input.removeClass("empty").data("url", url);
        button.prop("disabled", true);
        iframe.attr("src", url).load(function() {
          $(this).trigger("iframeloaded");
        });
    } else {
        input.addClass("empty");
        button.prop("disabled", false);
    }
});
```

Lastly, we can add an event handler for the custom `iframeloaded` event:

```
doc.on("iframeloaded", function () {

    var url = input.data("url");

    $.ajax({
        type: "POST",
        contentType: "application/json",
        url: "/heat-map.asmx/getClicks",
        dataType: "json",
        data: JSON.stringify({ url:url, layout: 4 }),
        converters: {
          "textjson": function (data) {
              var parsed = JSON.parse(data);

              returnparsed.d || parsed;
          }
        }
    });
});
```

Objective Complete - Mini Debriefing

We began, as we usually do, by setting some variables. We stored a reference to the `document` object wrapped in jQuery, which we can use to select any element on the page using this reference as a starting point, without creating a new jQuery object each time we select an element or bind an event handler.

We also stored a reference to the `<input>` element that will contain the URL of the page, a reference to the `<button>` next to the `<input>`, and the `<iframe>` that we'll render the requested page into. Lastly we set an undefined variable called canvas, which we'll use to store a reference to a `<canvas>` element that we create using JavaScript's `createElement()` function.

We could use jQuery to create this element of course, but we're only creating a single element as opposed to a complex DOM structure, so we may as well use plain JavaScript and get a performance boost at the same time.

As before we can use the `ajaxSetup()` method to set the `type`, `contentType`, and `dataType` options for the requests that we'll be making to the server. We also used a converter to transform the data that will be returned by the server.

The `converters` option takes an object where the data type the converter should be used for is specified as a key, and the function to use as the converter is specified as a value.

Some servers will return JSON data wrapped in an object and stored in the property `d` for security, while other servers do not do this. Usually the `text json` data type would be parsed using jQuery's `parseJSON()` method, but in this case our code would still need to extract the actual data from the object before it could be used.

Instead our converter parses the JSON using the browser's native JSON parser and then returns either the contents of `d` if it exists, or the parsed data. This means that the code which processes the data is the same regardless of whether the data is wrapped in an object or not.

While not critical in this particular example, converters can be extremely useful in situations where code is being distributed and the platform on which it will run is not known in advance.

Next we added a click handler to the `document` using jQuery's `on()` method in event-delegation mode. To add a delegated handler, we attach the handler to a parent element, in this case `document`, and use the second argument to `on()` to provide a selector that events should be filtered against.

Events bubble up the page, from the triggering element right up to the outer `window` object. The handler is only executed when the triggering element matches the selector passed as the second argument. The first argument is of course the type of event, and the third argument is the handler function itself.

Within the function we first prevent the default browser action for the event and then store the value of the `<input>` element in the variable `url`. We also set an undefined variable called `len`. We don't need to use that yet, but we will later on.

Next we check whether the `url` variable we set has a truthy value, like a string with length for example. If it does, we remove the class name `empty` if the `<input>` element has it, then set the contents of the `<input>` as the element's data using jQuery's `data()` method.

Associating the URL to the element in this way is a great way to persist the data so that it can be obtained from other functions in the code which do not have access to the event handler's scope. We also disable the `<button>` to prevent duplicate requests. We can enable it later on when the heat map has been painted to the screen.

We then added the URL that we obtained from the `<input>` element as the `src` property of the `<inframe>`, which causes the `<iframe>` to load the page the URL is for. We add a handler for the `load` event that will be fired by the `<iframe>` once the page has loaded. Inside this handler we fire a custom `iframeloaded` event using jQuery's `trigger()` method.

If the `url` variable does not contain a truthy value, we add the `empty` class to the `<input>` and enable the `<button>` once more.

Lastly we added an event handler for the custom `iframeloaded` event. Custom events will bubble up to the `document` just like regular events so we can attach the handler to our cached `<body>` element and it will still be triggered at the appropriate time.

Within this handler we get the URL for the page that has been loaded by recalling the data associated with the `<input>` element. We then make a request to the server using jQuery's `ajax()` method.

We've already set some of the required AJAX options as defaults using `ajaxSetup()` once again, so for this request we just set the `url` and the `data` options. This time the data we send is a stringified object containing the URL of the page, and the layout to get click data for. In response to this, we expect a JSON object containing a series of click objects, where each object contains `x` and `y` coordinates that refer to a specific point on the page.

Note that at this point, we're hardcoding which layout to load into the request, which we set to number `4`. We'll come back to this in the next part and allow the user to select which layout to view.

Displaying a heat map

We're all set to display a heat map. In this task we'll process the click data in order to generate the heat map, and then display it using the `<canvas>` element on top of the `<iframe>`.

Engage Thrusters

First of all we can add a success handler for the AJAX request we made at the end of the last task. We can do this by chaining the `done()` method to the `ajax()` method:

```
}).done(function (clicks) {

    var loadedHeight = $("html", iframe[0].contentDocument)
.outerHeight();

    doc.find("section").height(loadedHeight);

    canvas.width = doc.width();
    canvas.height = loadedHeight;
    $(canvas).appendTo(doc.find("section"))
            .trigger("canvasready", { clicks: clicks });

});
```

We can then add a handler for the custom `canvasready` event. This should be added directly after the `iframeloaded` event handler:

```
doc.on("canvasready", function (e, clickdata) {

    var docWidth = canvas.width,
        docHeight = canvas.height,
        ctx = canvas.getContext("2d") || null;

    if (ctx) {

        ctx.fillStyle = "rgba(0,0,255,0.5)";

        $.each(clickdata.clicks, function (i, click) {

            var x = Math.ceil(click.x * docWidth / 100),
                y = Math.ceil(click.y * docHeight / 100);

            ctx.beginPath();
            ctx.arc(x, y, 10, 0, (Math.PI/180)*360, true);
            ctx.closePath();
            ctx.fill();

        });
    }

    button.prop("disabled", false);

});
```

Objective Complete - Mini Debriefing

Once the AJAX request has completed, we first store the height of the document that has been loaded in the `<iframe>`. The jQuery method may be passed a second argument after the selector, which sets the context that should be searched to match the selector. We can set the context to be the `contentDocument` object of the first `<iframe>` on the page, which we can access using `frame[0]`.

Setting the `height` of the `<section>` element will automatically make the `<iframe>` and the `<canvas>` element that we created earlier the `width` and `height` of the `<section>` so that the page can be viewed full size.

Next we set the `width` and `height` properties of the `<canvas>` element we created in the last task. We haven't set the `width` or `height` attributes of the `<canvas>` element yet, so by default it will only be 300 x 300 pixels in size, regardless of its visible size as set by the CSS. We therefore set the attributes to the correct sizes.

We can then append the new `<canvas>` to the `<section>` element on the page, and then fire the custom `canvasready` event. We're going to want to use the data passed by the server in an event handler for this event, so we pass this to the handler function using the second argument of the `trigger()` method.

We then added a handler for the `canvasready` event. This function receives the event object and the click data as parameters. Within the function we first get the `width` and `height` of the `<canvas>` element. We stored the click data as percentages and we'll need to convert them back to pixel values.

In order to paint on the `<canvas>`, we'll need to get a context. We can get a 2D context for the `<canvas>` and store it in a variable using the `getContext()` function of the canvas object. If the `<canvas>` element isn't supported, the `ctx` variable will be set to `null`. We can then only proceed to interact with the canvas if the context is not `null`.

If `ctx` is not `null`, we first clear the `<canvas>` using the `clearRect()` function of the canvas API and then set the color that we'll be painting on the canvas. We can set it to the RGBA (Red, Green, Blue, Alpha) string `0,0,255,.05` which is a semi-transparent blue. This only needs to be set once.

We then iterate over the click data returned by the server using jQuery's `each()` method. The iterator function, which will be executed for the number of items in the clicks array, is passed the index of the current item in the array and the `click` object.

We first store the `x` and `y` positions of each pixel that was clicked. These figures are currently percentages, so we need to convert them back to pixel values. This is just the opposite calculation that we performed in the client part of the heat map. We just multiply the percentage by the `width` or `height` of the `<canvas>` and then divide that figure by `100`.

We can then paint a dot on the `<canvas>` where the click occurred. We do this by starting a new path using the `beginPath()` method of the canvas object. The dot is drawn using the `arc()` method, which is passed a number of arguments. The first two are the coordinates of the center of the arc, which we set to the `x` and `y` values we've just calculated.

The third argument is the radius of the circle. If we set the dot to be a single pixel the data would be quite difficult to interpret, so using a large dot instead of a single pixel improves the appearance of the heat map dramatically.

The third and fourth arguments are the angles to start and stop the arc at, and are in radians not degrees. We can paint a complete circle by starting at zero radians and ending on about 6.5 radians.

Once the arc has been defined, we can close the path using the `closePath()` method and fill the arc with color using the `fill()` method. At this point we should be able to run the console in a browser, enter the URL of one of the template pages, and see the page with dots on it corresponding to the clicks.

Allowing different layouts to be selected

In this task of the project, we need to allow the user to select each layout supported by the page. We can do this by using a `<select>` box which we populate at page load with each of the different layouts.

Engage Thrusters

First of all we can add the `<select>` element to the page. This can go in between the search field and the button at the top of the page in `console.html`:

```
<select id="layouts"></select>
```

Next we need to make a request at page load to populate the `<select>`element with an `<option>` for each of the different layouts. We can do this in the click handler for the `<button>` that we added in `console.js` earlier.

It will need to go into the first branch of the conditional that checks a URL has been entered into the `<input>`, directly before where we set the `src` of the `<iframe>`:

```
$.ajax({
    url: "/heat-map.asmx/getLayouts",
    data: JSON.stringify({ url: url })
}).done(function (layouts) {

    var option = $("<option/>"),
        max;

    len = layouts.length;

    function optText(type, i, min, max) {

        var s,
            t1 = "layout ";

        switch (type) {
            case "normal":
```

```
                    s = [t1, i + 1, " (", min, "px - ", max, "px)"];
                    break;
                case "lastNoMax":
                    s = [t1, len + 1, " (", min, "px)"];
                    break;
                case "lastWithMax":
                    s = [t1, len + 1, " (", max, "px+)"];
                    break;
            }

        return s.join("");
    }


    $.each(layouts, function (i, layout) {

        var lMin = layout.min,
            lMax = layout.max,
            text = optText("normal", i, lMin, lMax);

        if (i === len - 1) {
            if (lMax === "none") {
                text = optText("lastNoMax", null, lMin, null);
            } else {
                max = lMax;
            }
        }

        option.clone()
                .text(text)
                .val(i + 1)
                .appendTo("#layouts");
    });

    if (max) {

        var fText = optText("lastWithMax", null, null, max);

        option.clone()
                .text(fText)
                .val(len + 1)
                .prop("selected",true)
                .appendTo("#layouts");
    }
});
```

We can also add a little CSS for our new `<select>` element. We can just drop this into the bottom of `console.css`:

```
.jqheat select {
    width:175px; height:36px; padding:5px;
    margin:0 .25em 0 .5em; border:1px solid #707070;
    border-radius:3px;
}
```

Objective Complete - Mini Debriefing

First of all, we make the request to the server to get the layout information. The `url` is set to a web service that returns the layouts and the `data` is the URL of the page we'd like the layouts for.

We set a success handler using the `done()` method as is the recommended technique for adding success handlers to promise objects for when they become resolved. Within the handler we first set some variables.

We create an `<option>` element as we'll need one of these for each layout and so can clone it as many times as we need by using the `clone()` method. We also update the `len` variable that we created earlier but left undefined, to the number of layouts, which is the `length` of the array the function will receive, and an undefined variable called `max`.

Next we define a function called `optText()` that we can use to generate the text for each `<option>` element we create. This function will accept the type of string to create, the index, and the min and max values.

Inside this function we set a couple of variables. The first, called `s`, is undefined at this point. The second variable `t1` is used to store some simple text that is used in each variant of the string.

Then we use a `switch` conditional to determine which string to build based on the type, which will be passed into the function as the first parameter and will be set to `normal`, `lastNoMax`, or `lastWithMax`, and which should account for the different types of media query that may be found.

In the `normal case`, we specify the `min` and `max` values. When there is no `max` value, we build the string using the `min` value and when there is a `max` value, we build the string using the `max` value.

Each string is constructed using an array, then at the end of the function we return a string by joining whichever array was created.

We then use jQuery's `each()` method to iterate over the `layouts` object returned by the server. As always, the iterator function is passed the index of the current item and the current item itself as parameters.

Within the iterator function, we set our variables, which in this case are the `min` and `max` property values from the current layout object, and the normal variant of the text string, which we're definitely going to use at least once. We call our `optText()` function and store the result for later use.

We then check whether we're on the last iteration, which we'll know when the index is equal to the length of the `layouts` array, which we stored earlier, minus 1. If we are on the last iteration we then check whether the `max` value is equal to the string `none`. If it is, we call our `optText()` function again and set the text to the `lastNoMax` type, which generates the required text string for us. If it isn't we set the `max` variable, which we initially declared as undefined to the `max` value of the current object. Lastly, we create the `<option>` element required for each object in the `layouts` array. The `<option>` is given the text that we've set, and the value of the index plus 1. Once created, the `<option>` is appended to the `<select>` element.

Lastly we check whether the `max` variable has a truthy value. If it does, we call our `optText()` function once more, this time using the `lastWithMax` type, and create another `<option>` element, which we set as the selected item. This is required because we have one more layout than we have objects in the `layouts` array.

When we run the page in a browser now, we should find that as soon as we enter a URL into the `<input>` and hit the load page, the `<select>` element becomes populated with an `<option>` for each of the layouts.

Classified Intel

The middle `case` (`lastNoMax`) in the `switch` statement in our `optText()` function actually won't be used in this example because of how the media queries in the template we're using are structured. In this example the media query for the last break point is `769px` to `1024px`. Sometimes, media queries may be structured so that the final breakpoint contains just a `min-width`.

I've included this `case` of the `switch` to make the code support this other type of media query format as it is quite common and you're likely to run into it when using media queries yourself.

Showing heat maps for each layout

Now that we have each of the layouts in the `<select>` element, we can wire it up so that when the selected layout is changed, the page is updated to show the heat map for that layout.

Engage Thrusters

In this task we'll need to modify some of the code written in a previous task. We need to change the click handler for the `<button>` so that the layout isn't hardcoded into the request.

First of all we need to pass the `len` variable to the handler for the `iframeloaded` event. We can do this by adding a second argument to the `trigger()` method:

```
$(this).trigger("iframeloaded", { len: len });
```

Now we need to update the callback function so that this object is received by the function:

```
doc.on("iframeloaded", function (e, maxLayouts) {
```

Now, we can change the bit where we hardcoded layout `4` into the data passed to the server when making the request for click data:

```
data: JSON.stringify({ url: url, layout: maxLayouts.len + 1 }),
```

Now we're ready to update the heat map when `<select>` is changed. Add the following code directly after the `canvasready` handler in `console.js`:

```
doc.on("change", "#layouts", function () {

    var url = input.data("url"),
        el = $(this),
        layout = el.val();

    $.ajax({
        url: "/heat-map.asmx/getClicks",
        data: JSON.stringify({ url: url, layout: layout })
    }).done(function (clicks) {

        doc.find("canvas").remove();

        var width,
            loadedHeight,
            opt = el.find("option").eq(layout - 1),
            text = opt.text(),
            min = text.split("(")[1].split("px")[0],
            section = doc.find("section"),
```

```
                        newCanvas = document.createElement("canvas");

                if (parseInt(layout, 10) === el.children().length) {
                    width = doc.width();
                } else if (parseInt(min, 10) > 0) {
                    width = min;
                } else {
                    width = text.split("- ")[1].split("px")[0];
                }

                section.width(width);
                newCanvas.width = width;

                loadedHeight = $("html",
                iframe[0].contentDocument).outerHeight();

                section.height(loadedHeight);
                newCanvas.height = loadedHeight;

                canvas = newCanvas;

                $(newCanvas).appendTo(section).trigger("canvasready", {
                    clicks: clicks });
                });
            });
```

Objective Complete - Mini Debriefing

We begin by delegating our handler to the document as we have with most of our other event handlers. This time we're listening for the change event triggered by the element with an id of layouts, which is the <select> element we added in the last task.

We then continue following the previous form by setting a few variables. We get the URL saved as the data of the <input> element. We also cache the <select> element and the value of the selected <option>.

Next we need to make an AJAX request to get the heat map for the selected layout. We set the url to a web service that will return this information, and send the url we want the heat map for, and the layout, as part of the request. Don't forget that this request will also use the defaults we set using ajaxSetup().

We use the `done()` method once again to add a success handler for the request. When the response is received we first remove the existing `<canvas>` element from the page, and then set some more variables.

The first two variables are undefined to begin with; we'll populate these in just a moment. We store the `<option>` that was selected so that we can get its text, which is stored in the next variable. We get the minimum width of the breakpoint by splitting the text that we've just stored, and then cache a reference to the `<section>` on the page. Lastly we create a new `<canvas>` element to display the new heat map.

The conditional if statement that follows the variable deals with setting the first of our undefined variables – `width`. The first branch tests whether the layout requested is the last layout, and if so, sets the new `<canvas>` to the width of the screen.

If the last layout was not requested, the next branch of the conditional checks whether the minimum width of the layout is greater than 0. If it is, the `width` variable is set to the minimum breakpoint.

The final branch is used when the minimum width of the breakpoint is 0. If the minimum width is 0, we use the maximum `width` of the breakpoint instead, which we can obtain by splitting the text of the `<option>` once more.

We then set the width of the `<section>` element and the new `<canvas>` element using the width that we've just computed.

Following this we can define our second undefined variable – `loadedHeight`. This is calculated in the same way as it was before, by reaching into the document loaded into the `<iframe>` and getting the height of its `document` object using jQuery's `outerHeight()` method, which includes any padding the element may have. Once we have this value, we can then set the height of the `<section>` element and the new `<canvas>` element.

We're about to trigger our `canvasready` event once more, as this will consume the click data and generate the heat map. Before we do that however, we just need to save the newly created `<canvas>` element back to the `canvas` variable that we set right at the top of `console.js`.

At this point we should be able to load the default heat map for a URL, then use the `<select>` element to view the heat map for another layout:

Classified Intel

I've used an **MS SQL** database to store the data, and a **c#** web service containing various web methods required for this project. Included in the code download accompanying this book is a backup of the database and a copy of the web service file for you to use if you wish.

MS SQL express is a free version of SQL server which the database can be restored to, and Visual Studio 2012 for web, which is also free, will happily run the web service through its built-in development server.

If you don't have these products installed, and you have access to a Windows machine, I'd strongly recommend you install them so that you can see the code used in this project in action. The open source alternatives PHP and MySQL could also be used just as easily, although you'll need to write this code yourself.

Mission Accomplished

In this project we built a simple heat map generator that captured click data on web pages built using responsive techniques. We built two parts to the heat map generator – some code that runs in the browsers of the visitors of the website to capture every click on the screen, and a part that is used in conjunction with a simple management console in which the URL of the page the heat map is for, and the layout to display can be selected.

While we have to allow a margin of error to account for the pixel-to-percentage conversion and back again, different screen resolutions, and the range between different breakpoints, this easy-to-implement heat map can still give us valuable information about how our site is used, which features are popular, and which features are wasted screen space.

You Ready To Go Gung HO?
A Hotshot Challenge

One thing we haven't dealt with is color. Our heat map is built by dots of a uniform blue. As they're semi-opaque, they get darker as more dots appear in a condensed area, but with enough data, we should aim to change the color, going through red, yellow, and right up to white for the most-clicked areas. See if you can add this functionality yourself to really top the project off.

Project 10

A Sortable, Paged Table with Knockout.js

Knockout.js is a fantastic JavaScript **Model-View-ViewModel (MVVM)** framework that can help you save time when writing complex, interactive user interfaces. It works very well with jQuery and even has built-in basic templating support for building repeated elements that show different data.

Mission Briefing

In this project we'll build a paged table from data using jQuery and Knockout.js. Client-side paging itself is a great feature, but we'll also allow the table to be sorted by providing clickable table headings, and add some additional features such as filtering the data based on a particular property.

By the end of this mission we'll have built something that looks like the following screenshot:

Name	Atomic Number	Symbol	Atomic Weight	Discovered
Hydrogen	1	H	1.00794	1766
Helium	2	He	4.002602	1895
Lithium	3	Li	6.941	1817
Beryllium	4	Be	9.012182	1797
Boron	5	B	10.811	1808
Carbon	6	C	12.0107	Antiquity
Nitrogen	7	N	14.0067	1772
Oxygen	8	O	15.9994	1774
Flourine	9	F	18.9984032	1886
Neon	10	Ne	20.1797	1898

Items per page: 10 ▾   1 2 3 4 5 6 7 8 9 10 11 12 »   Filter by ▾

Why Is It Awesome?

Building complex UIs that respond rapidly to user interaction is hard. It takes time, and the more complex or interactive an application is, the longer it takes and the more code it requires. And the more code an application requires, the harder it is to keep it organized and maintainable.

While jQuery is good at helping us to write concise code, it was never designed with building large-scale, dynamic, and interactive applications in mind. It's powerful, and great at what it does and what it was designed to do; it just wasn't designed to build entire applications with.

Something else is needed when building large-scale applications, something that provides a framework within which we can keep code organized and maintainable. Knockout.js is one such framework designed to do just that.

Knockout.js is known as an MVVM framework, which is based on three core components – the **Model**, the **View**, and the **ViewModel**. This is similar to the better-known MVC pattern. The intent of these and other similar patterns is to provide a clear separation of the visual part of an application and the code required to manage the data.

The **Model** can be thought of as the data for the application. Really, the actual data is a result of the Model, but when working on the client side, we can forget about how the data is accessed by the server-side code because usually we just make an AJAX request and the data is delivered to us.

The **View** is the visual representation of that data, the actual HTML and CSS used to present the Model to the user. When using Knockout.js, this part of the application can also include bindings, which map elements on the page to specific bits of data.

The **ViewModel** sits between the Model and the View, and is quite literally a model of the View – a simplified representation of the state of the View. It manages the user interaction, makes and handles requests for data, and then feeds the data back to the user interface.

Your Hotshot Objectives

The tasks needed to complete this mission are listed below:

- ▶ Rendering the initial table
- ▶ Sorting the table
- ▶ Setting the page size
- ▶ Adding Previous and Next links
- ▶ Adding numerical page links
- ▶ Managing class names

- ▸ Resetting the page
- ▸ Filtering the table

Mission Checklist

We'll be using Knockout.js in this project, so you'll need to grab a copy of it now. The latest version, 2.2.1 at the time this book went to print, can be downloaded from: `http://knockoutjs.com/downloads/index.html`. This should be saved in the `js` directory within the main `jquery-hotshots` project folder as `knockout-2.2.1.js`.

We also need some data for this project. We'll need to use a reasonably large data set consisting of data that can be ordered in a variety of ways. We'll be using the periodic table of elements, in JSON format, as our data source.

I've provided a file as part of this example called `table-data.js`, which contains an object with a property called `elements`. The value of this property is an array of objects, where each object represents an element. The objects are in the following format:

```
{
    name: "Hydrogen",
    number: 1,
    symbol: "H",
    weight: 1.00794,
    discovered: 1766,
    state: "Gas"
}
```

Rendering the initial table

In our first task of the project, we'll build a super-simple ViewModel, add a basic View, and render the Model into a bare `<table>` without any enhancements or additional functionality. This will allow us to familiarize ourselves with some of the basic principles of Knockout, without dropping us in at the deep end.

Prepare for Lift Off

At this point we create the files we'll be using in this project. Save a copy of the template file as `sortable-table.html` in the root project directory.

We'll also need a style sheet called `sortable-table.css`, which we should save in the `css` folder, and a JavaScript file called `sortable-table.js`, which should of course be saved in the `js` directory.

The HTML file should link to each of these resources, as well as the knockout-2.2.1.js file. The style sheet should be linked to directly after common.css, which we've used in most of the projects in the book so far, while knockout.js, table-data.js, and the custom script file for this project (sortable-table.js) should come after the link to jQuery, in that order.

Engage Thrusters

First of all we can build the ViewModel. In sortable-table.js, add the following code:

```
$(function () {

    var vm = {
        elements: ko.observableArray(data.elements)
    }

    ko.applyBindings(vm);

});
```

Next, we can add the View, which is built from some simple HTML. Add the following markup to the <body> of sortable-table.html, before the <script> elements:

```
<table>
    <thead>
        <tr>
            <th>Name</th>
            <th>Atomic Number</th>
            <th>Symbol</th>
            <th>Atomic Weight</th>
            <th>Discovered</th>
        </tr>
    </thead>
    <tbody data-bind="foreach: elements">
        <tr>
            <td data-bind="text: name"></td>
            <td data-bind="text: number"></td>
            <td data-bind="text: symbol"></td>
            <td data-bind="text: weight"></td>
            <td data-bind="text: discovered"></td>
        </tr>
    </tbody>
</table>
```

Lastly, we can add some basic styling to our `<table>` and its contents by adding the following code to `sortable-table.css`:

```css
table {
    width:650px; margin:auto; border-collapse:collapse;
}
tbody { border-bottom:2px solid #000; }
tbodytr:nth-child(odd) td { background-color:#e6e6e6; }
th, td {
    padding:10px 50px 10px 0; border:none; cursor:default;
}
th {
    border-bottom:2px solid #000;cursor:pointer;
    position:relative;
}
td:first-child, th:first-child { padding-left:10px; }
td:last-child { padding-right:10px; }
```

Objective Complete - Mini Debriefing

In our script, we first added the usual callback function to be executed when the document loads. Within this we created the ViewModel using an object literal stored in the variable `vm`.

The only property this object has is `elements`, the value of which is set using a Knockout method. Knockout adds a global `ko` object that we can use to call methods. One of these methods is `observableArray()`. This method accepts an array as an argument, and the array passed in to the method becomes observable. This is the data for our application.

In Knockout, primitives such as strings or numbers can be observable and this allows them to notify subscribers when their values change. Observable arrays are similar, except that they are used with arrays. Whenever a value is added or removed from an observable array, it will notify any subscribers.

After defining our ViewModel, we need to apply any bindings that may be present in the View. We'll look at the bindings in just a moment; for now just be aware that until we call Knockout's `applyBindings()` method, any bindings we add to our View won't be applied.

The HTML we added is almost unremarkable, it's just a simple `<table>`, with a column for each property of an element. If you take a look inside the `table-data.js` file, you'll see the properties of each element in the array match the `<th>` elements.

The first interesting thing is the `data-bind` attribute we added to the `<tbody>` element. This is the mechanism Knockout uses to implement declarative binding. This is how we connect elements in the View to properties of the ViewModel.

The value of the `data-bind` attribute consists of two parts – the binding and the ViewModel property to connect to. The first part is the binding, which we set to `foreach`. This is one of Knockout's flow-control bindings, and acts in a similar way to a standard `for` loop in regular JavaScript.

The second part of the binding is the ViewModel property to bind to. The one property our ViewModel has at present is `elements`, which contains an observable array. The `foreach` binding maps to an array and then renders any child elements it has for each item in the array.

The child elements that this element has are a `<tr>` and a series of `<td>` elements, so we'll get a row in the table for each item in the `elements` array. In order to populate the `<td>` elements with content we'll use another Knockout binding – the `text` binding.

The `text` binding binds to a single observable property, so we have a `<td>` that is bound to each property in the objects within the `elements` array. The text of each `<td>` will be set to the value of each property in the current array item.

The CSS we added at the end of the task was purely for presentational purposes and contains nothing relevant to Knockout or jQuery. At this point we should be able to run the page in a browser and see the data from `table-data.js` displayed in a neat `<table>`.

Classified Intel

The binding between elements of the View and properties of the ViewModel are at the heart of Knockout. The ViewModel is a simplified version of the state of the UI. Because of the bindings, any time the underlying ViewModel changes, the view will be updated to reflect those changes.

So if we programmatically add a new element object to the observable array, the `<table>` will instantly be updated to show the new element. Similarly, if we remove an item from the array in the ViewModel, the corresponding `<tr>` will be immediately removed.

Sorting the table

In this task we can change the `<th>` elements so that they are clickable. When one of them is clicked, we can then sort the table rows by the column that was clicked.

Engage Thrusters

First of all we can update the `<tr>`and the `<th>` elements that it contains in
`sortable-table.html`:

```html
<tr data-bind="click: sort">
    <th data-bind="css: nameOrder">Name</th>
    <th data-bind="css: numberOrder">Atomic Number</th>
    <th data-bind="css: symbolOrder">Symbol</th>
    <th data-bind="css: weightOrder">Atomic Weight</th>
    <th data-bind="css: discoveredOrder">Discovered</th>
</tr>
```

Next we can add some new observable properties to our ViewModel in
`sortable-table.js`:

```js
nameOrder: ko.observable("ascending"),
numberOrder: ko.observable("ascending"),
symbolOrder: ko.observable("ascending"),
weightOrder: ko.observable("ascending"),
discoveredOrder: ko.observable("ascending"),
```

We also add a new method called `sort`:

```js
sort: function (viewmodel, e) {

    var orderProp = $(e.target).attr("data-bind")
                                .split(" ")[1],

        orderVal = viewmodel[orderProp](),
        comparatorProp = orderProp.split("O")[0];

    viewmodel.elements.sort(function (a, b) {

        var propA = a[comparatorProp],
            propB = b[comparatorProp];

        if (typeof (propA) !== typeof (propB)) {

            propA = (typeof (propA) === "string") ? 0 :propA;
            propB = (typeof (propB) === "string") ? 0 :propB;
        }

        if (orderVal === "ascending") {
```

```
                    return (propA === propB) ? 0 : (propA<propB) ? -1 : 1;

            } else {
                return (propA === propB) ? 0 : (propA<propB) ? 1 : -1;

            }

        });

        orderVal = (orderVal === "ascending") ? "descending" :
        "ascending";



        viewmodel[orderProp](orderVal);

        for (prop in viewmodel) {
            if (prop.indexOf("Order") !== -1 && prop !== orderProp) {
                viewmodel[prop]("ascending");
            }
        }
    }
```

Lastly, we can add some additional CSS to style our clickable `<th>` elements:

```
.ascending:hover:after {
    content:""; display:block; border-width:7px;
    border-style:solid; border-left-color:transparent;
    border-right-color:transparent; border-top-color:#000;
    border-bottom:none; position:absolute; margin-top:-3px;
    right:15px; top:50%;
}
.descending:hover:after {
    content:""; display:block; border-width:7px;
    border-style:solid; border-left-color:transparent;
    border-right-color:transparent; border-bottom-color:#000;
    border-top:none; position:absolute; margin-top:-3px;
    right:15px; top:50%;
}
```

Objective Complete - Mini Debriefing

We first updated our HTML with some more bindings. First we added the `click` binding using the `data-bind` attribute on the parent `<tr>`. The `click` binding is used to add an event handler to any HTML element.

The handler function can be a ViewModel method or any regular JavaScript function. In this example, we bound the handler to a function called `sort`, which will be a method of our ViewModel.

Note also that we've added the binding to the parent `<tr>` and not the individual `<th>` elements. We can exploit the fact that events bubble up to their parent elements to implement a very simple and computationally cheap form of event delegation.

We also added the `css` binding to each of the `<th>` elements. The `css` binding is used to add a class name to an element. So the class name that the element acquires depends on the ViewModel property it is bound to. Each of our `<th>` elements is bound to a different ViewModel property and will be used as part of our sorting.

Next we made some changes to our script file. First we added a series of new observable properties. We added the following properties:

- `nameOrder`
- `numberOrder`
- `symbolOrder`
- `weightOrder`
- `discoveredOrder`

Each of these properties is observable, which is required to allow the `<th>` element's class names to update automatically when any of the properties change. Each of the properties are initially set to the string `ascending` so this is the class name that each `<th>`element will be given.

Sorting the data

Next we added our `sort` method to the ViewModel. Because this method is part of an event-handling binding (the `click` binding we added to the `<tr>`), the method will automatically be passed two arguments – the ViewModel as the first, and an event object as the second. We can make use of both of these within the function.

First we define some variables. We use jQuery to select whichever `<th>` element was clicked. We can determine this using the `target` property of the event object, which we wrap in jQuery so that we can call jQuery methods on the selected element.

We can then get the `data-bind` attribute of the element using jQuery's `attr()` method, which we can then split on the space between the binding name and the property it is bound to. So for example, if we were to click on the `<th>` containing **Name** in a browser our first variable, `orderProp`, would be set to `nameOrder`.

The next variable `orderVal` is set to the current value of the ViewModel property that the `orderProp` variable points to. Knockout provides a simple way to get or set any ViewModel property programmatically.

If we want to get the value of a property, we call the property as if it were a function, as follows:

```
property();
```

If we want to set the property, we still call it like a function, but we pass in the value we would like to set as an argument:

```
property(value);
```

So, continuing the example of when the `<th>` containing **Name** is clicked, the `orderVal` variable would have the value `ascending`, because this is the default value of each of the `...Order` properties. Notice how we get the correct value using the `orderProp` variable and square-bracket notation.

Our last variable, `comparatorProp`, is convenient to store the property of the objects within the `elements` array that we are going to sort by. Our ViewModel properties have the string `Order` at the end of them, but the properties inside the objects in the `elements` array do not. So to get the correct property we just have to split the string on the uppercase `O` and take the first item from the array returned by `split()`.

observableArray

Next we use the `sort()` method to perform the sort. It looks like we're using JavaScript's regular `sort()` function for this, but actually, we aren't. Don't forget, the `elements` array isn't just a regular array; it's an **observableArray**, so while we could get the underlying array out of the element's `viewModel` property, and then call the regular JavaScript `sort()` function on it, Knockout gives us a better way.

Knockout provides a range of standard array functions from JavaScript that we can call on observable arrays. For the most part these work in very similar ways to their original JavaScript counterparts, but it's almost always better to use the Knockout variants where possible because they are better supported across browsers, especially legacy browsers, than the original JavaScript versions. Some of the Knockout methods also give us little extra bits of functionality or convenience too.

One example of this is with Knockout's `sort()` method. This isn't the reason we've used the method here, but it is an example of how Knockout can improve the original JavaScript function.

JavaScript's built-in default `sort()` function does not sort numbers very well, because it automatically converts numbers into strings and then performs the sort based on the string instead of the number, leading to results that we do not expect.

Knockout's `sort()` method does not do this, and can sort arrays of strings or numbers equally as successfully. We don't know at this point whether we'll be sorting strings, numbers, or both because the objects in the `elements` array contains both strings and numbers, sometimes in the same properties.

Like the JavaScript `sort()` function, a function passed to Knockout's `sort()` method will automatically be passed two values, which are the current items to sort. Also like JavaScript's `sort()` function, Knockout's `sort()` method should return 0 if the values being compared are equal, a negative number if the first value is lower, or a positive number if the first value is higher.

Within the function passed to `sort()`, we first get the values we're going to compare from the objects. Both of the values passed to the function will be objects, but we only want to compare a property from within each of these objects, so we store the properties we'll be comparing in the `propA` and `propB` variables for convenience.

Comparing different value types

I mentioned a moment ago that sometimes we might be comparing values of different types. This could occur if we are sorting by the date column, which may contain a number in the form of a year, or it may be the string `Antiquity`, which some of the objects have.

So we check whether the two values being compared are of the same type using JavaScript's `typeof` operator and a regular `if` statement. If they aren't the same type we check whether each property is a string, and if so, convert its value to the number 0. Within the `if` statement, we use JavaScript's ternary statement for conciseness.

Checking the order

We then check whether the `orderProp` variable we set a moment ago is set to ascending. If it is, we perform a standard sort. We check whether the two values are equal and if so, return 0. If the two values are not equal we can then check whether the first value is less than the second and return -1 if it is, or 1 if it isn't. To keep this entire statement on a single line we can use a compound ternary.

If the order is not `ascending`, it must be `descending`, so we can perform a descending sort instead. The code for this is almost identical, except that we return 1 if the first value is less than the second value, and -1 if not, the reverse of the statement in the first branch of the conditional.

We then need to update the value of the ...Order property for the column we have just sorted. This piece of code acts like a simple toggle switch – if the value is currently set to ascending, we set it to descending. If it's set to descending, we simply set it to ascending. The behavior that this allows is that when a <th> element is clicked for the first time, it will perform the default ascending sort. If it is clicked a second time, it will perform a descending sort.

Lastly we want to reset any other ...Order properties of our ViewModel if they have been changed. We use a simple JavaScript for in loop to iterate over the properties of our ViewModel. For each property we check whether it contains the string Order, and that it is not the property that we've just updated.

Provided both of these conditions pass, we reset the value of the current property to the default value ascending.

Adding icons

The CSS we added is used to add a little sort icon to each <th> element when it is hovered. We can exploit the CSS shape technique to create a down pointing arrow for ascending, and an up pointing arrow for descending. We also use the :after CSS pseudo selector to avoid hardcoding a non-semantic element, such as <span> or similar, to display the shape. Which arrow is display is determined by the class name that we bound to the ...Order properties of our ViewModel.

If you've never used CSS shapes before, I'd strongly recommend that you look into them because they are a fantastic way of creating icons without requiring non-semantic placeholder elements, or HTTP-heavy images. For more information, check out the CSS shapes guide at http://css-tricks.com/examples/ShapesOfCSS/.

At this point we should be able to run the page in a browser and click on any of the headings once to perform an ascending sort, or click twice to perform a descending sort:

Name ▲	Atomic Number	Symbol	Atomic Weight	Discovered
Actinium	89	Ac	227	1899
Aluminium	13	Al	26.9815386	1825
Americium	95	Am	243	1944
Antimony	51	Sb	121.76	Antiquity
Argon	18	Ar	39.948	1894
Arsenic	33	As	74.9216	1250
Astatine	85	At	210	1940
Barium	56	Ba	137.327	1808
Berkelium	97	Bk	247	1949
Beryllium	4	Be	9.012182	1797

Items per page: 10 ▼   1 2 3 4 5 6 7 8 9 10 11 12 »   Filter by ▼

Setting the page size

So the sorting functionality we added is pretty awesome. But the <table> is still quite large and unwieldy – too large in fact to be seen on the page in its entirety. So it's perfect for paging.

One thing we need to do is determine how many items should constitute a single page of data. We could hardcode a value into our script for the number of items to show per page, but a better way is to add a facility to the UI so that the users can set the number of items to display per page themselves. This is what we'll do in this task.

Engage Thrusters

We can start by adding some additional markup. Add the following elements directly after the <tbody> element:

```
<tfoot>
    <tr>
        <tdcolspan="5">
            <div id="paging" class="clearfix">
                <label for="perPage">Items per page:</label>
                <select id="perPage" data-bind="value: pageSize">
                    <option value="10">10</option>
                    <option value="30">30</option>
                    <option value="all">All</option>
                </select>
            </div>
        </td>
    </tr>
</tfoot>
```

We also need to make a minor change to the <tbody> element. It currently has a foreach binding to the observed array of elements. We're going to add a new property to our ViewModel in a moment and we need to update the binding in sortable-table.html so that it is linked to this new property:

```
<tbody data-bind="foreach: elementsPaged">
```

Next we can add a few new ViewModel properties in sortable-table.js:

```
pageSize: ko.observable(10),
currentPage: ko.observable(0),
elementsPaged: ko.observableArray(),
```

Lastly, we can add a special new variable known as a **computed observable**. This should come after the vm variable:

```
vm.createPage = ko.computed(function () {

    if (this.pageSize() === "all") {
        this.elementsPaged(this.elements.slice(0));
    } else {
        var pagesize = parseInt(this.pageSize(), 10),
            startIndex = pagesize * this.currentPage(),
            endIndex = startIndex + pagesize;

        this.elementsPaged(this.elements.slice(startIndex,
        endIndex));
    }

}, vm);
```

Objective Complete - Mini Debriefing

We started out in this task by adding a <tfoot> element containing a row and a single cell. Inside the cell is a container for our paging elements. We then have a <label> and a <select> element.

The <select> element contains a few options for showing different numbers of items, including an option to see all the data. It also uses Knockout's value data-bind attribute to link the value of the <select> element to a property on our ViewModel called pageSize. This binding means that any time the <select> element's value changes, such as when a user makes a selection, the ViewModel property will be updated automatically.

This binding goes both ways, so if we were to update the pageSize property programmatically in our script, the element on the page would automatically be updated.

We then linked the <tbody>foreach binding to a new property on our VeiwModel called elementsPaged. We'll use this new property to store a subset of the items in the elements array. The actual items in this property will constitute a single page of data.

Next we added some new properties to the object literal stored in the vm variable, also known as our ViewModel. These properties include currentPage, pageSize, and elementsPaged properties that we just discussed.

The last thing we do is add a Knockout feature called a computed observable. This is an extremely useful facility that lets us monitor one or more variables and execute code whenever any of the observables change values.

We use the `ko.computed()` method to set up the computed observable as a method of the ViewModel, passing in a function as the first argument. The ViewModel is passed in as the second argument. We're not within a method attached to our ViewModel now, so we need to pass the ViewModel in to the `computed()` method in order to have this set to the ViewModel.

Within the function passed as the first argument we reference the three new ViewModel properties we just added. Any ViewModel properties referenced within this function will be monitored for changes and the function invoked whenever this occurs.

All the function does is check whether the `pageSize()` property is equal to the string `all`. If it is, it simply adds all of the objects in the elements array to the `elementsPaged` array. It does this by taking a slice of the `elements` array that starts at the very first item. When `slice()` is used with a single argument it will slice to the end of the array, which is exactly what we need to get the entire array.

If `pageSize` does not equal the string `all`, we first need to make sure it's an integer. Because this ViewModel property is linked to the `<select>` element on the page, sometimes the value might be a string of the number instead of an actual number. We can ensure it's always a number by using the `parseInt()` JavaScript function on the property and storing it in the variable `pagesize` for use throughout the rest of the function.

Next we need to determine what the start index passed as the first argument to `slice()` should be. To work this out we just multiply the value of the `pageSize` property by the `currentPage` property, which is initially set to `0`.

We can then populate the `elementsPaged` array with a slice of the `elements` array starting at the `startIndex` value we just determined and ending at the `endIndex` value, which will be the `startIndex` plus the number of items per page.

When we run the page in our browser, the `<select>` box will initially have the value 10 set, which will trigger our computed observable, selecting the first 10 items in the `elements` array, and display them in the `<table>`.

We should find that we can use the `<select>` to change how many items are displayed dynamically.

Classified Intel

In this task we used the `slice()` Knockout method. You may have thought that we were using JavaScript's native `Array.slice()` method, but actually we were using the Knockout version and there's an easy way to spot this.

Usually when we want to get the value inside an observable property, we invoke the property like a function. So when we wanted to get the `pageSize` property of the ViewModel, we used `this.pageSize()`.

When we called the `slice()` method however, we didn't invoke the elements property like a function, so the actual array within the property wasn't returned. The `slice()` method was called directly on the observable.

Knockout re-implements a range of native methods that can be called on arrays, including `push()`, `pop()`, `unshift()`, `shift()`, `reverse()`, and `sort()`, which we used in the last task.

It's recommended to use the Knockout versions of these methods rather than the native JavaScript ones because they are supported across all browsers that Knockout supports, and so that dependency tracking is maintained and the UI of your application is kept in sync.

Adding Previous and Next Links

At this point our page is now only displaying the first 10 items. We need to add an interface that allows the user to navigate to other pages of data. In this task we can add **Next** and **Previous** links so that the pages can be viewed in a linear sequence.

Engage Thrusters

We'll start out once again by adding the HTML component of this feature. Directly after the `<select>` element within the `<tfoot>` element, add the following new markup:

```
<nav>
    <a href="#" title="Previous page"
    data-bind="click: goToPrevPage">&laquo;</a>

    <a href="#" title="Next page"
    data-bind="click: goToNextPage">&raquo;</a>
</nav>
```

Next we can add some new methods to our ViewModel. These can go directly after the `sort` method that we added earlier in `sortable-table.js`:

```
totalPages: function () {
    var totalPages = this.elements().length / this.pageSize() || 1;
        return Math.ceil(totalPages);
},
goToNextPage: function () {
    if (this.currentPage() < this.totalPages() - 1) {
        this.currentPage(this.currentPage() + 1);
    }
},
goToPrevPage: function () {
```

```
    if (this.currentPage() > 0) {
        this.currentPage(this.currentPage() - 1);
    }
}
```

Lastly, we can add a little CSS to tidy up the new elements we added in this part, as well as the ones we added in the last part by adding the following code to `sortable-table.css`:

```
tfoot label, tfoot select, tfootnav {
    margin-right:4px; float: left; line-height:24px;
}
tfoot select { margin-right:20px; }
tfootnav a {
    display:inline-block; font-size:30px; line-height:20px;
    text-decoration:none; color:#000;
}
```

Objective Complete - Mini Debriefing

We started out by adding a `<nav>` element containing two `<a>` elements to the page, which make the **Previous** and **Next** links. We add data bindings to the links that connect the **Previous** link to the `goToPrevPage()` method, and the **Next** link to the `goToNextPage()` method.

We then added a small utility method, as well as these two new methods to our ViewModel. Our methods don't have to accept parameters like the `sort()` method did, and we can access our ViewModel within the methods using `this`.

The first method `totalPages()` simply returns the total number of pages by dividing the total number of items in the `elements` array by the value held in the `pageSize` property.

Sometimes the `currentPage` property will equal the string `all`, which will return `NaN` when used in a Math operation, so we can add the double-bar OR (`||`) to return `1` when this is the case. We also use `Math.ceil()` to ensure we get a whole number, so when there are 11.8 pages of data (the default based on 10 items per page), the method will return 12. The `Ceil()` function will always round up, because we can't have part of a page.

The `createPage` computed observable that we added in the last task actually does most of the work for us. The next two methods simply update the `currentPage` property, which in turn automatically triggers the `createPage()` computed observable.

In the `goToNextPage()` method we first check that we aren't already on the last page, and as long as we aren't, we increase the `currentPage` property by one. We use the `totalPages()` method when we check whether we're on the last page.

The `goToPrevPage()` method is just as simple. This time we check that we aren't already on the first page of data (if `currentPage` is equal to 0), and if we aren't, we decrease the value of `currentPage` by 1.

The tiny bit of CSS we added simply tidies up the elements in the `<tfoot>` element, allowing them to float alongside each other, and makes the new links a little bigger than they would be by default.

Adding numerical page links

We can now add as many links as are required in order to allow the user to visit any of the pages directly. These are the numerical page links that link to each single page directly.

Engage Thrusters

First of all we need to add a new observable property to our ViewModel, directly after the existing observables in `sortable-table.js`:

```
pages: ko.observableArray(),
```

After this we can add a new method to our ViewModel. This can be added after the `goToPrevPage()` method, within the `vm` object literal:

```
changePage: function (obj, e) {
    var el = $(e.target),
        newPage = parseInt(el.text(), 10) - 1;

    vm.currentPage(newPage);
}
```

Don't forget to add a comma after the `goToPrevPage()` method! We can then add a new computed observable, in the same way that we have previously. This can come directly after the `createPage` computed observable that we added in the last task:

```
vm.createPages = ko.computed(function () {

    var tmp = [];

    for (var x = 0; x < this.totalPages(); x++) {
        tmp.push({ num: x + 1 });
    }

    this.pages(tmp);

}, vm);
```

Next, we need to add some new markup to the HTML page. This should be added between the **Previous** and **Next** links that we added in the last task:

```
<ul id="pages" data-bind="foreach: pages">
    <li>
        <a href="#" data-bind="text: num,
        click: $parent.changePage"></a>
    </li>
</ul>
```

Lastly we can add a little CSS to position the new elements in `sortable-table.css`:

```
tfoot nav ul { margin:3px 0 0 10px; }
tfoot nav ul, tfootnav li { float:left; }
tfoot nav li { margin-right:10px; }
tfoot nav li a { font-size:20px; }
```

Objective Complete - Mini Debriefing

First of all we added a new `pages` observable array to our ViewModel. We didn't give it an array to begin with; we'll add this dynamically at the appropriate time.

The computed observable we added as `createPages` is used to build an array where each item in the array represents a page of data. We can get the total number of pages using our `totalPages()` method as we did before.

Once this has been determined, which will be whenever the `pageSize()` observable changes, we can then populate the observable array that we just added.

The objects added to the array are created using a simple `for` loop to create an object and push it into an array. Once we've built an object for each page we can then set the array as the value of the `pages` property.

Each object we create has just a single property, called `num`, the value of which is the current value of the `x` counter variable used by the loop.

In the HTML page, we used the `foreach` data binding to iterate over the array we added to the `pages` array. For each object in the array, we create an `<li>` element and an `<a>` element. The `<a>` has two bindings specified using the `data-bind` attribute.

The first is the `text` binding, which sets the text of the element. In this case, we set the text to be the value of the `num` property that each object has.

The second binding is a click binding, which calls a method called `changePage`. However, within the `foreach` binding, the context is set to the current object in the `pages` array, so we need to use the special `$parent` context property to access the method on the ViewModel.

Lastly we added the `changePage` method used by the `<a>` elements. All we need to do in this simple method is get the text of the element that was clicked, remove `1` from its value because the actual page numbers are zero-based, and update the `currentPage` observable property of our ViewModel. Inside this method for some reason the value of `this` is not set to the element that was clicked, as we would expect from our encounters with the `sort()` method that we added earlier.

Because the `<a>` elements that will trigger the `changePage` method are created within a `foreach` binding, the first argument passed to `changePage` will be the object within the pages array that the `<a>` element is associated with. Luckily we can still access the ViewModel using the variable `vm`.

The CSS we added simply floats the list items alongside each other, spaces them out a little, and sets the color and size of the text.

Classified Intel

As well as the `$parent` context property that allows us to access the parent object of the ViewModel property being iterated in a `foreach` binding, we can also make use of `$data`, which points to the array being iterated.

As well as this, there is also an `$index` property that allows us to access the current iteration index, which we could have used in this example, instead of setting the `num` property on each object.

Managing class names

In this task we can show feedback to the user to describe which page is currently being viewed. We can also disable the **Previous** or **Next** links if we're on the first or last page of data. We can do all this using a little bit more script and some simple CSS.

Engage Thrusters

First we need to add another method to our ViewModel, directly after the existing ones in `sortable-table.js`:

```
manageClasses: function () {
    var nav = $("#paging").find("nav"),
        currentpage = this.currentPage();

    nav.find("a.active")
        .removeClass("active")
        .end()
        .find("a.disabled")
```

```
            .removeClass("disabled");

    if (currentpage === 0) {
       nav.children(":first-child").addClass("disabled");
    } else if (currentpage === this.totalPages() - 1) {
        nav.children(":last-child").addClass("disabled");
    }

    $("#pages").find("a")
              .eq(currentpage)
              .addClass("active");
}
```

We then need to call this method from several places in our existing code. First, we need to call it at the end of the `createPage()` and `createPages()` computed observables, by adding the following code to the end of the last line in each function (the line that begins with `this`):

```
.manageClasses();
```

Then, in order to add the initial class names before the table is interacted with, we need to call it after the `applyBindings()` method after the ViewModel:

```
vm.manageClasses();
```

Lastly, we can add the additional CSS that I mentioned in the task introduction:

```
tfoot nav a.disabled, tfoot nav a.disabled:hover {
    opacity: .25; cursor: default; color:#aaa;
}
tfoot nav li a.active, tfoot a:hover { color:#aaa; }
```

Objective Complete - Mini Debriefing

The first thing we did in this task was to add a new method to our ViewModel – the `manageClasses()` method. This method is responsible for adding or removing the `disabled` class from the **Previous** and **Next** links, and for adding the active class to the numbered link corresponding to the current page.

Inside the method, we first cache a selector for the containing `<nav>` element so that we can access the elements we need to update as efficiently as possible. We also get the `curentPage` ViewModel property as we'll be comparing its value a few times.

We then find the elements that have the `disabled` and `active` classes, and remove them. Notice how we use jQuery's `end()` method after removing the `active` class to get back to the original `<nav>` selection.

All we need to do now is to put the classes back onto the appropriate elements. If the currentPage is 0, we add the disabled class to the first link in the <nav> using jQuery's :first-child selector in conjunction with the children() method.

Alternatively, if we're on the last page, we add the disabled class to the last child of the <nav> instead, this time using the :last-child selector.

Selecting the element to apply the active class to is done easily using the jQuery eq() method, which reduces a selection of elements down to a single element as the specified index. We use the currentpage as the index of the element to retain in the selection.

The CSS was added purely to give the elements with the class names different styling so it was easy to see when the classes are added and removed.

When we run the page in a browser now, we should find that the **Previous** link is disabled to begin with, and the number 1 is active. If we visit any of the pages, that number will gain the active class.

Resetting the page

Now that we've wired up our numeric paging links, a problem has become apparent. Sometimes, when changing the number of items per page, an empty table is displayed.

We can fix this by adding another binding to the <select> element that resets the current page whenever the <select>element's value changes.

Engage Thrusters

First of all we can add the new binding to the HTML. Change the <select> element so that it appears as follows:

```
<select id="perPage" data-bind="value: pageSize, event: {
    change: goToFirstPage
}">
```

Now we can add the goToFirstPage() method to the ViewModel:

```
goToFirstPage: function () {
    this.currentPage(0);
}
```

Objective Complete - Mini Debriefing

First of all we added the `event` binding as a second binding to the `<select>` element responsible for setting the number of items per page. The format of this binding is slightly different than other bindings we've used in this project.

After the name of the binding, `event` in this case, we specify the name of the event and the handler to call when the event occurs within curly braces. The reason why this format is used is because if we want, we are able to specify multiple events and handlers within the braces.

We then added the new event handler, `goToFirstPage()`, as a method of our ViewModel. All we need to do within the handler is set the `currentPage` observable to `0`, which will automatically move us back to the first page of results. This will occur whenever the `<select>` element's value changes.

Filtering the table

To finish off the project we can add filtering so that the different types of elements can be shown. The data for the table contains a column we haven't used yet – the `state` of the element (the actual physical element, not an HTML element!)

In this task, we can add a `<select>` element that allows us to filter elements by their state.

Engage Thrusters

First we need to add a new observable array to the ViewModel, which will be used to store objects that represent the different states an element can be:

```
states: ko.observableArray(),
```

We can also add a simple non-observable property to the ViewModel:

```
originalElements: null,
```

Next we need to populate the new array. We can do this outside of our ViewModel, directly after where we call `vm.manageClasses()`:

```
var tmpArr = [],
    refObj = {};

tmpArr.push({ state: "Filter by..." });

$.each(vm.elements(), function(i, item) {

    var state = item.state;
```

```
        if (!refObj.hasOwnProperty(state)) {

            var tmpObj = {state: state};
            refObj[state] = state;
            tmpArr.push(tmpObj);
        }
    });

    vm.states(tmpArr);
```

Then we can add the new HTML that will create the `<select>` element used to filter the `<table>` data:

```
<div class="filter clearfix">
    <label for="states">Filter by:</label>
    <select id="states" data-bind="foreach: states, event: {
        change: filterStates
    }">
        <option data-bind="value: state, text: state">
        </option>
    </select>
</div>
```

Now we need to add a final method to our ViewModel that will actually filter the data when a selection is made:

```
filterStates: function (obj, e) {

    if (e.originalEvent.target.selectedIndex !== 0) {

        var vm = this,
            tmpArr = [],
            state = e.originalEvent.target.value;

        vm.originalElements = vm.elements();

        $.each(vm.elements(), function (i, item) {
            if (item.state === state) {
                tmpArr.push(item);
            }
        });

        vm.elements(tmpArr).currentPage(0);

        var label = $("<span/>", {
```

```
            "class": "filter-label",
            text: state
        });
        $("<a/>", {
            text: "x",
            href: "#",
            title: "Remove this filter"
        }).appendTo(label).on("click", function () {

            $(this).parent().remove();
            $("#states").show().prop("selectedIndex", 0);
            vm.elements(vm.originalElements).currentPage(0);

        });

        label.insertBefore("#states").next().hide();
    }
}
```

Lastly, we can add just a little CSS to `sortable-table.css`, just to tidy up the new elements:

```
tfoot .filter { float:right; }
tfoot .filter label {
    display:inline-block; height:0; line-height:0;
    text-indent:-9999em; overflow:hidden;
}
tfoot .filter select { margin-right:0; float:right; }
tfoot .filter span {
    display:block; padding:0 7px; border:1px solid #abadb3;
    border-radius:3px; float:right; line-height:24px;
}
tfoot .filter span a {
    display:inline-block; margin-left:4px; color:#ff0000;
    text-decoration:none; font-weight:bold;
}
```

Objective Complete - Mini Debriefing

First we added a new observable array called `states` that will be used to contain the different states of the elements that make up our data. These states are solid, liquid, gas, or unknown.

We also added a simple property to the ViewModel called `originalElements`, which will be used to store the complete collection of elements. This property is just a regular object property because we don't need to observe its value.

Populating the states array

Next we populate the states array with all of the unique states found in the data. We only need to populate this array once, so it can appear outside of the ViewModel. We start out by creating an empty array and an empty object.

We then add a single item to the array which will be used for the first `<option>` element within the `<select>` element and will function as a label before the `<select>` box is interacted with.

We can then use jQuery's `each()` method to iterate the `elements` array. For each item in the array (which if you remember, will be an object representing a single element) we get its `state` and check whether this is stored in the reference object. We can check this using the `hasOwnProperty()` JavaScript function.

If the state doesn't already exist in the object, we add it. If it does already exist, we don't need to do anything. If the object doesn't contain the state, we also push the state into the empty array.

Once the `each()` loop has finished, we should then have an array that contains a single instance of each `state` found in the data, so we can add this array as the value of the `states` observable array.

Building the <select> box

The underlying markup for the filtering feature is quite straightforward. We added a container `<div>` with a couple of class names, a `<label>` and a `<select>`. The `<label>` class name is just added for accessibility, we won't display it because the first `<option>` of the `<select>` element will function as a label.

The `<select>` element has several Knockout bindings. We use the `foreach` binding, which is connected to the states array, so once this is populated, the `<option>` elements for the `<select>` will be added automatically.

We also used the `event` binding once again to add a handler for the `change` event, which will be fired whenever the `<select>` box is interacted with.

Inside the `<select>` element, we add a template for the `<option>` elements. Each option will be given the `text` and `value` of the `state` property of the current object in the `states` array.

Filtering the data

We then added the method to our ViewModel responsible for filtering the data displayed in the `<table>`. The first thing we do in the method is check that the first `<option>` has not been selected, because this is just a label and doesn't correlate to a state.

We can determine this by looking at the `selectedIndex` property of the `target` element (`<select>`), which is available in the `originalEvent` object. This itself is part of the event object that is passed to our event handler automatically.

Because we're going to be changing the `elements` observable array (in order to trigger the paging of the filtered elements) we want to store the original elements for later. We can store them in the `originalElements` property of the ViewModel.

Next, we need to build a new array that contains only the elements that have the `state` that was selected in the `<select>` element. To do this we can create an empty array and then iterate over the `elements` array and check the `state` of each element. If it matches, we push it into the new array.

We can get the `state` that was selected from the `<select>` element again using the event object passed to our event handler. This time we use the `value` property of the `target` element in the `originalEvent` object.

Once the new array has been populated, we update the `elements` array so that it contains just the new array we have just created, and then set the `currentPage` to 0.

The filters that we've added are mutually exclusive, so only one filter can be applied at any one time. Once a filter has been selected, we want to hide the `<select>` box so that another filter cannot be selected.

We can also create a label that shows which filter is currently being applied. This label is made from a `<span>` element which shows the text of the filter, and also contains an `<a>` element that can be used to remove the filter and return the `<table>` back to its initial state of showing all of the elements.

We can use jQuery's `on()` method to attach the handler for the `<a>` element as soon as it is created and appended to the page. Within the handler, we simply set the `elements` property of the ViewModel back to the array saved in the `originalEvents` property and again reset the `<table>` back to the first page by setting the `currentPage` property to 0.

We should now find that we can select one of the options in the `<select>` box, see just the filtered data and the filter label, then click on the red cross sign in the filter label to go back to the initial `<table>`. A filtered selection of the data and the filter label is shown in the following screenshot:

Name	Atomic Number	Symbol	Atomic Weight	Discovered
Argon	18	Ar	39.948	1894
Chlorine	17	Cl	35.453	1774
Flourine	9	F	18.9984032	1886
Helium	2	He	4.002602	1895
Hydrogen	1	H	1.00794	1766
Krypton	36	Kr	83.798	1898
Neon	10	Ne	20.1797	1898
Nitrogen	7	N	14.0067	1772
Oxygen	8	O	15.9994	1774
Radon	86	Rn	222	1900

Items per page: 10 ⏷   « 1 **2** »   Gas x

Mission Accomplished

Our application runs mostly on Knockout functionality, which allows us to easily populate dynamic elements with content, add event handlers, and generally manage the state of the application. We use jQuery too, mostly in a DOM selection capacity, and also occasionally when we wish to use a utility, such as the `$.each()` method that we leveraged several times.

It would have been equally as possible to build this application purely using jQuery and without using Knockout at all; however, jQuery itself was never designed nor intended to be the complete solution to building complex dynamic applications.

What we generally find when we try to build complex dynamic applications using jQuery alone, is that our script very quickly becomes a bloated mess of event handlers that is neither easy to read, or maintain, or update at a future point.

Using Knockout to handle maintaining the state of an application, and using jQuery to fulfill the role it was intended for, gives us the ideal toolkit for building highly dynamic, data-driven, complex applications using very little code.

Throughout this example, I've tried to keep individual methods as simple as possible and have them do one thing well and one thing only. Keeping individual units of functionality isolated in this way helps to keep our code maintainable because it is easy to see what each existing function does, and easy to add new features without breaking what already exists.

You Ready To Go Gung HO? A Hotshot Challenge

Knockout makes it easy to build a `<table>` from an array of data, and because the data is dynamic, it's easy to edit it or add new items to it, and have the data in our application updated. Although the data is stored locally in a file in this example, it would be trivial to store the data on the server and populate our elements array at page load using a simple AJAX function.

This would be the first thing to do if you wanted to take this example further. Once this has been done, why not see if you can make the table cells editable so that their values can be changed, or add a feature that allows you to insert new rows into the `<table>`. Once you've done this, you'll want to post the new data back to the server so that it can be stored permanently.

Index

Thank you for buying
jQuery Hotshot

About Packt Publishing

Packt, pronounced 'packed', published its first book "*Mastering phpMyAdmin for Effective MySQL Management*" in April 2004 and subsequently continued to specialize in publishing highly focused books on specific technologies and solutions.

Our books and publications share the experiences of your fellow IT professionals in adapting and customizing today's systems, applications, and frameworks. Our solution based books give you the knowledge and power to customize the software and technologies you're using to get the job done. Packt books are more specific and less general than the IT books you have seen in the past. Our unique business model allows us to bring you more focused information, giving you more of what you need to know, and less of what you don't.

Packt is a modern, yet unique publishing company, which focuses on producing quality, cutting-edge books for communities of developers, administrators, and newbies alike. For more information, please visit our website: www.packtpub.com.

About Packt Open Source

In 2010, Packt launched two new brands, Packt Open Source and Packt Enterprise, in order to continue its focus on specialization. This book is part of the Packt Open Source brand, home to books published on software built around Open Source licences, and offering information to anybody from advanced developers to budding web designers. The Open Source brand also runs Packt's Open Source Royalty Scheme, by which Packt gives a royalty to each Open Source project about whose software a book is sold.

Writing for Packt

We welcome all inquiries from people who are interested in authoring. Book proposals should be sent to author@packtpub.com. If your book idea is still at an early stage and you would like to discuss it first before writing a formal book proposal, contact us; one of our commissioning editors will get in touch with you.

We're not just looking for published authors; if you have strong technical skills but no writing experience, our experienced editors can help you develop a writing career, or simply get some additional reward for your expertise.

jQuery UI 1.8: The User Interface Library for jQuery

ISBN: 978-1-84951-652-5   Paperback: 424 pages

Build highly interactive web applications with ready-to-use widgets from the jQuery User Interface Library

1. Packed with examples and clear explanations of how to easily design elegant and powerful front-end interfaces for your web applications

2. A section covering the widget factory including an in-depth example on how to build a custom jQuery UI widget

3. Updated code with significant changes and fixes to the previous edition

jQuery Mobile Web Development Essentials

ISBN: 978-1-84951-726-3   Paperback: 246 pages

Learn to use the touch-optimized, cross-device, cross-platform, jQM web framework for smartphones and tables

1. Create websites that work beautifully on a wide range of mobile devices with jQuery mobile

2. Learn to prepare your jQuery mobile project by learning through three sample applications

3. Packed with easy to follow examples and clear explanations of how to easily build mobile-optimized websites

Please check **www.PacktPub.com** for information on our titles

Responsive Web Design with HTML5 and CSS3

ISBN: 978-1-84969-318-9   Paperback: 324 pages

Learn responsive design using HTML5 and CSS3 to adapt websites to any browser or screen size

1. Everything needed to code websites in HTML5 and CSS3 that are responsive to every device or screen size

2. Learn the main new features of HTML5 and use CSS3's stunning new capabilities including animations, transitions and transformations

3. Real world examples show how to progressively enhance a responsive design while providing fall backs for older browsers

Git: Version Control for Everyone

ISBN: 978-1-84951-752-2   Paperback: 180 pages

The non-coder's guide to everyday version control for increased efficiency and productivity

1. A complete beginner's workflow for version control of common documents and content

2. Examples used are from non-techie, day to day computing activities we all engage in

3. Learn through multiple modes – readers learn theory to understand the concept and reinforce it by practical tutorials.

4. Ideal for users on Windows, Linux, and Mac OS X

Please check **www.PacktPub.com** for information on our titles